●

CRISIS
ESCALATION
WAR

●

CRISIS
ESCALATION
WAR

OLE R. HOLSTI

●

McGILL–QUEEN'S UNIVERSITY PRESS

MONTREAL AND LONDON 1972

●

© McGill-Queen's University Press 1972
International Standard Book Number 0-7735-0117-7
Library of Congress Catalog Card Number 73-179879

Legal Deposit first Quarter 1972

*This book has been published with the help of a grant
from the Social Science Research Council of Canada,
using funds provided by the Canada Council.*

PRINTED IN THE U.S.A. BY
VAIL-BALLOU PRESS INC.

●

TO
BOB
NORTH

●

TABLE OF CONTENTS

PREFACE

FOR HIGH DRAMA few periods in history can match the six weeks preceding the outbreak of World War I. The shots fired at Sarajevo ended a royal marriage with enough romance and intrigue to fill several Hollywood scripts. During the following weeks the Balkan crisis became intertwined with the sensational Caillaux murder trial in Paris; the threat of civil war in Ireland; the assassination of the French Socialist leader, Jean Jaurès; and a state visit by the French president to St. Petersburg. But July 1914 was not merely a period of intense drama. With the advantage of hindsight it is clear that 1914 marked the beginning of the end for a civilization with its economic and political centre in Europe.

It is thus scarcely surprising that the events culminating in World War I have been examined many times and for a multitude of purposes. The earliest studies were often single-minded searches for culprits upon whom to lay full blame for the war; among them were influential tracts written by Lenin and Hitler. As foreign-office archives were opened and the passions aroused by the war subsided, polemicists writing merely to indict or justify one nation or another were superseded by the "revisionists" who sought to demonstrate the injustice of assigning all war guilt to the Central Powers, as had been done in Article 231 of the Versailles Treaty; books by Count Max Montgelas (1925), Harry Elmer Barnes (1926), and George Peabody Gooch (1938) are representative of the best of these. Among the diplomatic histories of the period, the multivolume studies of Sidney B. Fay (1930), Luigi Albertini (1953), and Pierre Renouvin (1955) stand out. Finally, with publication of A. J. P. Taylor's *The Struggle for Mastery of Europe* (1954) and Fritz Fischer's *Griff nach der Weltmacht* (1961), severe indictments of German policy, the process has come full circle. In short, the historical literature on the crisis is voluminous and it has probably come close to exhausting the archival materials.

The Cuban missile crisis was no less dramatic and, although it is too soon to make any conclusive assessment, it too may have given rise to wide-ranging international consequences, including a deepening rift between the USSR and China, some limited areas of accommodation between Moscow and Washington and, perhaps, some disastrous misapplications of the "lessons of Cuba" to Vietnam by the Johnson and Nixon administrations. The events of 1962 have also been analysed for a wide variety of purposes. These range from essays which attempt to show that President Kennedy was a coward or a warmonger, to some exceptionally thoughtful studies by Graham Allison, Cyril Black, Alexander George, Robert Jervis, Albert Wohlstetter and Roberta Wohlstetter, and Oran Young in which the Cuban episode serves as the basis for discussing questions of continuing significance.

My purpose has not been to write another diplomatic history of the pre-World War I and Cuban crises. Brief narrative descriptions appear in Chapters 2 and 7, but only to provide an overview of the two episodes. Rather, I have tried to use 1914 and 1962 as instances of intense international crises—one resulting in general war, the other in de-escalation—which may be used to explore several aspects of policy making in high-stress situations. I have done so largely out of a conviction that there are lessons of contemporary significance to be drawn from these crises. The primary goal, then, is to shed light on some widely held assumptions about national security policy, strategy, and crisis management. I have felt free, in the concluding chapter, to speculate rather widely about a number of these issues, on occasion going beyond the evidence presented in the earlier chapters.

A second purpose has been an attempt to demonstrate that there is no inherent incompatibility between history, the social sciences, and concern for important social issues. Several recent essays have asserted that social scientific study of international politics is *and must be* "ahistorical," "irrelevant," and "in support of the status quo"—these are among the more temperate charges.* If this book contributes in some small way to refuting these charges I will be pleased.

I have been urged to re-open the issue of who was to blame for the catastrophe of 1914, but I explicitly disavow this goal. In the first place, this issue is quite peripheral to my central theme that intense and protracted stress tends to erode almost everyone's ability to carry out complex tasks effectively. Moreover, each re-reading of the evidence impresses on me further that the search for culprits—either individuals or nations—is both theoretically sterile and practically without any redeeming social value.

Searches for villains will always be popular—and expecially so in times of conflict and turmoil such as the present—because they inevitably lead the investigator to the conclusion that angels have the wisdom to be on his side; moreover, they require a very low ratio of intellectual to emotional energy.† But such enterprises are not merely trivial if they divert our attention from real dangers. To put it somewhat differently, the issue of whether the kaiser was or was not "guilty"—as well as other questions of that genre—are of underwhelming importance, whereas the problems of policy making in crises are significant by virtually any criterion.

Rejecting Manichean theories of politics is not, however, to argue that political science—or any work that purports to be a contribution to that discipline—is "value free." Nor does it re-

---

* Much of the continuing debate on this and related issues has been conducted at a high level and is thus to be welcomed. But some of it has been reminiscent of the most irresponsible forms of McCarthyism. Consider the "case" developed by one critic: he found that of seventeen political scientists signing an anti-adminis-tration statement on Vietnam, "only" two (12%) were so-called behaviouralists, whereas one of the six (17%) political scientists with the names on the letterhead of a pro-administration organization was a behaviouralist. On this "evidence" the critic concluded that such scholars "are unable to make useful policy recommendations." Illogical charges of this type against traditionalists or any other group would, of course, be equally reprehensible.

† The first principle of the "demonological" school is that behind every disapproved event there must be evil men and corrupt institutions; the second principle is that if substantial evidence in support of the first cannot be found, this only proves how cleverly the machinations of the power elite are camouflaged.

quire one to be a moral eunuch or to view all policy alternatives as equal. One need not, for example, assess the proposal to use atomic weapons during the missile crisis as the ethical equivalent of a blockade in which not a single life was lost. Those who would search through these events for heroes and villains, however, may do well to consider the case of Senator J. William Fulbright, who has served in the House and Senate with considerable distinction for more than a quarter of a century. Senator Fulbright had advised against the Bay of Pigs invasion in 1961, correctly forecasting that it would result in a political and military disaster. Eighteen months later, however, he demanded bombing and invasion of Cuba. Or, consider the case of General Douglas MacArthur, whose military and political judgment after the brilliant Inchon landing in Korea left a good deal to be desired. Yet a decade later MacArthur warned with acute prescience against increasing American commitments to South Vietnam. The limited categories of hero and villain do not seem adequate to encompass these not untypical cases.

A few words about the plan of the book may be in order. Chapter 1 introduces the question—"How does intense stress affect performance?"—and surveys a wide range of evidence from laboratory research. Chapter 2 provides a brief overview of the 1914 crisis and describes an approach to studying the effects of stress in historical settings. Two experiments to test the validity of this approach are described in Chapter 3, which readers with a limited interest in this problem may wish to skip. Evidence about the consequences of stress for decision making in 1914 is presented in Chapters 4, 5, and 6; detailed tables and discussions of methodology relating to these chapters may be found in the appendix. Chapter 7 examines the Cuban missile confrontation in the light of findings from the 1914 crisis. The most important question is how Kennedy and Khrushchev avoided war when their counterparts forty-eight years earlier were not able to do so. The final chapter is a speculative effort to adduce some practical lessons and policy guidelines from the crisis studies.

While preparing this book I have become indebted to many persons. Elizabeth Hart, Jean Heflin, William Moul, Donald Munton, and John Terry assisted in some coding and scaling of the data. Arlee Ellis and Violet Lofgren typed many preliminary drafts and also assisted me in more ways than I can enumerate. The final draft was ably typed by Joan Ippen. Early versions of papers and chapters have been improved by the criticisms and suggestions of Hayward Alker, Nazli Choucri, David Elkins, Richard Fagen, Jean Laponce, Todd LaPorte, Stephen Milne, Richard Snyder, Lois Swirsky, and Dina Zinnes. Critical reviews by Gordon Hilton, Robert Jervis, and John Mueller of several earlier crisis studies pointed to shortcomings that I have attempted to rectify here. Lancelot L. Farrar, Alexander George, K. J. Holsti, Robert Jervis, Fern Miller, and Mark Zacher kindly read the entire manuscript and contributed many valuable suggestions. Less tangible but no less real are my intellectual debts to Charles Hermann, James Robinson, and Richard Snyder, pioneers in the study of crisis decision making. The Canada Council and the Dean's Committee on Research, University of British Columbia, generously provided financial support for preparation of this book. Initial stages of the research contributing to this book was supported by a grant from the Ford Foundation. That foundation is not, however, the author, owner, publisher, or proprietor of this publication, and is not to be understood as approving by virtue of its grant any of the statements made or views expressed. The UBC Computation Centre contributed computer time, and David Malcolm and Frank Flynn assisted in processing my data. To all the above I can only express my thanks, my hopes that they will not be disappointed by the final product to which they have so kindly contributed, and the traditional release from responsibility for any errors of fact or interpretation that may remain.

My special thanks to Ann for typing the tables, to Eric for checking many of my computations and for helping to prepare the index, and to Maija for occasionally keeping her nimble fingers off my typewriter and out of my desk for several hours at a time; they also have my gratitude for other reasons.

This book is gratefully dedicated to Robert North, for whom the phrase "scholar and gentleman" might have been invented.

Chapter One

CRISIS, STRESS, AND DECISION MAKING

Crisis and Stress

"WHAT IS RELEVANT FOR POLICY" in times of crisis, according to Henry Kissinger, President Nixon's principal foreign-policy adviser, "depends not only on academic truths but also on what can be implemented under stress."[1] Observations by others who have experienced or studied international crises vary widely. Consider the following:

Hence, a decision-maker may, in a crisis, be able to invent or work out easily and quickly what seems in normal times to both the "academic" scholar and the layman to be hypothetical, unreal, complex or otherwise difficult.[2]

In every case, the decision [to go to war] is based upon a careful weighing of the chances and of anticipating consequences. . . . In no case is the decision precipitated by emotional tensions, sentimentality, crowd-behavior, or other irrational motivations.[3]

We have faith that man, who has been endowed with the wit to devise the means of his self-destruction, also has enough wit to keep those means under effective control.[4]

We create and enjoy crises. . . . Why? I don't know. I wish I knew. But all of us like them. I know I enjoy them. . . . There is a sense of elation that comes with crises.[5]

You see a poor, rather stupid fellow behind a desk and you wonder why he couldn't do better than that [in crisis situations]. Unfortunately, that picture comes up too often.[6]

I saw first-hand, during the long days and nights of the Cuban crisis, how brutally physical and mental fatigue can numb the good sense as well as the senses of normally articulate men.[7]

How *do* individuals and groups respond to the pressures and tensions of a crisis? Do we tend to approach such situations with high motivations, a keen sense of purpose, extraordinary energy and enhanced creativity? Is necessity, as Kahn suggests, the mother of invention? Or, is our capacity for coping with the problem impaired, perhaps even to the point suggested by Neustadt's phrase, "the paranoid reaction characteristic of crisis behavior"?[8] When under intense pressure do we characteristically take the more cautious path, or are we more prone to taking high risks? Is our sense of what constitutes risk in any way altered?

The answers to these questions are always important for persons who find themselves faced with a crisis. They assume extraordinarily wide significance when the individuals are national leaders and the context is that of a contemporary international crisis: upon the ability of national leaders to cope with situations of intense stress may depend the lives of millions, if not the future of mankind. Despite the importance of these questions, many descriptive or prescriptive theories of international politics either ignore them or assume that the answers are self-evident. Consider, for instance, some of the basic premises of deterrence theories: that decisions by the nation to be deterred, as well as all others, will be based on dispassionate calculations of probable costs and gains, accurate evaluations of the situation, and careful assessments of relative capabilities;° that the value hierarchies of national leaders are similar at least to the point that each places the avoidance of war at or near the top; and that all nations maintain tight centralized control over decisions which might involve or provoke the use of force.

Deterrence thus presupposes rational and predictable decision processes. No system of deterrence, however powerful the weap-

---

° An argument for "assured second-strike capabilities" is that it reduces the burdens of careful calculation for the adversary; that is, it should be clear to the enemy that even if his calculations are far off the mark, a decision for war will still lead to disaster.

ons, is likely to prove effective against a nation led by a trigger-happy paranoid, or by someone seeking personal or national self-destruction or martyrdom, or by decision makers willing to play a form of international Russian roulette, or by leaders whose information about and communication with an adversary are so incomplete that their decision-making processes are dominated by guesswork, or by those who regard the loss of most of their nation's population and resources as a reasonable cost for the achievement of foreign-policy goals.

Clearly the assumptions of deterrence are valid most of the time and under most circumstances, even in relations of considerable enmity such as "cold wars." Otherwise, we would be at war almost continuously. Most deterrence theories further assume, however, that threats and ultimata not only effectively influence an adversary's behaviour, but also enhance calculation, control, and caution while inhibiting recklessness and risk-taking. There may be a recognition that "the rationality upon which deterrence must be based is frangible," [9] but there is also a tendency to assume that these rationalistic premises require little if any modification for crisis situations. Deterrence theorists, in short, tend to be sanguine about the ability of policy makers to be creative when the situation requires it—even when they are under stress.[10] To be sure, they often recognize some special features of crisis—for example, the difficulties of normal communication between adversaries.[11] But the lesson drawn from such examples is usually that lack of control over the situation may be used as a bargaining asset to force the adversary into a disadvantageous position, not only once, but in repeated encounters.

This is an oversimplified summary of the rich literature on deterrence, a topic to which we shall return in the concluding chapter. Nevertheless, there is a substantial element of truth in one critics's assertion that "the theory of deterrence . . . first proposes that we should frustrate our opponents by frightening them very badly and that we should then rely on their cool-headed rationality for our survival." [12]

The more general question is how crisis—defined here as *a situation of unanticipated threat to important values and restricted decision time* [13]—is likely to affect policy processes and outcomes. What are the probable effects of crisis upon abilities which are generally considered essential to effective decision making? These include the ability to:

Identify major alternative courses of action.
Estimate the probable costs and gains of each alternative course.
Resist premature cognitive closure.
Distinguish between the possible and the probable.
Assess the situation from the perspective of other parties.
Discriminate between relevant and irrelevant information.
Tolerate ambiguity.
Resist premature action.
Make adjustments to meet real changes in the situation (and, as a corollary, to distinguish real from apparent changes).

This list is by no means exhaustive.[14] Nor does it establish an unrealistic standard. It does, however, give us a checklist against which we can evaluate the probable consequences of stress on aspects of human performance relevant to foreign-policy decisions.

The most important aspect of crises for our purposes is that these situations are characterized by high stress for the individuals and organizations involved. That a threat to important values is stress-inducing requires little elaboration. The element of surprise is also a contributing factor; there is evidence that unanticipated and novel situations are generally viewed as more threatening.[15] Finally, crises are often marked by almost around-the-clock work schedules, owing to both the severity of the situation and the absence of extended decision time. During the Cuban missile confrontation, for instance, many American officials slept in their office for the duration of the crisis: "We had to go on a twenty-four hour basis here in the Department of State."[16] Premier Khrushchev also appears to have had little sleep during that week: "I must confess that I slept one night in my studio fully dressed on the sofa. I did not want to be in the position of one western diplomat who, during the Suez crisis, rushed to the telephone without his trousers."[17] Even during the much less intense Middle East situation created by the "Six Day War" in 1967 the Soviet Politburo had at least one all-night meeting.[18] Lack of rest and excessively long working hours are likely to magnify the stresses inherent in the situation.

Stress and Performance: The Evidence from Psychology

The central concern of this book is to explore the possible consequences of crisis-induced stress on those aspects of individual and organizational performance that are most likely to affect the processes and outcomes of foreign-policy making. In this book stress is viewed as *the result of a situation that threatens important goals or values.* For reasons to be discussed later, we shall measure stress by subjective responses to the situation rather than by attributes of the situation itself.°

As a starting point we shall turn to the rich and voluminous body of theory and evidence from experimental psychology.† The advantages of precise measurement, easy replication, and tight control over the experimental variables have permitted psychologists to probe many aspects of human performance in various types of situations. Some emphasis will be placed on the consequences of stress for the identification of alternatives and processes of choosing from among them, assessments of time factors, and patterns of communication. We shall also consider how time pressure, the number of perceived alternatives, and the volume of communications may affect the level of stress in a situation, and examine other relations between these variables as well —for example, between patterns of communications and identification of policy options. Theories and research on crises have generally demonstrated the importance of these variables.[19]

Some degree of stress is an integral and necessary precondition for individual or organizational problem-solving; in its absence

---

° An operational definition of stress is developed in Chapter 2 and an experiment to test its validity is described in Chapter 3.

† It should be noted that there is a lack of consensus on operational measures of stress among authors of the studies reviewed here. Some define it as the stimulus (e.g. a severe threat), whereas others view it as the perceptual and behavioural response to threat. We shall adopt the latter position, but the review in this chapter is not restricted to any single measure of stress. For further discussions, see Raymond B. Cattell and Ivan H. Scheier, "Stimuli Related to Stress, Neuroticism, Excitation, and Anxiety Response Patterns," *Journal of Abnormal and Social Psychology*, LX (1960), 195–204; Richard S. Lazarus, *Psychological Stress and the Coping Process* (New York: McGraw-Hill, 1966); and Margaret G. Hermann, "Testing a Model of Psychological Stress," *Journal of Personality*, XXXIV (1966), 381–396.

we lack any motivation to act. Low levels of pressure alert us to the presence of a situation requiring our attention, increase our vigilance and our preparedness to cope with it.* Increasing stress to moderate levels may heighten our propensity and ability to find a satisfactory solution to the problem. A study of research scientists revealed, for example, that an environment of moderate stress, characterized by "uncertainty without anxiety," is the most conducive to creative work.[20] Indeed, for some elementary tasks a rather high degree of stress may increase performance, at least for limited periods of time. If the problem is qualitatively simple and performance is measured by quantitative criteria, stress can increase output. The threat of a severe flood may result in exceptional physical performance by emergency work crews who are filling and stacking sandbags, and a severe international crisis might give rise to improved output by foreign-office clerical staffs.

Our present concern, however, is not with the effects of crisis on persons engaged in manual or clerical tasks, but with its consequences on the performance of top-ranking foreign-policy officials. Foreign-policy issues are nearly always marked by complexity, ambiguity, and the absence of stability; they usually demand responses which are judged by qualitative rather than quantitative criteria. It is precisely these qualitative aspects of performance that are most likely to suffer under high stress.[21]

Most research findings indicate a curvilinear relation between stress and the performance of individuals and groups. A moderate level of anxiety can be beneficial, but at higher levels it disrupts decision processes.[22] On the basis of a series of experiments, Birch determined that intermediate—rather than high or low motivation—was most conducive to the efficient solution of problems requiring both high and low insight. A related finding is that persons with moderate fear were better able to cope with the problems arising from major surgery than were those with

---

* There are some research findings which indicate that just as "some degree of stress in infancy is necessary for the development of normal, adaptive, behavior, so the information we now have on the operation of the pituitary-adrenal system indicates that in many situations effective behavior in adult life may depend on exposure to some optimal level of stress." Seymour Levine, "Stress and Behavior," *Scientific American*, CCXXIV (January 1971), 26–31.

high or low fear.[23] These results have been supported by other studies.[24] Lanzetta, in an analysis of group behaviour, found that "under increased stress there was a decrease in initiating behaviors, mainly in terms of 'diagnoses situation, makes interpretation' kinds of behavior; and an increase in more 'general discussions of the task' kind of behavior."[25] Following their analysis of the effects of stress on perception, Postman and Bruner concluded: "Perceptual behavior is disrupted, becomes less well controlled than under normal conditions, and hence is less adaptive. The major dimensions of perceptual function are affected: selection of percepts from a complex field becomes less adequate and sense is less well differentiated from nonsense; there is maladaptive accentuation in the direction of aggression and escape; untested hypotheses are fixated recklessly."[26]

Other effects of stress which have been found in experimental research include: increased random behaviour; increased rate of error; regression to simpler and more primitive modes of response; problem-solving rigidity; diminished focus of attention, across both time and space; reduced ability to discriminate the dangerous from the trivial; diminished scope of complex perceptual activity; loss of abstract ability; disorientation of visual-motor coordination; and loss of complexity in the dimensions of political cognition.[27] A finding of special relevance for international crises is that tolerance for ambiguity is reduced when there is high stress. Under these conditions individuals made decisions before adequate information was available, with the result that they performed much less capably than those working under normal conditions. The combination of stress and uncertainty leads some persons to feel that "the worst would be better than this."[28]

To summarize, in situations of high stress "there is a narrowing of the cognitive organization at the moment; the individual loses broader perspective, he is no longer able to 'see' essential aspects of the situation and his behavior becomes, consequently, less adaptive."[29]

Some experimental studies have been criticized on both conceptual and methodological grounds, but the general conclusion that high stress inhibits rather than facilitates most aspects of human performance appears to be unassailable. Moreover, the capabilities which may be enhanced by moderate-to-high stress tend to have limited relevance in formulating foreign policy, whereas the skills which are inhibited under these conditions are usually crucial for such complex tasks.

A related aspect of international crises is the existence of time pressures which may become accentuated if either party believes that there are advantages to acting first. It should be pointed out that time pressure is not only a matter of clock time, but also of the complexity and importance of the task to be accomplished. Given five minutes within which to choose between playing golf or mowing the lawn on Sunday a person may feel no particular pressure, but a five week deadline for deciding whether to change jobs may give rise to intense feelings of short decision time. Moreover, it is apparently the *perceptions* of time that are crucial: "The effects of a time limit appear to be due to perceived pressure rather than actual pressure brought on by an impossible time limit." [30]

Time perspectives are affected by high stress. For example, the ability to judge time is impaired in situations which increase anxiety.[31] Thus there appears to be a two-way relation between time and stress. On the one hand the common use during crisis of such techniques as ultimata and threats with built-in deadlines is likely to increase the stress under which the recipient must operate. On the other hand, increasing levels of stress tend to heighten the salience of time and to distort judgments about it. It has been found in "real life" crisis situations as well as experimentally that as danger increases there is a significant overestimation of how fast time is passing.[32] This suggests not only that short decision time distinguishes crises from other types of situations, but also that increasing stress will further heighten the salience of time.

Perceived time pressure may affect the search for alternatives in several ways. Foreign-policy issues are rarely if ever analogous to the familiar multiple-choice question in which the universe of options is neatly outlined. The theoretically possible choices far exceed the number that can or will be considered. Especially in unanticipated situations such as crises it is necessary to search out and perhaps create alternatives. A number of studies indicate that some time pressure can enhance creativity as well as the rate of performance, but most of the evidence suggests that beyond a moderate level it has adverse effects. Because complex tasks requiring feats of memory and inference suffer more from time pressure,[33] its effects on foreign-policy decisions—which are usually marked by complexity—are likely to be particularly harmful. In such situations there is a tendency to fix upon a single approach, to continue using it whether or not it proves effective, and to hang on to familiar solutions, applying them even to problems that may be substantially different.[34]

Experimental research has shown that under severe time pressure normal subjects produce errors similar to those committed by schizophrenics. Another study revealed that, although a moderate increase in time pressure can increase the productivity of groups, an increase from low to high pressure has an adverse effect. Mackworth and Mackworth report that increasing the number of decisions required in a given period of time by a factor of five led to a fifteenfold rise in decision errors. There is, in addition, evidence that time pressure increases the propensity to rely upon stereotypes, disrupts both individual and group problem-solving, narrows the focus of attention, and impedes the use of available information. Finally, short decision time tends to create early group agreement, thereby reducing incentives to search for and weigh other options.[35]

When decision time is short, the ability to estimate the range of possible consequences arising from a particular policy choice is likely to be impaired. There are several reasons why this should be so. Both experimental and field research indicate that severe stress is likely to give rise to a single-minded concern for the present and immediate future at the sacrifice of attention to longer-range considerations.[36] The uncertainties attending severe crisis make it exceptionally difficult to follow outcomes from a sequence of actions and responses very far into the future. Increasing stress also tends to narrow the focus of attention, thereby further limiting perceptions of time to the more immediate future. During the Korean war, for instance, it was observed that combat troops "cannot exercise complex functions involving the scanning of a large number of factors or long-term foresight because the stress is too massive and time too short for anything but the immediately relevant."[37] Moreover, if the present situation is perceived as extremely dangerous, the more distant future may appear to have little or no relevance unless a satisfactory solution can be found for the immediate problems. This may well be true and placing a priority on the immediate often makes sense. After a drowning man has been pulled out of icy waters it would be foolish to take medical steps directed at warding off the longer-range dangers of pneumonia before giving artificial respiration to revive the victim.

There are also potential difficulties, however, in an overly developed sense of concern for the immediate. Present actions alter future options, and decisions which provide immediate advantages may carry with them unduly heavy costs later. The price may be worth paying but the balance sheet can scarcely be evaluated effectively if attention is fixed solely on the short-run benefits. There is also something seductively appealing about the belief that, "If I can just solve the problem of the moment the future will take care of itself." This reasoning appears to have contributed to both Neville Chamberlain's actions during the Czech crisis of 1938 and to Lyndon Johnson's policies during the war in Vietnam.

Sustained time pressure may also give rise to significant changes in goals. The authors of a bargaining experiment concluded that "the meaning of time changed as time passed without the bargainers reaching an agreement. Initially the passage of time seemed to place the players under pressure to come to an agreement before their costs mounted sufficiently to destroy their profit. With the continued passage of time, however, their mounting losses strengthened their resolution not to yield to the other player. They comment: 'I've lost so much I'll be damned if I give in now. At least I'll have the satisfaction of doing better than she does.' " [38] This assertion and its underlying rationale are not unlike one of Kaiser Wilhelm's marginal notes, written when he finally recognized that his hopes of British neutrality in the rapidly approaching war were a delusion: "If we are to be bled to death, England shall at least lose India." [39]

The extent of the search for satisfactory solutions to a problem depends in part on the belief that the environment is benign and that such options in fact exist. But it is in the nature of crisis that most, if not all, policy alternatives are likely to be perceived as undesirable. The frying pan and the fire rather than Burian's ass (who starved to death when unable to choose between equally delectable bales of hay) is the appropriate metaphor for choices in an international crisis. As noted earlier, when stress increases, problem solving tends to become more rigid: the ability to improvise declines; previously established decision rules are adhered to more tenaciously, whether appropriate to the circumstances or not; and the ability to "resist the pull of closure" is reduced.[40] The evidence thus suggests the paradox that as the intensity of a crisis increases it makes creative policy making both more important and less likely.

Identification of alternatives can also be related to the element of surprise in crises. Snyder has suggested that more options will be considered when the need for a decision is anticipated rather than suddenly imposed from without.[41] By the definition used here, crises are unanticipated, for at least one of the parties. Thus this attribute of the situation is itself likely to restrict inquiry and, as the crisis becomes more severe and stress increases, the search for options is likely to be further attenuated. In circumstances such as existed after the attack on Pearl Harbor we would not expect a lengthy review of potential responses by decision makers. Even during the Korean crisis of 1950, in which the situation was somewhat more ambiguous, only a single alternative course of action was considered: "The decision-making process in the Korean case was not characterized by the consideration of multiple alternatives at each stage. Rather a single proposed course of action emerged from the definition of the situation." [42]

The extreme situation occurs when only one course is perceived and the policy-making process is reduced to resigning oneself to the inevitable. If decision makers perceive that their options are reduced to only those with potentially high penalties —for example, "We have no alternative but to go to war"— considerable dissonance may be generated. The dissonance between what the decision maker does (pursues policies that are known to carry a high risk of war) and what he knows (that war can lead to disaster) can be reduced by absolving himself from responsibility for the decision. This solution has been described by Festinger: "It is possible, however, to reduce or even eliminate the dissonance by revoking the decision psychologically.

This would consist of admitting to having made the wrong choice *or insisting that really no choice had been made for which the person had any responsibility.* Thus, a person who has just accepted a new job might immediately feel he had done the wrong thing and, if he had it to do over again, might do something different. Or he might persuade himself that *the choice had not been his; circumstances and his boss conspired to force the action on him.*" [43] This process may also be related to the widespread inability to perceive and appreciate the dilemmas and difficulties of others: "The grass is always greener on the other side of the fence." This has been noted with respect to the motives, general capabilities, and military strength ascribed to the adversary. [44]

One method of dissonance reduction is to believe that the only options which offer a way out of the dilemma rest with the opponent—only the other side can prevent the impending disaster. For example, during the frantic last-minute correspondence between the kaiser and the tsar, Wilhelm wrote: "The responsibility for the disaster which is now threatening the whole civilized world will not be laid at my door. In this moment it still lies in your [Nicholas] power to avert it." [45] Although it may at times be difficult to appreciate fully the dilemmas and difficulties of friends [46] there is likely to be greater empathy with allies than with enemies. One way of coping with dissonance is to persuade oneself that the adversary is free from the very situational constraints which restrict the options available to self and allies.

What, finally, is the relation between crisis-induced stress, communication, and policy making? The adequacy of communication both in the physical sense of open channels of communication and in the sense of "pragmatics"—the correspondence between the sender's intent and the recipient's decoding—has been a major concern in studies of decision making. In this respect Heise and Miller have found that "the performance of a small group depends upon the channels of communication open to its members, the task which the group must handle, and the stress under which they work." [47]

Inadequate communications has received the greatest share of attention in crisis studies, with less concern for the effects of information overload.[48] Study of the latter appears to have been confined mostly to the laboratory rather than to historical situations. Yet information overload does appear to be an important consideration. The inception of a crisis usually gives rise to a sharply increased pace of individual and bureaucratic activities, virtually all of which are likely to increase the volume of diplomatic communication.

We noted earlier that high-stress situations tend to increase selective perception and to impair the ability to discriminate between sense and nonsense, the relevant and the irrelevant. Aside from the effects of stress, there are limits on our ability to process information. An experimental study of complex situations revealed that increased information loads resulted in fewer strategic integrated decisions and more unintegrated and simple retaliatory decisions.[49] As the volume of information directed at policy makers rises, the search for information within the communication system will tend to become less thorough, and selectivity in what is read, believed, and retained takes on increasing importance. Unpleasant information and that which does not support preferences and expectations is most likely to fall by the wayside, unless it is of such an unambiguous nature that it cannot be disregarded. The experimental finding that selective filtering is often used at levels ranging from cells to human groups to cope with an unmanageable amount of information is apparently also valid for governmental organizations: "All Presidents, at least in modern times, have complained about their reading pile, and few have been able to cope with it. There is a temptation, consequently, to cut out all that is unpleasant."[50] Thus, more communication may in fact result in less useful and valid information available to policy makers.

Although the volume of communication may rise during crises, the increase is likely to be uneven; there may be considerable disruption of communication with potential adversaries. In a simulation study, Brody found that as perceived threat rose, the proportion of intra-alliance communication—as compared to inter-alliance messages—increased.[51] At the same time, both incoming and outgoing messages are likely to reflect increasingly simple and stereotyped assessments of the situation. If these expectations regarding changes, patterns, and content of communication in crisis are valid, the number of options which decision makers will consider is correspondingly restricted.

Certain other aspects of communications in a crisis may restrict the search for alternatives. There is a general tendency for a reduction in size of decision-making groups in such situations.° Technological and other factors have reduced decision time to a point where broad consultation with legislatures and other important groups may be virtually impossible. The limited membership of the "Excom," in which the decisions regarding missiles in Cuba were made, is a case in point. Decision groups in the crises concerning Korea (1950), Indo-China (1954), Vietnam (1965), Cambodia (1970), and others were similarly restricted in size.[52]

There may be, moreover, a tendency to consult others less as the pressure of time increases, as well as to rely more heavily upon those who support the prevailing "wisdom." In his study of a governmental department, Pruitt found a significant reduction in the number of people consulted by persons responsible for solving problems when time pressure increased.[53] One of the key decisions in the crisis leading up to World War I—the German decision to grant Vienna a blank cheque in support of the plan to punish Serbia—was made without any extended consultation.

On 5 July the Kaiser went for a stroll in the park at Potsdam with his chancellor, that bearded, sad-eyed giant Theobald von Bethmann-Hollweg, whom irreverent young officers called 'Lanky Theobald', and Under-Secretary Zimmermann of the Foreign Office. By the time the walk was over, the Kaiser had made up his mind. Not another man had been consulted. The Foreign Minister was on his honeymoon and had not been recalled. The experienced, too subtle, too

---

° This consequence of crisis may, however, actually improve some aspects of policy making: "The greater the emergency, the more likely is decision-making to be concentrated among high officials whose commitments are to the over-all system. Thus it may be, paradoxically, that the model of means-ends rationality will be more closely approximated in an emergency when the time for careful deliberation is limited. Though fewer alternatives will be considered the values invoked during the decision period will tend to be fewer and more consistent, and decisions will less likely be the result of bargaining within a coalition." Sidney Verba, "Assumptions of Rationality and Non-rationality in Models of the International System," *World Politics*, XIV (1961), 115. A more general argument along the same lines appears in Theodore J. Lowi, *The End of Liberalism: Ideology, Policy, and the Crisis of Public Authority* (New York: W. W. Norton, 1969), pp. 158–160.

slippery ex-chancellor Bernhard von Bülow had not been called in. There in the park with Bethmann-Hollweg, whose judgment he despised, and Zimmermann, an official, the Kaiser reached his decision. He told the Austrian ambassador in Berlin that Germany would cover Austria should Russia intervene.[54]

Similarly, John Foster Dulles's decision to cancel a loan for the Aswan Dam, precipitating the 1956 Suez crisis, was made virtually on his own. He refused to consult with, much less accept the advice of, the American ambassador to Egypt, Henry Byroade, whose assessment of the situation—a correct one as it turned out—did not correspond to his own. During the months that followed Dulles's action, Anthony Eden believed that Nasser couldn't keep the Suez Canal open because European pilots would quit and there were no trained Egyptians to replace them. In contrast to the Norwegian government, which had learned from captains who had been through the canal that little training or skill was required to become a pilot, Eden made no effort to confirm or disconfirm his erroneous belief.[55]

Increasing stress may produce one potentially counteracting change in communication. In his studies of information overload, Miller found that one of the widely used coping mechanisms is the use of parallel channels of communication, particularly in higher-level systems such as groups or organizations, as opposed to cells, organs, or individuals.[56] Decision makers may seek to bypass both the effects of information input overload and of distortion of content in transmission by the use of improvised *ad hoc* channels of communication. These may take many forms, including direct communication between heads of governments and employment of special emissaries, or mediators.

It has been noted at various points that the rate of diplomatic and other activities tends to increase sharply during a crisis.[57] It remains to consider whether high stress increases risk-taking, aggressiveness, and related aspects of foreign policy. Are we led to a position closely akin to the frustration-aggression hypotheses? The evidence is mixed. In some instances stress has resulted in higher risk-taking; in other cases persons in such situations have become more cautious because they demanded greater certainty before committing themselves.[58] Assessments of what constitutes high and low risk may, however, change in circumstances of severe stress. During the tense days preceding the outbreak of World War I, many European statesmen came to believe that rapid mobilization of their armies was the "safe" choice, even though they may have recognized that doing so might be considered equivalent to an act of war. Or, to cite a more recent example, Dean Acheson, William Fulbright, and Richard Russell argued in October 1962 that President Kennedy's decision to blockade Cuba represented a far higher risk than their preferred strategy of bombing or invading to remove the Soviet missiles.

Thus, high-stress situations may result in more aggressive policy choices, but the evidence presented here suggests a somewhat more complex process: crisis-induced stress gives rise to certain changes in perceptions of time, definition of alternatives, and patterns of communication. These, in turn, may reduce the effectiveness of both decision-making processes and the consequent policy choices, but not necessarily in the direction of higher risk taking.

It would be useful to specify the circumstances under which stress leads to aggression, appeasement, capitulation, attempts to withdraw from the situation, or other types of response. Unfortunately it is virtually impossible to do more than suggest some highly tentative hypotheses. For example, because stress often leads to a reduced ability to make fine distinctions, there may be a heightened tendency to see similarities between the present situation and previous events with which the decision makers have been associated. When faced with an intransigent Egypt in 1956, Anthony Eden drew an analogy between Nasser and Hitler. Harry Truman likewise saw a basic similarity between the Communist invasion of South Korea in 1950 and the expansion of other totalitarian systems during the 1930s. In these examples Eden and Truman drew upon the history of the 1930s—the period in which each reached national prominence—as a source of guidance, the latter far more successfully than the former.

A second very tentative hypothesis is that under conditions of high stress there will be a heightened tendency to maintain existing policies. This may appear to be a trite observation because there are always bureaucratic and other constraints which tend to act against sudden changes of policy. But because high-stress situations are often marked by reduced creativity and group pressures for conformity, we might suspect that only the presence of almost incontrovertible evidence of failure will give rise to substantial policy changes. It took the Nazi invasion of an already truncated Czechoslovakia in 1939 to cause Britain to abandon its conciliatory policy toward Hitler. Similarly, it was not until a conjunction of the Tet offensive, demands by General Westmoreland for 206,000 additional troops in Vietnam, and evidence from the New Hampshire primary election of massive public dissatisfaction that a basic shift in American policy in Southeast Asia occurred. Note, however, that in the first example the change was from a policy of negotiation and conciliation toward a more aggressive stance, whereas the reverse was true of the second.

Conclusion

The evidence suggests that policy making under circumstances of crisis-induced stress is likely to differ in a number of respects from decision-making processes in other situations. More important, to the extent that such differences exist they are likely to inhibit rather than facilitate the effectiveness of those engaged in the complex tasks of making foreign-policy choices.* Certainly this conclusion is consistent with the findings from experimental research.

While this literature is not lacking in empirical and quantitative findings, it is not wholly free from conceptual and operational problems. It cannot merely be assumed, for example, that results obtained with experimental subjects—usually students—are necessarily valid for persons of different age, culture, experience, and the like.† Nor is the usual technique of asking subjects

---

* An alternative view is that "decision-makers do not perceive or behave differently in a crisis." That is, "they do not perceive hostility where none exists, and they express hostility directly in terms of their perception of hostility." Dina A. Zinnes, Joseph Zinnes, and R. D. McClure, "Hostility in Diplomatic Communication: A Study of the 1914 Crisis," in Charles F. Hermann (ed.), *Contemporary Research in International Crisis* (New York: The Free Press, forthcoming). This does not demonstrate, however, that many other aspects of perception and behaviour may not change in crisis situations. Moreover, their conclusion does not rule out the possibility that mutual perceptions of hostility may be sustained and magnified beyond their original causes.

† Nor, of course, can it be assumed that they are *not* valid, or that the *converse* of the experimental findings are true.

to find the best answer to a problem or puzzle quite analogous to the task of the policy maker who may be confronted with a situation in which there is no single correct answer.

Perhaps an even more important question might be raised about the experimenter's ability to create a truly credible situation of high stress.[59] When human subjects are used, the stress situation in the laboratory must of necessity be relatively benign and of short duration. It is usually induced by leading the subject to believe that he has failed at his assigned task. In contrast, a foreign-policy official may perceive a crisis situation as a genuine threat to the continued existence of self, family, nation, or even mankind. Clearly the ethical experimenter cannot create an identical situation in the laboratory.

In short, these experimental findings suggest some questions about the "conventional wisdom" underlying several aspects of strategy and diplomacy in crises. But the answers can only be found in the real world of international crises, not in the laboratory.

The crisis leading up to the outbreak of World War I in 1914 provides an almost ideal situation in which to assess the effects of stress on policy-making processes. As Horvath points out in discussing the limitations of experimental research, the knotty problem of defining stress operationally poses fewer difficulties when one studies a situation "which seems obviously stressful to most individuals." [60] Even a cursory reading of diaries, memoirs, and other eyewitness accounts of events during the culminating days of the crisis reveals the intense stress under which all European leaders were making foreign-policy decisions. Admiral von Tirpitz wrote of his colleagues: "I have never seen a more tragic, more ravaged face than that of our Emperor during those days," and, "Since the Russian mobilization the Chancellor gave one the impression of a drowning man." [61] Walter Hines Page, the American ambassador in London, described even more vividly the effects of the crisis on Prince Lichnowsky: "I went to see the German Ambassador at 3 o'clock in the afternoon [August 5]. He came down in his pyjamas, a crazy man. I feared he might literally go mad. . . . the poor man had not slept for several nights." [62] Moreover, the rather widespread optimism about peace during the initial weeks after the assassination of the

Austrian archduke, Franz Ferdinand, provides an opportunity to compare differences between circumstances of relatively high and low stress.

Nineteen fourteen is also an almost classic example of a diplomatic crisis which very rapidly escalated beyond the calculations and control of those responsible for making foreign-policy decisions. This is not to say that in 1914 European nations were governed by monarchs, prime ministers, parliaments, and parties with a deep and unalterable devotion to peace. Nor is it to deny that competing imperial ambitions, trade rivalries, arms races, alliances, and rigid military plans may have been underlying sources of international instability; although these and many other attributes of the international system in 1914 were potent factors in shaping and constraining European diplomacy, the outbreak of war was the result of decisions which were made —or not made—by statesmen in Vienna, Belgrade, Berlin, St. Petersburg, Paris, and London. And the evidence indicates that general war in 1914 was not the goal of any European leaders, not even those who were willing to engage in diplomatic brinksmanship, or who sought the fruits of limited conflict, or who may have cherished long-range ambitions which could only be achieved by ultimate recourse to arms.°

Finally, the documentation on the crisis probably surpasses in quality and quantity that of any comparable event in history. Thus the events of 1914 provide an exceptional opportunity for examining the effects of stress on selected aspects of policy making.

° Fritz Fischer has demonstrated that German war aims, as they developed during 1914–1918, were imperialistic. No doubt the goals of other belligerents also expanded during the war, if only to justify the dreadful costs of the conflict. But I find quite unconvincing his severe indictment of German intentions during the prewar crisis. Fritz Fischer, Germany's Aims in the First World War (New York: W. W. Norton, 1967), ch. 2.

Chapter Two

THE 1914 CRISIS

1914: A Brief Overview

AS SUMMER APPROACHED the pace of diplomatic activity in Europe slowed perceptibly. Parliaments would soon be adjourning, statesmen and diplomats would be going on holiday and Europe seemed markedly free of diplomatic controversy, even in the Balkans. The threat of war between Greece and Turkey seemed to be passing, the Baghdad agreement between Germany and Great Britain had been initialled in May and the controversy between Germany and Russia on armaments appeared to have faded. Indeed, there were prospects that in contrast to the serious July crises of the three previous years July 1914 would be at least a peaceful interlude, if not a permanent respite from the threat of war.[1]

On 28 June, however, Archduke Franz Ferdinand, heir to the throne of Austria-Hungary, was assassinated in Sarajevo by a young Serbian nationalist. Although Franz Ferdinand was widely distrusted in Vienna because of his morganatic marriage and his somewhat liberal political views, his death was regarded by many Austrians as perhaps the last good opportunity to eliminate the "Greater Serbia" menace to the multinational Dual Monarchy.

At a meeting with top German officials a week later, a delegation of high-ranking Austrians was promised the full support of the Berlin government for a policy of severe punishment of Serbia. Indeed, instead of counselling restraint the Germans urged

Austria-Hungary to act quickly against Serbia while world opinion was still focused on the royal murder.

Thus encouraged by support from Berlin the Austrian Crown Council, after some initial dissent by Hungarian Premier Istvan Tisza, agreed to present Serbia with an ultimatum of almost unprecedented severity. War would follow in the likely case that all demands were not met. Originally scheduled for delivery in Belgrade on 20 July, the ultimatum was held back for three days in order not to coincide with a visit to Russia—Serbia's "protector"—by the French president and premier. For fear that the German foreign office would disapprove and counsel restraint, the text of the note to Serbia was kept secret from Germany until the day of delivery.

Any inclinations in Belgrade to accede to the entire ultimatum were dispelled by promises, albeit vague ones, of support from Russia. Before responding to the Austrian note Serbia mobilized. The Serbian reply, although conciliatory in tone, was evasive on several points and rejected one of them outright. Following carefully worded instructions from Vienna, the Austrian ambassador immediately deemed the Serbian reply unacceptable. Diplomatic relations with Serbia were severed and the entire Austrian diplomatic staff left Belgrade within the hour. Austria-Hungary also ordered a partial mobilization. Figures on the magnitude of these and other mobilizations are presented in Tables 1 and 2.

When the text of the Serbian reply became public there were widespread feelings that this latest Balkan crisis would pass without severe consequences. Kaiser Wilhelm, vacationing on his yacht in the North Sea, was exuberant that his ally had won a major diplomatic victory. He was also relieved that the need for further aggressive action had apparently vanished. Although Russian military preparations had begun on 25 July, two days later the tsar found little reason to worry about the peace of Europe. Lloyd George recalled that as late as 27 July every cabinet minister was convinced that the means to avoid a general European war would be found.[2] Even the "hawkish" British first lord of the admiralty, Winston Churchill, was confident that Serbia's response to the ultimatum marked the end of the war threat. Ironically, the aged and nearly senile Emperor Franz Joseph of Austria-Hungary was one of the few who foresaw the actual

TABLE 1

Mobilization of Armies in 1914

	Great Britain	France	Russia	Serbia	Monte-negro	Belgium	Austria-Hungary	Germany	Turkey
25 July				180,000			200,000[a]		
26 July									
27 July									
28 July					40,000				
29 July									
30 July			800,000[b]						
31 July			4,100,000[c]			186,000[d]	538,000[e]		
1 August		1,091,000[f]						4,000,000[g]	300,000[j]
2 August									
3 August									
4 August	420,000[h]	50,000[i]							

[a] 8 of 16 corps of the Imperial Army ordered mobilized: 3rd, 4th, 7th, 8th, 9th, 13th, 15th, 16th.

[b] Mobilization of following army corps: Odessa: 7th, 8th; Moscow: 5th, 13th, 17th, 25th, grenadiers; Kiev: 9th, 10th, 11th, 12th, 21st; Kazan: 16th, 24th. (500,000 regular troops, augmented by 300,000 reserves.)

[c] General mobilization includes remaining regular army units (an additional 900,000 men), plus all reserves.

[d] Includes field army of six divisions and one cavalry division (117,000), plus fortress troops in Antwerp, Liege, and Namur (69,000).

[e] Remaining 8 corps of the Imperial Army mobilized (250,000). One Landwehr (State army) division of 18,000 is attached to each army corps (288,000). In addition, the Landsturm (militia) is called up for the first time since 1866 (figures unavailable, thus total Austrian mobilization actually involved more men than 538,000).

[f] 5 French armies totalled 1,071,000 men, including reserve divisions. 20,000 additional troops readied in Tangiers for embarkation to France.

[g] The seven German armies (1st, 2nd, 3rd, 4th, 5th, 6th, 7th) participating in the Schlieffen plan totalled 1,700,000 men. Eastern front units included 5 corps (1st, 17th, 20th, 1st Reserve, 3rd Reserve), 1st Cavalry Division, 5 Ersatz divisions and 5 Landwehr brigades, totalling 314,500 men. One source, however, gives total German strength mobilized as 4,000,000 men. The remaining troops were probably Landwehr and Landsturm personnel.

[h] Regular army of six divisions and one cavalry division (120,000), plus Territorial Force of 14 divisions (300,000).

[i] Troops recalled from Morocco.

[j] General mobilization on 2 August. A dispatch quoted in Albertini (III, p. 614) cites the figure 300,000.

TABLE 2

Naval Mobilizations in 1914

Date	Nation	Type
15 July	Great Britain	Routine test mobilization [a]
24 July	Great Britain	Reservists dismissed [a]
25 July	Germany	Fleet ordered alerted by kaiser [b]
25 July	Russia	Baltic Fleet mobilized [c]
27 July	Great Britain	First and Second Fleets alerted by Churchill [d]
28 July	Great Britain	First Fleet ordered to Scapa Flow [e]
29 July	Germany	Fleet moves from Norway to home ports [f]
30 July	Great Britain	Churchill sends mobilization telegram without cabinet permission [g]
31 July	Russia	Baltic Fleet ordered to stay on high seas [c]
31 July	Austria-Hungary	Fleet mobilized [h]
1 August	France	Fleet ready [i]
2 August	Great Britain	Fleet mobilized; all reserves under fifty-five called [g]
3 August	France	Fleet sails from Toulon [i]

[a] 20,000 men   [b] 638,165 tons   [c] 196,100 tons   [d] 1.267,425 tons   [e] 881,715 tons
[f] 610,615 tons   [g] 1,722,610 tons   [h] 216,087 tons   [i] 697,108 tons

course of events. After Germany had promised Austria-Hungary full support he remarked, "Now we can no longer turn back. It will be a terrible war." The reaction of Arthur Nicolson, British under-secretary of state for foreign affairs, was more typical: "I have my doubts as to whether Austria will take any action of serious character and I expect the storm will blow over." [3]

As it became clear that these initial assessments were overly sanguine, several diplomatic moves were initiated to forestall war or, failing that, to keep it from spreading beyond the Balkans. Edward Grey, British foreign minister, proposed a four-power conference to settle the Austro-Serbian issue. Vienna and Berlin were willing to accept a conference to deal with the differences between Russia and Austria-Hungary, but they maintained that the Serbian issue was a question of "national honour" to be settled on Austria's terms, not those of an international body.

A second proposal, the "Halt in Belgrade" plan, was advanced almost simultaneously by several European statesmen as a means of satisfying Vienna's desire for a military as well as a diplomatic triumph. The proposal called for military activity to be limited to the occupation of the Serbian capital. Belgrade would, in effect, become a hostage to guarantee Serbian compliance with the Austrian ultimatum.

In the midst of these diplomatic efforts, Austria-Hungary declared war on Serbia and, on 29 July, began the bombardment of Belgrade. That evening a series of almost desperate telegrams was dispatched from Berlin to Vienna. Urgently but unsuccessfully they requested acceptance of the "Halt in Belgrade" plan.

Behind the belated German efforts to regain some control over Austrian policy was the spectre of Russian action to prevent the subjugation of Serbia. Earlier that day Russia had ordered a general mobilization, an act widely considered as tantamount to a declaration of war. At the last minute the tsar intervened and a partial mobilization of the southern military districts facing Austria-Hungary was ordered instead. Despite German warnings, however, the general mobilization of Russian forces was reinstated the next day. Russian generals, well aware that any effort to put into effect a partial mobilization would have made it impossible to undertake a full-scale call to arms in the near future, persuaded the tsar to change his mind once again.

The Berlin government proclaimed a "state of threatening danger of war" and dispatched to St. Petersburg a twelve-hour ultimatum which demanded cessation of Russian military preparations on the German frontier. On 1 August Germany mobilized. Having failed to receive an answer to the ultimatum, Germany declared war on Russia later that evening.

In the meanwhile the German ambassador in Paris had demanded to know what France's attitude would be in case war broke out between Germany and France's ally, Russia. The French reply—"France will be guided by her own interests"—coincided with orders for general mobilization in Paris and Berlin, as well as the German declaration of war on Russia.

Germany's long-standing strategy for a two-front war, the Schlieffen plan, called for a holding action against Russia and a rapid victory in the west by means of an invasion of France through Belgium. A German request to cross Belgium, in exchange for a guarantee of Belgian territorial integrity, was re-

TABLE 3
Summary of Major Events, June–August 1914

Date	Event
28 June	Archduke Franz Ferdinand of Austria-Hungary assassinated by a member of a Serbian terrorist organization
5 July	Germany assures Austria-Hungary of complete support in measures to be taken against Serbia (the "blank cheque")
7 July	Premier Tisza of Hungary opposes war against Serbia at Austrian Crown Council
13 July	Baron von Wiesner reports inability to find proof of Serbian government complicity in assassination
14 July	At Austrian Crown Council, Tisza won over to war policy
20–23 July	French president and premier visit Russia
23 July	Austria-Hungary presents Serbia with a ten-point ultimatum, to be answered within forty-eight hours
24 July	Russia warns that Serbia is not to be devoured by Austria-Hungary
25 July	Serbia mobilizes
	Serbia replies to ultimatum, accepting some demands, rejecting or evading others
	Austria-Hungary rejects Serbian reply and breaks diplomatic relations
	Austria-Hungary orders partial mobilization
	Russian Ministerial Council agrees to take military measures preparatory to mobilization
	Austria-Hungary assures Russia that no Serbian territory will be annexed
	France assures Russia of support
26 July	Grey of Great Britain proposes conference to deal with Balkan issue, but Austria-Hungary refuses to submit a question of "national honour" to judgment of others
27 July	France begins military preparations
	British fleet ordered not to disband following exercises
	Grey promises diplomatic support to Russia
28 July	Austria-Hungary declares war on Serbia
	End of talks between Austria-Hungary and Russia on Balkan crisis
	France renews expressions of support to Russia
29 July	Germany warns Russia not to mobilize
	Russia orders, then cancels, general mobilization
	Russia orders partial mobilization, against Austria-Hungary
	Austro-Hungarian bombardment of Belgrade begins

Table 3 (*continued*)

Date		Event
29	July	Germany repeatedly requests Austria-Hungary to accept "Halt in Belgrade" plan, but without success
30	July	Russia orders general mobilization
		Talks between Russia and Austria-Hungary resume
31	July	Austria-Hungary orders general mobilization
		Germany declares "state of threatening danger of war"
		Germany issues twelve-hour ultimatum to Russia to stop military measures on the German frontier
		In answer to British inquiry, Germany refuses to guarantee respect of Belgian neutrality
		Germany inquires about French attitude in case of Russo-German war
1	August	France informs Germany: "France will be guided by her own interests"
		France orders general mobilization
		Germany orders general mobilization
		Germany declares war on Russia
2	August	Germany requests permission to cross Belgian territory; Belgium rejects this
		British cabinet votes to protect French coast against German attack
		Germany invades Luxembourg
3	August	Germany invades Belgium
		Germany declares war on France
4	August	Great Britain issues twelve-hour ultimatum to Germany; when no reply is received, Great Britain declares war on Germany

jected by Brussels. The Schlieffen plan had already been put into motion, however; within hours Germany invaded Luxembourg and Belgium, and declared war on France.

Although allied to France and Russia, Great Britain's position throughout the crisis had been equivocal. Until the end of July many British officials were more concerned with the threat of civil war over the Irish question than with the Balkan situation. Several somewhat ambiguous messages transmitted by unofficial sources to Berlin sustained the kaiser's hopes that Britain might stay out of the conflict altogether; the accurate warnings of Prince Lichnowsky, German ambassador in London, were largely disregarded. The British cabinet was badly divided and sentiment within the financial community and influential parts of the press was decidedly against steps which might lead to war. Some military measures, including mobilization of the fleet, were taken but urgent French requests for full British support were rebuffed.

The German invasion of Belgium, however, provided Grey with a sufficient issue around which to unite virtually the entire cabinet. On 4 August a twelve-hour ultimatum was sent to Germany. When, at midnight, Berlin had failed to answer, Great Britain declared war on Germany.

Thus, less than six weeks after the assassination and only seven days after a "minor" war had broken out between Austria-Hungary and Serbia, every major power in Europe was at war (see Table 3 for a more detailed summary of these developments). The diplomacy of July had failed to prevent a general war, the "guns of August" [4] would fail to provide either side with a quick victory, and during the next four years an additional fifty-six declarations of war brought into the conflict a large part of the world, including China, Japan, Italy, Turkey, Brazil, and the United States. When fighting finally stopped in November 1918, Austria-Hungary was in dissolution, Germany was on the edge of civil war and the Bolshevik revolution had destroyed the Russian monarchy. France and Great Britain had emerged on the side of the victors, but at a cost more frightful than even the most pessimistic would have foreseen in August 1914.

Escalation of this diplomatic crisis into a general war can be described more systematically by examining the political, economic, military, and other actions of European nations during the summer of 1914. Sources for these data included monographs, histories, and contemporary newspapers. In addition to international actions a number of domestic events with obvious external implications (declarations of martial law in frontier towns, requisitions of food for the military, and the like) were coded.

Each discrete action was coded and recorded in a uniform format, with identification of the *acting nation*, the *action*, and the *target*. The coding yielded 448 actions, of which the following are examples.

DATE	ACTING NATION	ACTION	TARGET
10 July	France	Chamber approves three-year military law	General
14 July	Germany	Armaments budget increased by $250,000,000	General
24 July	Russia	Russian foreign minister accuses Austrian ambassador: "The fact is, you want war and have burned your bridges"	Austria-Hungary
26 July	Germany	German ambassador gives Russian foreign minister a friendly but firm warning, "concerning the news according to which it is supposed that mobilization orders have been issued"	Russia
29 July	Serbia	Serbia withdraws troops from Bulgarian border (because Bulgaria declares neutrality)	Bulgaria
4 August	Great Britain	Great Britain declares war on Germany	Germany

These data were then rated for *intensity of threat* on a fixed-distribution scale of 1 (lowest intensity) to 9 (highest intensity).[*] The crisis-related actions of all countries are summarized in Figure 1 (the data for each nation are reported in the appendix). The results indicate that the frequency of actions increased six-fold between the first month and the final week of the crisis pe-

[*] This method of scaling, the Q-sort, is described further in the appendix. The intercoder reliability for the action data was .853.

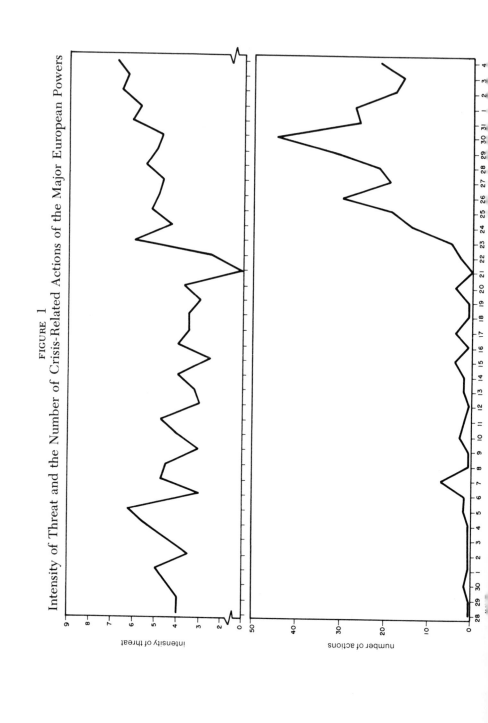

FIGURE 1

Intensity of Threat and the Number of Crisis-Related Actions of the Major European Powers

riod.* The rise in the intensity of threat was much less regular. There were isolated instances of violence (e.g. border skirmishes between Serbia and Bulgaria) even before Austria-Hungary declared war on Serbia. Nor was the final week characterized solely by ultimata, mobilizations, declarations of war, and invasions. Through the end of July there were continued diplomatic efforts to contain the escalation—for example, the steady stream of telegrams from Berlin to Vienna and St. Petersburg on the night of 29–30 July, trying to forestall an Austro-Russian war in which Germany would certainly become involved.†

The Measurement of Stress

This brief overview suggests that the 1914 crisis satisfies the most widely used definition of a stressful situation—one that "seems to be threatening to most people." [5] For present purposes, however, this definition is not sufficiently precise to be very useful. Aside from its ambiguity it fails to provide any guidelines for measuring stress. Moreover, it is of little assistance for assessing *changing levels of stress* within the crisis period.

The latter problem could be overcome by examining the level of threat at various points within the crisis period. The data described in Figure 1 could serve as an index if we assume that for any given action an "objective" assessment of threat will correspond to the subjective interpretations of policy makers in 1914.

There is ample evidence, however, that this assumption may not always be tenable. Many actions can be interpreted in several ways. Indeed, a single event can give rise to quite contradictory interpretations even by persons working within the same national, cultural, and organizational environment. When the

---

* This may be in part an artifact of the sources. Dramatic events such as mobilizations and declarations of war are more likely to be reported by newspapers and historians than are the normal transactions which constitute the bulk of international relations. Even allowing for this, however, the almost around-the-clock schedules in many foreign and war offices attests to the unusually hectic pace of events during the climactic stages of the crisis period.

† For a different interpretation of these diplomatic efforts, see Fritz Fischer, *Germany's Aims in the First World War* (New York: Norton, 1967), chs. 1–2. Fischer argued that these were merely cynical attempts to make Germany appear the victim rather than the instigator of a European war.

Soviet Union reduced its armed forces by 1.2 million men in 1956, this was viewed as a conciliatory action by Harold Stassen and as a threat by John Foster Dulles, who regarded it as a sign that the Soviets would place greater reliance upon nuclear weapons. Even a casual survey of events during the summer of 1914 reveals some surprising interpretations of events by European statesmen. Kaiser Wilhelm viewed the presence of a few Russian torpedo boats in the North Sea as a severe threat to his navy, for example, and a senior official in the British foreign office perceived the situation arising from the assassination as a series of inconsequential events which would soon "blow away." For present purposes it is these views of "reality" which are of interest; whether or not such interpretations were accurate is of less importance.

The most useful approach, then, is one which takes into account how foreign-policy officials perceived and interpreted the situation during the crisis period. In order to avoid the problem of circularity the measure of stress and its predicted effects must also be independent. We cannot, for instance, use perceptions of time pressure as evidence of stress and then test the proposition that increasing stress will give rise to feelings of time pressure. *Perceptions of international hostility* provide an index which satisfies all the above criteria. The relevance of this measure also receives substantial support from a systematic study of thirty-two crises; correlations between perceptions of hostility and threats of violence, consideration of violent alternatives, and decisions to use violence were consistently high (over .50).[6]

Ideally we might gather data that reveal the perceptions and attitudes of statesmen during a period of interest by any of several standard methods, including observation, interviews, questionnaires, and the like. But, aside from the fact that the events in question occurred over a half-century ago, the nature of foreign-policy crises rules out virtually all direct methods of generating data.

Under these circumstances, the best and most revealing evidence is to be found in the documents written by policy makers at the time of the crisis. The primary sources of data in this and subsequent chapters are the British, French, Russian, German, and Austro-Hungarian collections of diplomatic documents written during the five and a half weeks following the assassination of Franz Ferdinand.[7] *

Immediately after the outbreak of war in August 1914 each of the major European governments published a collection of documents relating to the prewar crisis. Given the circumstances and motivations surrounding their publication, it is hardly surprising that these "colour books" are replete with alterations, omissions, and deletions, especially of materials which might have proved damaging to claims of innocence for the war. The most notorious of these is the French Yellow Book which is worthless save as an example of wartime propaganda.

After the war, however, respected archivists and historians were commissioned to collect, edit, and publish collections free of the glaring weakness that characterized the colour books. Although there may have been political motives for initiating some of these projects—both the Weimar and Soviet regimes, for instance, no doubt felt that the full disclosure would tend to discredit the prewar governments in those countries—the resulting collections are unquestionably authentic. For the crisis period they include almost six thousand documents totalling some 1.4 million words. Unfortunately, comparable materials are not available for Serbia. Neither the Serbian nor the Yugoslavian government has published such a collection, and their archives have remained inaccessible.

Examples of these documents appear in Figures 2 and 3. The first is a telegram from Edward Goschen, British ambassador in Berlin, to the foreign minister. In addition to the full text, the time of dispatch and receipt, and comments by other officials in the foreign office to whom the telegram was circulated (Eyre Crowe and Arthur Nicolson) are provided. Note also that a paraphrased † and incomplete version of the message has been published earlier as document no. 108 in the British Blue Book of 6 August 1914. The tsar's telegram to the kaiser includes the uninhibited and usually very revealing annotations by Wilhelm

---

* These collections are hereafter cited as Britain, France, Russia, Germany, and Austria-Hungary.

† Documents sent in code or cypher (including that in Figure 2) were paraphrased in the Blue Book to prevent cracking of the British code.

FIGURE 2

Telegram from the Ambassador in Berlin to the Foreign Minister,
with Comments by Sir Eyre Crowe and Arthur Nicolson

(35051)

No. 337.

Sir E. Goschen to Sir Edward Grey.
Berlin, July 31, 1914.
D. 11:55 A.M.
R. 1:45 P.M.

Tel. (No. 107.)
Austria and Servia. Chancellor informs me that he has just received news to the effect that Russia has burnt her cordon of houses
along German frontier, sealed her public offices in neighbourhood of
frontier and carried off her money chests into the interior. He has
been unable to get absolute confirmation of this intelligence, as Russo-
German frontier was now entirely closed, but if, as he thinks, it is true,
it can only mean that Russia looks upon war as certain, and that she
is now taking military measures on the German frontier. This news
reaches him, he said, just as the Tsar has appealed to the Emperor in
the name of their old friendship to mediate at Vienna, and when the
Emperor is doing so. Chancellor added that he himself had done
everything possible and even more perhaps than Austro-Hungarian
Government liked at Vienna to preach moderation and peace, but his
efforts had been seriously handicapped by the mobilisation of Russia against Austria. If now the news he had received proved true
and military measures were also being taken against Germany, he
could not remain quiet, as he could not leave his country defenceless
while other Powers were gaining time. He was now going to see
the Emperor and he wished me to tell you that it was quite possible
that in a very short time, perhaps even to-day, they would have to
take some very serious step.
(Repeated to Embassies.)

Published in BB No. 108 (*paraphrased and parts omitted*).
Cf. No. 677.

MINUTES.

This is an endeavour to throw the blame for military preparations on Russia. All
our information shows that short of the issue of actual "mobilization orders" in set
terms, German mobilization has for some time been actively proceeding on all three
German frontiers.—*E. A. C. July* 31.

Russia is taking very reasonable and sensible precautions, which should in no wise
be interpreted as provocative. Germany, of course, who has been steadily preparing
now wishes to throw the blame on Russia—a very thin pretext. However comments
are superfluous.—*A. N.*

Source: Great Britain, p. 214. Reprinted by permission.

FIGURE 3
Telegram from Tsar Nicholas to Kaiser Wilhelm

No. 390

The Czar to the Emperor [4]

Telegram (unnumbered). PETERHOF PALACE, *July 30, 1914.*[5]
To HIS MAJESTY THE EMPEROR, NEW PALACE.

Thank you heartily for your quick answer. Am sending Tatistcheff this evening with instructions. The *military measures which have now* [6] *come into force* [7] *were decided five days ago* [8] for reasons of *defense* [9] *on account of Austria's* [10] preparations.[11] I hope from all my heart that these measures *won't in any way interfere* with your part as mediator which I greatly value. *We need your strong pressure on Austria* [12] to come to an *understanding with us.*

NICKY.

°)
No!
No there is
no thought
of anything
of that sort!!!

° *Austria has only made a <u>partial</u> mobilization against <u>Serbia</u> in the south. On the strength of that the Czar—as is openly admitted by him here —instituted "mil. measures which have <u>now come into force</u>" against Austria and us and as a matter of fact five* [13] *days ago. Thus it is almost a week ahead of us. And these measures are for <u>defense</u> against <u>Austria, which is <u>in no way</u> attacking him!!!</u> I can not agree to any more mediation, since the Czar who requested it has at the same time secretly mobilized behind my back. It is only a maneuver, in order to hold us back and to increase the start they have already got. My work is at an end!*

W.

[4] From the corrected copy [in English] of the Telegraph Office at the New Palace. Cf. German White Book of May, 1915, p. 35, No. 22, VI. There the telegram is dated 1:20 p.m. See also Nos. 359 and 366. See further No. 413.

[5] Filed at Peterhof Palace at 1:20 a.m.; arrived at the Telegraph Office at the New Palace at 1:45 a.m.; receipt stamp of the Foreign Office, July 30, p.m.

[6] "now" twice underscored by the Emperor.

[7] "force" twice underscored by the Emperor.

[8] "five" thrice, "days" twice underscored by the Emperor.

[9] "defense" twice underscored by the Emperor.

[10] "Austria" twice underscored by the Emperor.

[11] Exclamation-point by the Emperor on the left margin.

[12] The words "strong . . . Austria" twice underscored by the Emperor.

[13] "five" twice underscored by the Emperor.

Source: Germany, p. 342. Reprinted by permission.

as well as footnotes by the editors adding further details about the message.

In no historical situation are we in possession of all relevant documents. The 1914 collections, although far richer than most, represent only a *sample* rather than the entire universe of communication within and between foreign offices.[8] The adequacy and representativeness of historical materials may depend on many factors.

Perhaps the most important reason for lack of completeness is that many communications—face-to-face and telephone conversations, meetings at which minutes were not kept, and the like— were not recorded.* The content of these messages, however, can often be determined and cross-checked for accuracy from memoirs, diaries, or other sources. In addition, many private letters were made available after the war to editors of the various collections.

Even early drafts of many documents were preserved, along with the annotations of various officials to whom they were circulated, but inevitably some of them have been lost. Missing data may also be attributed to mis-filing or destruction of documents, either intentionally or inadvertently, by personnel in the foreign offices.† Duplicate copies may exist, however. A message lost or destroyed by the sender can often be found within the recipient's files.

Finally, bias or carelessness by those commissioned to collect and edit documents could have seriously affected the representativeness of the data. The criteria of inclusion and exclusion used by the editors of the 1914 collections indicate that in the present instance this is not a major problem. According to J. W. Headlam-Morley, historical adviser to the British foreign office:

---

* Note Richard E. Neustadt's assessment of the impact of technology on historical records: "The telephone and copying machine combine to falsify the files as sources of historical reconstruction. The one may leave no record, while the other makes so many that few men entrust their full thoughts to papers." *Alliance Politics* (New York: Columbia University Press, 1970), p. 7. Copying machines were not, of course, available in 1914, and few statesmen of that period would have foreseen that their files would be published soon after the end of a catastrophic war.

† In any case, there does not appear to have been any deliberate attempt to destroy entire files of the 1914 documents, as Anthony Eden is reported to have done with records relating to the Suez invasion of 1956. *Ibid.*, p. xi.

When it had been determined that a new edition should be issued, the question had to be considered on what principle this should be prepared. It would have been possible simply to publish in its original and unparaphrased form the complete text of the documents already published [in the British Blue Book of August 1914] inserting those passages which had been omitted and adding to them such documents of obvious political importance as had not been included. This would not have been satisfactory. It certainly would not have satisfied the criticisms and stilled the suspicions which had been aroused. The only thing to do was to publish the whole correspondence, including every telegram and dispatch, however unimportant and incorrect, in any way relating to the origins of the war. This is the course which has been pursued, and *the reader has before him in this edition everything, within the specified dates, contained in the Foreign Office records which appeared to have a bearing on the origin and outbreak of the war. He is in possession of all the documentary material which the Secretary of State and his advisers had before them at the time.*[9]

Similar standards appear to have been used by those responsible for editing the other collections.

In summary, these documents represent a very substantial but nevertheless incomplete record of relevant diplomatic communications in 1914. Although the possibility that the missing evidence may be qualitatively different from these documents cannot be dismissed with absolute certainty, it appears reasonable to assume that the available data are a representative sample.°

With several exceptions,† the data reported in this and subsequent chapters are derived from a sub-set of these documents—those written by or on behalf of designated top-ranking foreign-policy officials during the period between 27 June and Great Britain's declaration of war on Germany at midnight, 4 August.‡ Persons occupying such positions as head of state,

° A wide variety of sources other than primary documents have also been consulted, including standard histories of the period, biographies, and monographic studies; diaries and memoirs of participants; contemporary newspapers and journals; and the like. These have been used primarily as sources of anecdotal evidence, details, and to cross-check information.

† For some parts of the present analysis additional materials were also used. The analysis of patterns of communication in Chapter 4 is based on *all* 5620 documents appearing in the five major collections, and a number of Serbian and ambassadorial reports were included in parts of the analysis in Chapter 3.

‡ No data for Austria-Hungary are available beyond 31 July, however, as its eight-volume collection ends on that date.

head of government, or foreign minister were included, unless there was a clear indication that they had no part whatsoever in the formulation of policies. Several other persons who played a prominent part during the crisis were added to this list. Excluded were the 2807 reports from ambassadors, consuls, and attachés to their foreign offices which represent almost exactly one-half of the documents in the 1914 collections. Although reports of diplomats serving abroad are of undeniable importance, these officials served primarily as channels of communication rather than as formulators of policy.

No further sampling within the set of documents meeting the criteria of authorship (Table 4 shows the foreign-policy officials who fall within this category) and time (27 June—4 August) was used. The entire verbatim text of these messages was subjected to content analysis, a technique for making inferences by objectively and systematically identifying specified characteristics of messages.[10]

For coding purposes a theme was defined as a unit of text with no more than one each of the following elements: a *perceiver,* a perceived *agent,* an *action* or *attitude,* and a *target.* For example, one of the kaiser's marginal notes on a telegram from the tsar read: "Austria has only made a partial mobilization against Serbia in the south. On the strength of that the Czar—as is openly admitted by him here—instituted 'mil [itary] measures which have now come into force' against Austria and us and as a matter of fact five days ago."[11] Three themes were coded from this passage.

PERCEIVER	AGENT	ACTION OR ATTITUDE	TARGET
Germany (Wilhelm)	Austria	has only made a partial mobilization against	Serbia
Germany (Wilhelm)	The tsar (Russia)	instituted mil [itary] measures which have now come into force against	Austria
Germany (Wilhelm)	The tsar (Russia)	instituted mil [itary] measures which have now come into force against	us (Germany)

TABLE 4

Foreign-Policy Officials, June–August 1914

Position°	Austria-Hungary	Germany	Great Britain	France	Russia
Head of State	Franz Joseph	Wilhelm II	George V	Poincaré	Nicholas II
Head of Government	Stürgkh°° Tisza	Bethmann-Hollweg	Asquith	Viviani	
Foreign Minister	Berchtold	Jagow	Grey	Viviani	Sazonov
Under-Secretary for Foreign Affairs / Other Officials in Foreign Office	Forgach Macchio Hoyos	Zimmermann Stumm	Nicolson	Bienvenu-Martin Berthelot Ferry	
Minister of War / Chief of General Staff	Conrad	Moltke		Messimy	Sukhomlinov
Others			Haldane°°°		

° Position refers to functionally equivalent roles, not to formal titles, which varied from nation to nation.

°° Stürgkh was Austro-Hungarian minister-president; Tisza was Hungarian prime minister.

°°° Lord Chancellor.

The 1914 documents yielded 5078 such themes, of which 1096 were coded as perceptions of hostility.[*] After masking, each theme was rated for *intensity* of perceived hostility by a series of judges on a scale of 1 to 9 with a distribution among categories which approximates a normal curve.

Data on perceptions of hostility during the 1914 crisis are summarized in Figure 4. (The data for each nation are reported in the appendix.) They reveal a consistent increase in the number of perceptions of hostility throughout the crisis period. Because the number of documents from which they were drawn also increased sharply [†] as war approached, the rising frequency of hostile perceptions might merely reflect the increasing volume of diplomatic communications. However, the mean intensity of perceived hostility is independent of the number of documents under analysis, and for that reason it will be used as the measure of stress.[‡]

Unlike the action data described in Figure 1, the intensity of perceived hostility increased virtually without interruption throughout the crisis period. This suggests that although there were a number of diplomatic efforts to reverse the escalation toward general war, these had relatively little impact on the manner in which European statemen defined the situation.

---

[*] The reliability coefficients for coding hostile themes and for scaling were .80 and .74 respectively. The other themes were coded as perceptions of friendship, frustration, satisfaction, and change of status quo. These data are reported in Ole R. Holsti, Robert C. North, and Richard A. Brody, "Perception and Action in the 1914 Crisis," in J. David Singer (ed.), *Quantitative International Politics: Insights and Evidence* (New York: The Free Press, 1968), pp. 146–148.

[†] For quantitative evidence on this point see Chapter 4.

[‡] If frequency and intensity of perceived hostility were highly correlated the choice between them would make little difference. This is not, however, the case. A measure of association for rank-ordered data (Goodman-Kruskal *gamma*) reveals the absence of a consistently strong relation between the frequency and intensity measures:

Austria-Hungary	.26
Germany	.53
France	.15
Great Britain	.25
Russia	.34

Intensity and Frequency of Perceptions of Hostility: All Nations

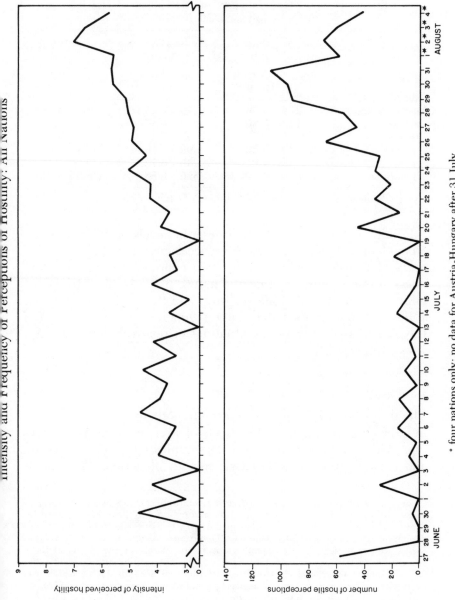

° four nations only; no data for Austria-Hungary after 31 July

TABLE 5
Frequency and Mean Intensity of Perceptions of Hostility
27 June–28 July and 29 July–4 August

	27 June–28 July		29 July–4 August		Entire Period	
	N	Mean Intensity	N	Mean Intensity	N	Mean Intensity
Austria-Hungary °	274	4.00	48	5.25	322	4.18
Germany	127	3.86	249	6.17	376	5.39
Great Britain	31	4.71	95	5.22	126	5.10
France	55	4.66	99	6.16	154	5.63
Russia	83	4.91	35	5.72	118	5.10
All Nations	570	4.20	526	5.88	1096	5.01

° Austro-Hungarian documents available through 31 July only.

Finally, in some cases we will describe levels of stress in terms other than daily changes. On these occasions we will compare aspects of decision making under two conditions—high and low stress. Table 5 indicates that the month prior to the outbreak of military hostilities (27 June–28 July) and the week during which a limited conflict escalated into a general European war (29 July–4 August) can serve as situations of relatively low and high stress, respectively.°

Conclusion

The discussion in Chapter 1 and the hypotheses to be considered in later chapters examine the effects of stress upon decision making, with special emphasis on communications, time pressure, and identification of alternative courses of action. The opera-

° The choice of 28–29 July as the dividing line between the two periods is, of course, arbitrary. The cases for 19–20 July and 27–28 July have been argued by Gordon Hilton, "The Stanford Studies of the 1914 Crisis: Some Comments" (London: mimeo., 1969); and John Mueller, "Deterrence, Numbers and History" (Security Studies Project, UCLA, 1969), respectively. Whatever the merits of these alternatives (which are also arbitrary choices), the 28–29 July cutting point satisfies two important criteria. The outbreak of war, the first full day of which was 29 July, is a clear and intuitively satisfying point at which to divide the crisis period. Secondly, both the intensity of threat in the action data ($Z = 3.14$, $p = .001$) and perceptions of hostility ($Z = 13.3$, $p < .0001$) were significantly higher during 29 July–4 August than during the earlier period.

tional definition of the independent variable—the level of stress —has been discussed above. Before defining the dependent variables more precisely and testing the hypotheses, however, it is worth considering two problems of validity. First, how much confidence can be placed in measures derived by content analyses of documentary data? Does the intensity of perceived hostility, for instance, actually measure the concept—stress—which it is purported to represent? The results summarized in Figure 4 seem reasonable. There appears to be a close correspondence, for example, between these data and the chronology of major events during the crisis period, as summarized in Tables 1–3. Thus the requirements of "face validity" seem to have been met. Because this study is so heavily dependent on content analysis data, however, it is important to take further and more systematic steps to explore the question of validity.

The second issue concerns the validity of aggregating data about individuals—the officials listed in Table 4—to test hypotheses about nations or even coalitions of nations. This procedure is valid only if it can be demonstrated that differences between individual policy makers within a given country are sufficiently small to permit aggregation without serious distortion. Stated differently, the more similar the parts (individuals) with respect to the variables in this analysis, the more validly we can represent the whole (nation) as the sum of the parts.

Chapter Three

DOCUMENTARY EVIDENCE IN THE STUDY OF CRISIS: TWO VALIDITY EXPERIMENTS

IN EXAMINING THE EFFECT of crisis-related stress on those who formulate foreign policies, we adopt the perspective of "decision-making" approaches to international politics and foreign policy: the nation is defined as the officials who are authorized to act on its behalf.° To recreate the situation as viewed by European leaders in 1914 we are relying very substantially on data derived from diplomatic documents. But can we assume the validity of the documentary evidence and the measures developed by content analysis? Is it valid to define the nation as the sum of a small group of individuals? This chapter describes two experiments designed to test these premises.

*Perceptions of Hostility and Financial
Indices in a Crisis*

When content analysis is used merely to describe certain attributes of documents, validity is rarely more than a minor problem once adequate steps have been taken to ensure the absence of

---

° *"State action is the action taken by those acting in the name of the state.* Hence, the state is its decision-makers. State X as *actor* is translated into its decision-makers as actors. It is also one of our basic choices to take as our prime analytical objective the re-creation of the 'world' of the decision-makers as *they* view it. The manner in which *they* define situations becomes another way of saying how the state oriented to action and why." Richard C. Snyder, H. W. Bruck, and Burton M. Sapin (eds.), *Foreign Policy Decision Making* (New York: The Free Press, 1962), p. 65.

systematic sampling and coding error. Because the 1914 documents are used to test hypotheses about the attitudes and perceptions of their authors, however, the question of validity is a critical one. Owing to possible differences in style, conscious efforts to deceive, and the like, the data are not self-validating. In order to draw conclusions about authors from the messages they produce, content data must therefore be validated, *directly* or *indirectly*, with independent indices.

Direct and systematic methods of validation—for example, interviewing or observing decision makers during the crisis—are rarely feasible in any circumstances, and certainly not when the events under analysis took place over a half century ago. Alternatively, one could search for eyewitness reports which would confirm or refute inferences drawn from the diplomatic documents. Reports drawn from diaries and memoirs of those who took part in the 1914 decisions are in fact consistent with the content data.° But at best such evidence is anecdotal and unsystematic; at times it may even be highly suspect, as in the case of memoirs written years after the actual events. In short, although it would have been desirable to have direct, systematic, and reliable evidence regarding the attitudes, perceptions, and values of decision makers in the various capitals of Europe during the summer of 1914, data of this type were not available.

An alternative strategy is the indirect approach to validation adopted here. The content data were compared with a series of financial indices, which met several criteria, and were available in quantitative form in sources of established authenticity. Several such sources, including major daily and financial newspapers were used.[1] They had to be reported on a daily basis; hence such otherwise useful data as trade statistics,† which are usually reported annually, quarterly, or monthly were of little

---

° See, for example, the descriptions of Kaiser Wilhelm, Bethmann-Hollweg, and Prince Lichnowsky that appear in Chapter 1.

† For example, Sino-Soviet trade figures since 1950 reveal a pattern of decreasing cooperation well *before* the open break between these two nations. See Ole R. Holsti and John D. Sullivan, "National-International Linkages: France and China as Non-Conforming Alliance Members," in James N. Rosenau (ed.), *Linkage Politics: Essays on the Convergence of National and International Systems* (New York: The Free Press, 1969), pp. 178–180.

value in this instance. And, most importantly, they had to be indices whose sensitivity to changes in the international political climate can be demonstrated. Figures on the international flow of gold, the prices of securities, commodities, currency, and the like satisfied the first two requirements. We shall return to the third one later.

The logic of this analysis, summarized in Figure 5, is as follows. International events are salient not only for political leaders. The financial community must also be sensitive to international developments because virtually all forms of investment are affected by them. The perceptions of political leaders have been measured by content analysis of documents; at issue is the validity of the findings. For this experiment our measure of stress—intensity of perceived hostility (as reported in Figure 4)—was selected because it will be used later for testing hypotheses. The attitudes of financial elites can be measured directly with a high degree of precision and reliability by changes in various financial indices. We may then compare the results. If we consistently find good correlations between the financial and content data, our confidence in the validity of the latter is enhanced; if not, the value of the content analysis data is open to serious question.

THE PRICES OF STOCKS AND BONDS

Marxist clichés to the contrary notwithstanding, the threat of war is rarely viewed favourably by the financial community. In common with most events that create widespread uncertainty about the future—for example the assassination of John F. Kennedy—the onset of a major international crisis very often sets off massive dumping of securities, driving their prices down precipitously. Even gilt-edged government bonds issued by prospective belligerents are likely to suffer, all the more so if there is any reason to suspect that the issuing government will not survive a protracted war. Anyone who sold tsarist Russian bonds for whatever price they might fetch in July 1914 showed keener foresight than those who purchased them. We may therefore expect securities to rise and fall in concert with optimism and pessimism about the prospects for peace.

In 1914 securities exchanges operated in the capitals of all the

FIGURE 5
Design of an Experiment to Test the Validity of
the 1914 Content-Analysis Data

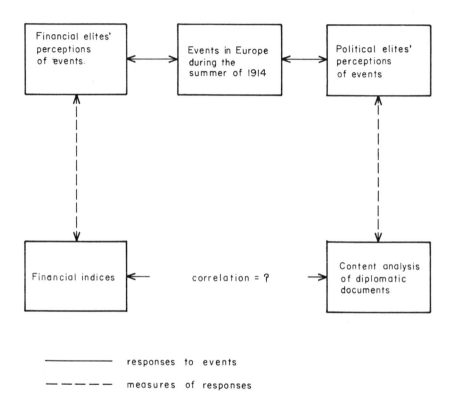

major European powers. The data used here consist of stocks and bonds traded on the London, St. Petersburg, Paris, Berlin, Vienna, and Brussels exchanges. Selection of stocks and bonds for analysis from among the many issues traded on various exchanges was somewhat arbitrary. None of the European exchanges had a standard index, comparable to the Dow-Jones or Standard and Poor's averages on the New York Stock Exchange, designed to summarize trends in price movements of all issues. It was thus necessary to devise a substitute. Twenty stocks and bonds issued in Serbia, Russia, Austria-Hungary, Germany, France, Great Britain, and Belgium were selected. Although Belgium was not directly involved in the crisis arising from the assassination, the Bank of Brussels stock was included because it was common knowledge that, in case of war between France and Germany, the Schlieffen plan called for a sweep of German armies through Belgium. An effort was made to select widely owned "blue chip" securities, the prices of which would be more likely to reflect widespread attitudes toward the future within the financial community, rather than more speculative issues whose prices might be responding to events other than international ones. To facilitate interpretation, the price of each security is given as a percentage of its value during the pre-crisis week (20–26 June). The index is the average value for the twenty securities.

Table 6 reveals that the pattern of changes in perceived hostility is matched by that in security prices. This is true when the *gamma* coefficient, a summary statistic, is calculated with the data grouped into nine periods,° as well as when the correlation is calculated on a daily basis.† When the composite index is compared to changes in the intensity of perceived hostility, the similarity is evident. It is interesting to note, for example, that the marked drop in perceived hostility on 27 July was matched by an improvement in stock prices. Some of the best gains were made by issues which would be most directly affected by the outbreak

---

° These periods were used in several earlier studies of the 1914 crisis because they each contained an approximately equal number of themes drawn from the diplomatic documents by content analysis.

† The Goodman-Kruskal *gamma* correlation coefficient is a measure of the association or agreement between two sets of rank-ordered data. This statistic is identical to the more familiar Kendall *tau* when there are no ties in the rankings of either variable. When there are tied ranks (as is often true in the data to be examined in this and other chapters), the value of *tau* cannot reach unity and, therefore, it does not have a simple interpretation. The range for *gamma*, on the other hand, is between ±1.00 and .00 even with tied scores. In the present instance a *gamma* coefficient of 1.00 indicates that the period with the highest stress also had the lowest security prices, the period with the second highest stress had the second lowest prices, and so on through the entire period. For a further discussion, see William L. Hays, *Statistics for Psychologists* (New York: Holt, Rinehart and Winston, 1963), pp. 647–656.

Probability levels are given only to assist in interpreting the results. The probability of .0006 for the analysis on a daily basis indicates that when there are 34 scores for each variable, a *gamma* coefficient of .44 or higher would occur by chance only 6 times out of 10,000.

TABLE 6

Securities of Prospective Belligerents

Security	27 June–2 July	3–16 July	17–20 July	21–25 July	26 July	27 July	28 July	29 July	30 July
Serbia: 4% Bonds	99.0	96.2	92.0	89.8	87.2	89.7	87.6	83.5	83.5
Serbia: Monopoles	98.8	98.0	98.9	97.3	96.6	95.5	93.6	92.5	92.5
Banque Internationale	98.8	97.8	95.6	91.2	89.0	89.0	85.8		
Baku	100.2	100.1	99.0	96.0	94.4	94.4	92.0		
Moscow: Kazan	97.2	96.0	93.3	92.6	93.1	93.1	88.6		
Russian 4½% 1909	99.8	99.9	98.0	95.8	91.5	94.0			
Russia: 4% Bonds	100.1	98.3	97.5	96.5	93.8	91.5	90.2	89.1	89.1
Austria: Credit Shares	99.5	97.8	97.2	95.5	92.8	94.5	93.5	94.3	92.7
Austria: 4% Gold	99.8	99.9	99.7	99.0	98.1				
Hungary: 4% Gold	99.6	98.5	98.0	97.5	94.3				
Hungarian Bonds	101.0	97.2	97.0	94.7	91.4	90.1	89.0	89.0	89.0
Germany: 3% Imperial	99.7	99.2	98.8	97.8	96.5	95.9	95.8	94.8	94.8
3% Prussian Consols	99.7	99.2	98.8	97.7	96.4	97.0	96.9	94.7	
General Electric	99.9	99.8	98.1	94.7	91.2	92.1	91.2	88.9	
France: 3% Loan	99.0	98.9	97.8	96.5	93.8	93.7	92.9	92.9	86.9
3½% French Loan	100.0	99.9	99.7	97.0	93.6	94.4	94.4	93.1	
Bank of France	100.0	99.4	98.7	98.0	97.5	97.5	97.5		
British Consols: 2½%	99.8	101.1	101.3	100.3	98.4	96.8	95.8	94.8	93.1
Port of London B 4%	100.3	100.8	99.0	98.9	98.5	97.9	97.9	94.8	
Bank of Brussels	99.9	99.5	98.5	97.6	97.0	97.0		95.9	95.9
INDEX	99.6	98.9	97.8	96.2	94.2	94.3	93.3	92.5	92.1

20–26 June = 100

Correlations, rising hostility and falling security prices:

	N	gamma	P
Data grouped as in this table	9	1.00	.0001
Daily	34	.44	.0006

of war in the Balkans, notably Serbian Bonds (2.5%) and Austrian Credit Shares (1.7%). During the preceding weekend many observers and participants, including the kaiser and Winston Churchill, had concluded that the Serbian reply to the ultimatum marked the end of the crisis. On the text of the Serbian reply to the Austro-Hungarian ultimatum, Wilhelm wrote: "A brilliant performance for a time limit of only forty-eight hours. This is more than one could have expected! A great moral victory for Vienna; but with it every reason for war drops away, and Giesl [Austro-Hungarian minister to Serbia] might have remained quietly in Belgrade! On the strength of this I should never have ordered mobilization." [2] Churchill recalled that, "On Saturday [July 25] afternoon the news came in that Serbia had accepted the ultimatum. I went to bed with a feeling things might blow over . . . we were still a long way, as it seemed, from any danger of war. Serbia had accepted the ultimatum, could Austria demand more?" [3]

Subsequently there was a virtual collapse in prices, corresponding to the rise in perceived hostility. The extent of the collapse during the last few days before general war is stated quite conservatively by our figures. In the first place, many of the quoted prices were, according to market observers, nominal and considerably higher than the actual selling price of securities—if indeed a buyer could be found at any price.[4] Secondly, for calculating the index the price of an issue which was no longer traded —usually because the exchange on which it was listed had been closed in response to the deepening European crisis—is carried through 30 July at the last quoted price. For example, the last recorded trade of the Russian 4½% Bonds was on 27 July, at 94% of its precrisis value. But for our index it was carried at the same price through 30 July. The closing dates of European exchanges were: Vienna (27 July), Budapest (27 July), Brussels (27 July), Berlin (29 July), Paris (30 July), St. Petersburg (30 July), and London (31 July). Differences in closing dates affected the losses described in Table 7. For example, Austrian losses are probably understated relative to those of Britain because the London Exchange remained open longer.

For reasons indicated earlier, validation of the content analysis data also requires evidence that the financial indices with which

TABLE 7
Securities of Prospective Neutrals and Comparison of Losses in Value with Securities of Prospective Belligerents

Security	27 June–2 July	3–16 July	17–20 July	21–25 July	26 July	27 July	28 July	29 July	30 July	31 July
Sweden 3%	100.0	100.0	100.0	100.0	100.0	100.0	100.0	100.0	100.0	100.0
Sweden 3½%	99.7	97.9	98.4	98.5	99.2	98.3	98.0	98.0	98.0	98.2
Switzerland										
Chemin de Fer	100.3	99.6	99.5	99.5	99.5	99.5	99.5	99.5	99.5	99.5
INDEX	100.00	99.17	99.30	99.33	99.57	99.27	99.17	99.17	99.17	99.23

20–26 June = 100

Correlations, rising hostility and falling security prices:

	N	gamma	P
Data grouped as in this table	10	.38	n.s.
Daily	34	.04	n.s.

Average Loss in Value of Securities:
Serbia 12.0%, Russia 10.1%, Hungary 8.4%, Germany 7.9%, France 6.4%, Great Britain 5.5%, Austria 4.6%, Belgium 3.0%, Sweden 0.9%, Switzerland 0.5%.

they are compared are in fact proper standards. That is, if financial data such as the price of securities, or any of the others examined in this chapter, are to serve as criteria with which to validate the data derived from diplomatic documents, it must also be shown that they varied systematically with international developments. If, for example, there had been widespread fears of a recession, we might have found that the prices of securities were falling, but for reasons that had nothing to do with the Balkan crisis. To guard against a possibility of this type, the prices of securities issued in traditionally neutral nations, Sweden and Switzerland, were examined. Table 7 reveals that their values remained quite stable, falling less than 1% during the entire crisis period. Such fluctuations as there were appear to have been unrelated to the international crisis; the average value of the Swiss and Swedish securities was slightly higher on the final day of July than it had been during the first two weeks of the month.

In contrast, the paper losses in values of the stocks and bonds of the major participants in the crisis were staggering. During the ten-day period ending with 30 July, the value of 387 representative British stocks fell by £188,000,000. By 25 July, the value of the securities of 23 German industrial firms had dropped from £79,000,000 to £65,900,000—and the worst was yet to come! In one sense the "cost" of the war reached catastrophic proportions even before the first shot was fired.[5] Some contemporary accounts describe something of the atmosphere in which trading took place: price losses "exceed anything that has happened in the past." "The Market has become completely demoralized, the chief factor being the Eastern situation." "A panic on the Bourse, on which prices fell below any recorded since 1895." [6] Thus the comparison of the securities of belligerents and neutrals during the crisis strongly suggests that security prices during July 1914 were in fact responding to international news.

THE FLOW OF GOLD

During major crises gold prices usually rise for the same reasons that security values decline. The latter have value in direct proportion to expectations that the issuing firms or nations will prosper. When the outlook is clouded by the prospect of war, security prices tend to fall. Because the value of gold lies in the metal itself, however, it is often in greatest demand when the value of paper, including securities and currencies, is in question. Not only are individuals likely to convert paper assets into gold, but governments will often seek to stockpile the metal to finance any anticipated war.

Any study of the international flow of gold in 1914 must centre on London—"the financial center and the free market for gold." [7] Whereas notes could be redeemed for gold to an unlimited extent in the Bank of England, the government banks in Berlin, St. Petersburg, and Paris had been hoarding gold for some time prior to the assassination of Franz Ferdinand. By the law of 3 July 1913, the Bank of Germany was authorized to build up a gold-silver war reserve of 240 million marks. At the same time the French were building up a counterpart to the German fund. In contrast, as late as 25 July 1914, the influential London *Economist* opposed demands from some British bankers that England take official steps to prevent a run on gold in times of panic.[8] Thus fluctuations in the influx or outflow of gold from London took place in a market free—until 31 July—of any governmental interference.

The daily average net flow of gold is summarized in Table 8. As the crisis developed the influx of gold first declined and then was followed by a wave of withdrawals when war broke out in the Balkans. The steady rise in perceived hostility starting on 28 July corresponds to the withdrawal of gold in quantities suggesting panic. Only on 1 August was there any abatement. Late in the previous day the bank rate had been raised to an almost unprecedented 8 per cent; on 1 August the rate was increased again to 10 per cent. Thus the drop in net outflow from £1,204,000 on 31 July to £60,000 was less the result of a restoration of confidence than of a consciously adopted policy on the part of the British to take remedial steps by what amounted to abolishing the free market in gold.

Is there any evidence that the purchases of gold were related to the European crisis? Recall that Table 8 had revealed a close correspondence between gold transactions with European nations and perceptions of international hostility. A more detailed view of all gold purchases and sales is provided in Table 9, which

TABLE 8
Gold Flow and Perceptions of International Hostility

Period	All Transactions	Transactions with European Nations	Mean Intensity of Perceived Hostility
20–26 June	+120.3	0.0	
27 June–2 July	+92.0	0.0	3.44
3–16 July	+71.0	+0.9	3.79
17–20 July	+9.8	−1.5	3.80
21–25 July	+6.0	0.0	4.43
26 July	0.0	0.0	4.94
27 July	+269.0	−50.0	4.48
28 July	−22.0	−22.0	5.10
29 July	−911.0	−696.0	5.19
30 July	−1034.0	−971.0	5.62
31 July	−1204.0	−1263.0	5.70
1 August	−60.0	−16.0	5.61
2 August	no market	no market	7.04
3 August	no market	no market	6.64
4 August	no market	no market	5.81

Net influx (+) net exflux (−) of gold (daily average in £ thousands)

Correlations, rising hostility and net exflux of gold:

	N	gamma	P
All Transactions:			
Data grouped as in this table	11	.82	<.001
Daily	31	.36	.02
Transactions with European Nations:			
Data grouped as in this table	11	.69	.002
Daily	31	.82	<.001

reveals that the great bulk of gold leaving London was in fact shipped to prospective belligerents on the continent. Net exports for the five weeks were worth £1,440,000; however, this takes into account British purchases of £1,703,000 in gold bars and the receipt of £803,000 from South American nations. For the entire period European nations, excluding neutral Switzerland, purchased £3,011,000 more gold than they sold; from 27 July to 1 August, a period encompassing the outbreak of war, the comparable figure was £3,018,000. Thus, gold shipments to Europe for

TABLE 9
Gold Purchases and Sales in London

Source or Destination	27 June–2 July	3–16 July	17–20 July	21–25 July	26 July	27 July	28 July	29 July	30 July	31 July	1 August	Net
France "Continent"			− 6				− 22	− 380	− 971	− 143	− 16	− 1538
Belgium		− 7						− 275		− 572		− 854
Within empire						− 50		− 41		− 548		− 639
Egypt	+ 185		+ 45	− 280				− 230	− 150	− 80	− 100	− 610
Switzerland								− 235	− 100			− 335
Germany									− 60			− 60
United States	+ 70	+ 20										+ 90
South America	+ 77	+ 165		+ 186		+ 201			+ 174			+ 803
Bars purchased	+ 128	+ 815	+ 39	+ 124	0	+ 118		+ 250	+ 73	+ 139	+ 56	+ 1703
NET	+ 460	+ 993	+ 39	+ 30	0	+ 269	− 22	− 911	− 1034	− 1204	− 60	− 1440
DAILY AVERAGE	+ 92.0	+ 71.0	+ 9.8	+ 6.0	0	+ 269.0	− 22.0	− 911.0	− 1034.0	− 1204.0	− 60.0	—

Net influx (+) net exflux (−) of gold (figures in £ sterling)

the entire period accounted for 75.0% of all gold purchases and for 211% of the surplus of exports over imports. From 27 July through 1 August shipments to Europe were responsible for 75.7% of all gold leaving London and for 100.2% of net exports. Again these figures may be stated conservatively; the final destination of gold shipped to Switzerland, for example, might well have been one of the nations that was on the verge of war.

Finally, there is strong, although indirect, evidence that much of the gold leaving Britain was recalled by national banks of the major powers involved in the crisis. The weekly statements of the European national banks (Table 10) reveal sharp increases in gold reserves during the crisis period. For some days prior to the

TABLE 10
Gold Reserves of National Banks
(in units of £1,000)

Bank of °	Gold Reserves	On	Gold Reserves	On	Net Change
France	£159,028.0	25 June	£165,654.0	30 July	+£ 6,626.0
Belgium	£ 13,451.0	25 June	£ 15,980.0	6 August	+£ 2,529.0
Germany	£ 63,712.2°°	2 July	£ 75,426.0	15 August	+£11,713.8
Russia	£159,575.0	29 June	£160,204.0	4 August	+£ 629.0

° No figures are available for the Austro-Hungarian Bank after 23 July 1914.
°° 1,306.1 million marks, converted in pounds at the rate of 20.50 M /£.

outbreak of war German banks paid only 20% of demands in gold; on the declaration of the "state of threatening danger of war" (31 July), payments in gold were stopped altogether. On 5 August the Austro-Hungarian Bank Act, which had required 40% gold backing for currency, was suspended.[9] Hence, while the figures in Table 10 undoubtedly reflect internal stockpiling of gold, they also suggest that major financial institutions on the continent had been in large part responsible for the run on gold in London.

WHEAT FUTURES

The threat or onset of a major international crisis often brings about widespread price increases in various commodities. Specu-

TABLE 11
December Wheat Futures and Perceived International Hostility

	Wheat Futures (shillings)	Mean Intensity of Perceived Hostility
20–26 June	6.90	
27 June–2 July	6.74	3.44
3–16 July	6.81	3.79
17–20 July	6.87	3.80
21–25 July	7.08	4.43
26 July	7.15	4.94
27 July	7.21	4.48
28 July	7.30	5.10
29 July	7.56	5.19
30 July	8.02	5.62
31 July	8.29	5.70
1 August	8.13	5.61
2 August	no market	7.04
3 August	no market	6.64
4 August	no market	5.81

Correlations, rising hostility and rising wheat prices:

	N	gamma	P
Data grouped as in this table	11	.93	<.0001
Daily	36	.54	<.0001

lators, anticipating panic buying, hoarding, and diminished supplies, would be expected to drive the price of commodity futures up as the crisis deepened. Table 11 reveals that during the month of July, wheat futures in London rose more than 20%. Moreover, the pattern of rising prices corresponds almost exactly to that of increasing hostility. Similar increases in prices took place on the Continent. In Berlin, for example, the price of rye rose from 172.5 Reichsmarks per sack to 176 RM between 27 July and 29 July; wheat rose from 202.25 to 207 RM and oats rose from 167.25 to 169.75 RM during the same period.[10]

EXCHANGE RATES

The standard against which all currencies were measured in 1914 was the British pound sterling; the value of any currency was stated in terms of how much sterling one could buy with it. Given the prospect of a war involving the Dual Alliance, we would expect a decline in the value relative to the pound of the German mark and Austrian krone, especially because there was a strong possibility that Britain would not be drawn into the conflict. Table 12 reveals that the value of both currencies did undergo a drastic decline and that fluctuation in their exchange rates were closely correlated to changes in perceived hostility. Although day-to-day figures on the Russian rouble are less readily available, the trend was the same. According to one source, the rouble, 95.6 of which were required to purchase a ten-pound note on 27 July, was quoted at 110-120 only three days later.[11]

TABLE 12

Exchange Rates and Perceptions of International Hostility

	German Mark		Austrian Krone		Intensity of Perceived Hostility
	Mark	Pfenning	Krone	Heller	
20–26 June	20	49.6	24	16.3	
27 June–2 July	20	49.7	24	15.2	3.44
3–16 July	20	49.3	24	16.6	3.79
17–20 July	20	48.9	24	17.3	3.80
21–25 July	20	50.1	24	21.2	4.43
26 July	20	52.5	24	23.5	4.94
27 July	20	52.0	24	29.0	4.48
28 July	20	53.0	24	30.0	5.10
29 July	20	55.0	24	40.0	5.19
30 July	20	82.0	26	50.0	5.62
31 July	no market				5.70
1 August	no market				5.61
2 August	no market				7.04
3 August	no market				6.64
4 August	no market				5.81

Correlations, rising hostility and falling currency values:

	N	gamma	P
German Mark:			
Data grouped as in this table	9	.83	.001
Daily	34	.39	.003
Austrian Krone:			
Data grouped as in this table	9	.89	.0005
Daily	34	.31	.02

The extent of the collapse of continental currencies is illustrated by the fact that the mark lost 1.6% of its value relative to the pound, the krone fell 9.7% and the rouble fell 24.5% during the short span of the crisis.

INTEREST RATES

Table 13 indicates that official bank rates and free-market money rates were also closely correlated to the fluctuations in perceived

TABLE 13
Interest Rates and Perceptions of International Hostility

	Official Money Rates °	Market Money Rates ° °	Intensity of Perceived Hostility
20–26 June	3.92%	2.63%	
27 June–2 July	3.92%	2.48%	3.44
3–16 July	3.92%	2.27%	3.79
17–20 July	3.92%	2.31%	3.80
21–25 July	3.92%	2.47%	4.43
26 July	4.08%	2.71%	4.94
27 July	4.25%	3.17%	4.48
28 July	4.58%	4.00%	5.10
29 July	4.58%	4.17%	5.19
30 July	4.92%	no market	5.62
31 July	5.92%	no market	5.70
1 August	6.50%	no market	5.61
2 August	6.83%	no market	7.04
3 August	7.17%	no market	6.64
4 August	7.17%	no market	5.81

Correlations, rising hostility and rising interest rates:

	N	gamma	P
Official rate:			
Data grouped as in this table	14	.88	<.0001
Daily	39	.96	<.0001
Market rate:			
Data grouped as in this table	8	.63	.015
Daily	33	.25	.06

° Average rates in London, Paris, Berlin, Vienna, St. Petersburg, and Brussels.

° ° Average rates in London, Paris, and Berlin.

hostility during the crisis. Although official rates were usually a highly stable figure—many of the rates at the outbreak of the crisis had not been changed since 1913 or earlier—every one of the major participants for which figures are available increased their rates at least once during the six-week period. Three increases in as many days brought the British figures from 3% on 29 July to an unprecedented 10% on 1 August. During a similar period the French rate rose from 3½% to 6%, in Vienna the interest rate increased from 4% to 8%, and that in Brussels rose from 4% to 7%. In each case the action on interest rates was a direct outgrowth of the European crisis; a primary reason was to ensure that gold would not flow out of the country. According to one contemporary account "the rise to 8 per cent [in England] marked a real panic. Almost the whole continent, from Paris to St. Petersburg, and from Amsterdam to Vienna and Rome, wants to convert paper into cash; and the great banks even in Paris and Berlin are, of course, hoarding gold against an emergency." [12]

The market money rate, unlike the official rate, fluctuated from day to day much as the price of securities or exchange rates. Although figures were not quoted in Paris, London, or Berlin after 29 July, interest rates on that day were almost double what they had been earlier in the month. As with the official interest figures, the market rate varied in concert with the level of hostility perceived by European political leaders.

One by-product of this analysis is a picture, albeit sketchy, of the collapse of an international economic system. That system, which Lenin had prophesied would lead to war and which many others had predicted would make future wars impossible was, in the words of the *Economist*, "staggering under a series of blows such as the delicate system of international credit has never before witnessed, or even imagined." [13] Hence, "In a single moment all this wonderful machinery was broken or thrown out of gear." [14] Gold became a weapon of war, and as a result the free movement of gold was in effect abolished as an expedient of war. Major securities exchanges were closed to prevent a more ruinous panic; not even the New York Stock Exchange was able to remain open in the face of war in Europe. The price of commodities came to depend on diplomatic and military manoeuvres rather than on the free market. Exchange rates reflected the results of ultimata and responses to them rather than the finely tuned system of international credit. The effects of the crisis on the shipping insurance industry were characteristic of the inability of existing institutions to cope with a crisis of such magnitude. British insurance rates for the last week of the crisis and the first week of the war are given in Table 14. Only the establishment of the government War Risks Office on 7 August, in effect replacing the old system with a new one, broke the virtual paralysis in the shipping insurance industry.

TABLE 14
Shipping Insurance Rates

Date	Rate per £100 value	Rate as % of value
28 July	5 shillings	0.25
31 July	60–80 shillings	3.0–4.0
4 August	10–15 guineas	10.5–15.8
6 August	20 guineas	21.0
7 August	10 guineas	10.5
9 August	8 guineas	8.4
12 August	4 guineas	4.2
14 August	3 guineas	3.1

Source: Economist, 15 August 1914, p. 304.

In the final days prior to the outbreak of general war, one observer, reflecting upon the closing of the London Stock Exchange, noted the inability of the financial institutions to cope with the situation: "Nothing, indeed, could have given a more dramatic touch, and nothing could have testified more clearly to the impossibility of running modern civilization and war together than this closing of the London Stock Exchange owing to a collapse of prices, produced not by the actual outbreak of a small war, but by the fear of war between some of the great powers of Europe." [15]

CONCLUSION

This experiment has attempted to assess the validity of data derived from a content analysis of diplomatic documents written during the 1914 crisis. In the absence of any feasible method of

establishing validity directly, we have taken an indirect approach. Multiple indicators of the attitudes of various financial
elites revealed a pattern of responses to developments in Europe
strikingly similar to the measure of stress derived by content
analysis of the diplomatic documents. There was, moreover, substantial evidence that when gold was purchased in London,
when stocks were sold at a loss, or when commodity futures were
purchased, it was done in response to increasing apprehension
about war in Europe. These results cannot, of course, establish
beyond all doubt that the content analysis of diplomatic documents yields valid measures of decision makers' attitudes and
perceptions of every event, but they do enhance the confidence
with which we can use the data for testing hypotheses in subsequent chapters.

One further question emerges from this analysis. If there is a
close correspondence between the attitudes of political elites (as
measured by content analysis of their messages) and the financial
community (as revealed by their behaviour on the stock exchange and elsewhere), why not rely on the latter as our indices
of stress, thereby foregoing the rather arduous task of content an-
alyzing diplomatic documents? [16] In the first place, financial indices of the type examined in this chapter respond to a variety of
factors—some economic, some social, and some political. The
stock market collapses of 1929, 1962, and 1966 in the United
States, for example, were probably more closely related to internal than to international factors. Sales of gold by the Soviet
Union in the early 1960s were largely a response to agricultural
difficulties, and the more recent gold sales by France were required to protect the franc against the effects of domestic disturbances during the spring of 1968. The evidence strongly suggests that during the summer of 1914 financial indices reflected
the state of international tensions, but this may not always be the
case. Moreover, while prices on the New York Stock Exchange or
the value of the Swiss franc may still respond to dramatic international developments,* such data can no longer be gathered in

---

* Note, for example, the extent to which news of Vietnam dominated stock
price movements in 1968. President Johnson's decision to limit the bombing of
North Vietnam and not to seek another term in the White House triggered off a
buying spree which shattered all volume records on the New York Stock Exchange. Since that time virtually every indication of peace in the Middle East or

many major world capitals—for example, in Moscow and Peking. Thus this experiment was only designed to be a partial and indirect check on the validity of content data from the 1914 documents. It was clearly *not* intended to provide a general-purpose index of tensions in the international system.

Individual Differences in "Definition of the Situation"

The decision to aggregate data about individuals to represent nations was not merely one of research convenience. Theory and evidence from several social sciences suggest that socialization and role requirements often outweigh, if not eliminate, the effect of personal factors in organization decision making.[*] The collective nature of much foreign-policy activity would appear to make these findings especially germane.

Questions have been raised, however, concerning the validity of aggregating individual data to test hypotheses about nations or alliances on the grounds that important individual differences may be overlooked.[17] The point is not a trivial one and it warrants far more systematic investigation than it is usually accorded in foreign-policy studies.[18] Unless we accept a simple-minded view of politics (for instance, the Marxist position that all American foreign-policy officials are the products of monopoly capitalism and are therefore interchangeable; or its right-wing counterpart, the "protracted conflict" school which views all Communist leaders as cut from the same unholy bolt of cloth), a substantial case can be developed for the viewpoint that differences in per-

---

Southeast Asia has been met by higher prices, whereas threats of war or of a widening war—for example the "Six Day War" in 1967 and the Cambodian operation in 1970—have resulted in selling of panic proportions and sharp declines in prices. See also the analysis of such financial indices during the Cuban missile crisis, in Ole R. Holsti, Richard A. Brody, and Robert C. North, "Measuring Affect and Action in International Reaction Models," *Peace Research Society, Papers*, II (1965), 170–190.

[*] This viewpoint is forcefully developed with respect to analyses of the international system and foreign-policy research by Sidney Verba, "Assumptions of Rationality and Non-Rationality in Models of the International System," *World Politics*, XIV (1961), 93–117; and J. David Singer and Paul Ray, "Decision-Making in Conflict: From Inter-Personal to International Relations," *Bulletin of the Menninger Clinic*, XXX (1966), 300–312.

sonality, background, experience, and the like may give rise to diverging ways of defining the situation. Thus, aggregating data about individuals and denoting the sum as the nation may lead us astray. We may, in the first place, bias the results by the assumption that extreme viewpoints are accurately represented by the mean position. It is not, for example, self-evident that a very hypothetical group composed of General Curtis LeMay (George Wallace's "superhawkish" ticket-mate in 1968), Senator Clifford Case (a liberal Republican), and Professor Herbert Aptheker (a Marxist theorist) would choose a policy towards the Soviet Union which represented the mean of their views. Secondly, we may be led to overlook the interesting and important political processes by which differences within nations are resolved.

The remainder of this chapter is intended to shed some light on this question, at least with respect to the 1914 crisis. More specifically, how much of the variation in the perceptions of statesmen may be explained by changes in the situation? By differences in the nations they represent? By personality and other idiosyncratic differences among individuals acting on behalf of the same nation?

To answer these questions we shall again use the data on perceptions of hostility. Each theme was recoded to include the author of the document from which it was drawn.* The absence of a complete collection of Serbian documents made it impossible to gather sufficient data to include Serbia in other analyses of the crisis. But several documents written by or on behalf of the regent and prime minister were coded and these data are included here. Nor were documents written by ambassadors part of the data reported in Chapter 2, but a number of messages by the British and Austro-Hungarian ambassadors to Berlin, Sir William Edward Goschen and Count Laszlo Szögyeny, had been coded and they are also included here. In all, the Serbian and ambassadorial data added 62 themes to the 1096 used in other analyses, for a total of 1158. As grouped in Table 15, the figures can be

---

* Drafts of many messages sent out over the signature of a prime minister, foreign minister, or other official were initially written by civil servants and perhaps revised by a number of persons prior to being released. Whenever possible, however, the author of comments and annotations—including the most famous of these, Kaiser Wilhelm's "marginal notes"—was identified in the coding.

TABLE 15
Effects of Situation, Nation, and Individual Differences
on Intensity of Perceived Hostility

	Mean Intensity of Perceived Hostility During:	
	27 June–28 July	29 July–4 August [°]
Austria-Hungary		
Franz Joseph (Monarch)	4.55	5.95
Berchtold (Foreign Minister)	4.28	5.20
Forgach (Division Chief, Foreign Office)	3.77	5.90
Szögyény (Ambassador to Germany)	4.11	4.47
Germany		
Government [°°]	5.53	5.87
Wilhelm II (Monarch)	4.40	5.78
Bethmann-Hollweg (Chancellor)	4.08	6.47
Jagow (Secretary of State, Foreign Affairs)	3.59	6.08
Great Britain		
Grey (Foreign Minister)	4.52	5.00
Nicolson (Under-Secretary, Foreign Affairs)	5.25	5.43
Goschen (Ambassador to Germany)	4.09	5.71
France		
Government [°°]	4.34	6.63
Viviani (Premier & Foreign Minister)	4.76	5.97
Bienvenu-Martin (Deputy Minister, Foreign Affairs)	4.51	5.85
Berthelot (Acting Director, Foreign Office)	5.00	7.30
Russia		
Nicholas II (Monarch)	7.00	5.86
Sazonov (Foreign Minister)	5.21	5.11
Serbia		
Paschich (Premier & Foreign Minister)	3.97	5.66
Alexander (Crown Prince & Regent)	4.23	7.67

Source of Variation	Sum of Squares	d.f.	Mean Squares	F Ratio	P
Between Groups					
Situation	16.08	1	16.08	39.22	<.001
Nation	4.12	5	0.82	2.00	n.s.
Situation x Nation	6.45	5	1.29	3.15	.05
Within Groups					
(Individual differences)	10.54	26	0.41		
TOTAL	37.19	37			

[°] Austro-Hungarian documents available only through 31 July 1914.

[°°] Documents issued by the government but author not identified.

used to examine three possible sources of variation: differences in *situations, nations,* and *individuals.*

The data were divided at 28–29 July to provide two different *situations.* The early period was marked by considerable diplomatic activity and rather widespread optimism that the crisis need not result in war; it ended with the outbreak of war between Serbia and Austria-Hungary. The later period was characterized by massive general mobilizations, ruptures of diplomatic relations, and declarations of war involving all the major European nations.

The second possible source of variation is the *nation.* The nineteen officials for whom documents were available during both the 27 June–28 July and 29 July–4 August periods include most of the top leaders in all six nations. Among those who were excluded for lack of data in one period or the other were: Tisza of Austria-Hungary; Zimmermann, Moltke, and Stumm of Germany; Ferry, Margerie, and Messimy of France; and Asquith of Great Britain. The latter would appear to be the most serious loss, given his position of prime minister, but there was only a single perception of hostility articulated by him during the entire crisis period. Excluding the Serbian and ambassadorial data, the figures in Table 15 represent 80.7% of the 1096 perceptions of hostility reported in the previous chapter.

Finally, *individual differences* in the definition of the situation are measured by variations in perceptions of hostility among all nineteen statesmen. It should be noted that no relation is made here to the specific event giving rise to each perception. Thus, on a given day Kaiser Wilhelm may have stated that German relations with Great Britain were developing less favourably than he had hoped (relatively low intensity in hostility), whereas Jagow may have indicated that Austria-Hungary was intent upon crushing Serbia once and for all (high intensity).* If such differences

---

* This fails to satisfy the suggestion that perceptions of each discrete event should be analysed separately. Robert Jervis, "The Costs of the Quantitative Study of International Relations," in Klaus Knorr and James N. Rosenau (eds.), *Contending Approaches to International Politics* (Princeton: Princeton University Press, 1969). Jervis' point is well taken, but because the crisis period encompassed literally hundreds of events—even the coding system used to produce Figure 1 yielded 448 discrete actions—this procedure would have resulted in data sliced so thinly as to defeat the purpose of the present experiment.

significantly affected the results, however, they *increased* rather than decreased the amount of variance accounted for by individual attributes.

The analysis of variance * reported in Table 15 reveals that by far the greatest amount of variation can be attributed to changes in the situation; there are far greater and more consistent differences in perceptions of international hostility between one time period and the other than there are between individuals in any nation, or indeed, between all European statesmen included here. Stated somewhat differently, the differences between the low-stress early period and the later high-stress period account for virtually all the variation in the scores; the "unexplained" part which might be attributed to personality or other individual differences is extremely small. Although there is a significant interaction between nation and situation, the amount of variation for which differences among nations may be responsible is very small. Moreover, even if we assume that *all* of the "within groups" variation is accounted for by differences in personal characteristics—for reasons indicated above, this would be a very generous premise indeed—the results strongly suggest that differences between officials are small enough to be disregarded. It is therefore reasonable to conclude that aggregation of individual data within nations (or even within alliances) will not do serious violence to the validity of our results.†

Several objections can be stated against the analysis to this point, however. First, it might be argued that dividing the data into only two periods may bias the results cancelling out differences

---

* Analysis of variance (ANOVA) is a statistical method which compares the mean (average) scores for data classified into two or more groups, with the mean for all the data. To oversimplify, the results in Table 15 indicate that classifying the data according to situation produced two groups of nineteen scores each that have significantly different means; that classifying the data by nation produced six groups whose means were not very different; and that the amount of difference among each of the nineteen individuals within either time period was negligible. Further descriptions of the logic and computation of ANOVA may be found in virtually any statistics text.

† Analysis of variance designs are typically used with controlled experiments in which individuals are randomly assigned to groups. The inability to assign leaders randomly to nations in this instance is obvious. Although this assumption of analysis of variance has been violated, there is no possible distribution of individuals in Table 15 that would substantially alter the present findings.

TABLE 16
Effects of Situation vs. Individual Differences
on Intensity of Perceived Hostility

Nation/Time Periods [*]	Source of Variation	Sum of Squares	d.f.	Mean Squares	F Ratio	P
Austria-Hungary 27 June–20 July 21–27 July 28–31 July	Between Groups (Situation)	3.22	2	1.61	3.29	.10
	Within Groups (Individual differences)	4.39	9	0.49		
	TOTAL	7.61	11			
Germany 27 June–20 July 21–28 July 29–30 July 31 July–4 August	Between Groups (Situation)	13.92	3	4.64	10.79	.001
	Within Groups (Individual differences)	5.19	12	0.43		
	TOTAL	19.11	15			
Great Britain 27 June–25 July 26–29 July 30 July–4 August	Between Groups (Situation)	1.53	2	0.77	4.64	.10
	Within Groups (Individual differences)	0.99	6	0.16		
	TOTAL	2.52	8			
France [**] 27 June–28 July 29–31 July 1–4 August	Between Groups (Situation)	7.04	2	3.52	8.38	.025
	Within Groups (Individual differences)	2.50	6	0.42		
	TOTAL	9.54	8			
Russia 27 June–27 July 28 July 29–31 July 1–4 August	Between Groups (Situation)	8.74	3	2.91	7.86	.05
	Within Groups (Individual differences)	1.47	4	0.37		
	TOTAL	10.21	7			

[*] Insufficient Serbian data to divide into more than 2 periods.

[**] Bienvenu-Martin dropped from analysis owing to lack of data for all three periods.

that exist at any given point in time. This is, of course, a two-edged sword; it may in fact accentuate rather than diminish individual differences. Among French leaders, for example, Bienvenu-Martin's initial statements came on 22 July (before the Austro-Hungarian ultimatum to Serbia), whereas the first data for Berthelot and Viviani occurred on 26 and 27 July, respectively (after the ultimatum and Serbia's response to it). The paucity of data for some individuals, especially for British, French, and Russian leaders during the first month after the assassination, ruled out the most desirable strategy—grouping the figures into periods of one day each. A feasible but not wholly satisfactory alternative was to divide the data for each nation into as many periods as possible without losing any individual for lack of data in a period. This method made it possible to get three or four periods for each country except Serbia. Because the cutting points were determined solely by the desire to maximize the number of situations, they are not the same for each nation. Even so, there was no way of dividing the French data into more than two periods without dropping Bienvenu-Martin from the analysis.

The results in Table 16 substantially confirm those of the earlier analysis. They reveal again that the changing situation rather than individual differences account for the greatest part of the variance in perceptions of hostility.

Secondly, we have failed to consider the possible effects of *role.** The present data are insufficient for a systematic examination of differences across bureaucracies, ministries, or coalitions within them. We can, however, consider whether persons holding a similar office (such as foreign minister) tended to view the situation differently from hereditary monarchs, ambassadors, or others. For this purpose the 1914 officials were classified into six categories:

---

* It is assumed that perceptions of hostility reflect international developments. But they may also serve as ammunition in internal bureaucratic competition for funds, prestige, and other scarce resources. In this case role differences would presumably be quite significant.

For excellent discussions of the effects of bureaucratic politics on foreign policy, see Graham Allison, "Conceptual Models and the Cuban Missile Crisis," *American Political Science Review*, LXIII (1969), 689–718; Richard E. Neustadt, *Alliance Politics* (New York: Columbia University Press, 1970); and Alexander L. George, "Political Decision-Making: Problems of Stress and Coping in Individual, Group and Organizational Contexts" (Stanford University: mimeographed, 1970).

Monarch	Prime Minister
Franz Joseph	Bethmann-Hollweg
Wilhelm II	Viviani
Nicholas II	Paschich
Alexander	

Foreign Minister	Deputy in Foreign Office
Berchtold	Forgach
Grey	Nicolson
Jagow	Bienvenu-Martin
Sazonov	Berthelot

"Government"	Ambassador
Germany	Szögyeny
France	Goschen

As indicated in Table 17, introducing role into the analysis does not alter the earlier conclusion that situational differences account for virtually all systematic variation in perceptions of hostility. That is, the manner in which European officials viewed crisis developments did not significantly depend on which office they held, any more than it did on individual differences.

An objection might also be made about using analysis of variance, a parametric statistic, when it is open to question whether

TABLE 17
Effects of Role on Intensity of Perceived Hostility

Source of Variation	Sum of Squares	d.f.	Mean Squares	F Ratio	P
Between Groups					
Situation	16.08	1	16.08	26.80	<.001
Role	4.89	5	0.98	1.63	n.s.
Situation x Role	0.74	5	0.15	0.25	n.s.
Within Groups (Individual differences)	15.48	26	0.60		
TOTAL	37.19	37			

Q-sorting yields data on an interval scale. Equivalent non-parametric tests for ranked scores (Mann-Whitney test for 2-sample cases, and the Kruskal-Wallis test for k-sample cases) were used with the same data. The results, summarized in Table 18, differ only slightly from earlier ones. The major exception is that they do not provide a test of the interaction between situation and nation that was found to be significant in Table 15.

These results indicate that aggregation of individual data for purposes of testing hypotheses about nations or alliances is a valid procedure with perceptions of hostility during the 1914 crisis. It would be claiming far too much, however, to assert that it has given us license to disregard individual factors in the analysis of foreign policy and international politics. Although we cannot generalize beyond the 1914 data on the basis of the evidence presented here, it is possible to speculate about the results with a view to decision making in general. For example, at least three interpretations of these results might be advanced.

First, the range of differences among foreign-policy leaders on *politically relevant attributes* is quite restricted. Without necessarily falling prey to simplistic views about the nature of politics, the premise that the range of individual variations among foreign-policy elites is smaller than that of the general population is eminently reasonable. Yet even if we consider such well-established factors as selective recruitment, group pressures for conformity, and the like, this interpretation is not wholly satisfactory. To rely too much upon it would be to deny, in effect, that the process of making external policy is a political one, often marked by conflict among those with different assessments of the situation, values, goals, and preferences among strategies.

Secondly, if the situation is "objectively" unambiguous, we might expect all persons (barring those with severe pathological disabilities) to perceive it similarly. But this interpretation is insufficient to explain the 1914 findings. As was pointed out previously, there was considerable doubt about the intentions of many countries almost up to the outbreak of war.

Finally, perhaps the results indicate that perceptions of the situation will tend to become more similar as stress increases. There is evidence that both the tendency to stereotype and group pressures towards defining the situation similarly are greater as stress

TABLE 18
Results of Non-parametric Tests

Leaders	Effects of	Test	Results	P
All	Situation	Mann-Whitney	$U = 35.5$ $n_1 = 19,$ $n_2 = 19$	$< .00003$
All	Individual Differences	Kruskal-Wallis	$H = 8.94$ 18 d.f.	n.s.
All, Aggregated by Nation	Situation	Mann-Whitney	$U = 4$ $n_1 = 6,$ $n_2 = 6$	.008
All, Aggregated by Nation	Nation	Kruskal-Wallis	$H = 2.44$ 5 d.f.	n.s.
All, Aggregated by Role	Situation	Mann-Whitney	$U = 0$ $n_1 = 6,$ $n_2 = 6$	.001
All, Aggregated by Role	Role	Kruskal-Wallis	$H = 2.61$ 5 d.f.	n.s.
Austro-Hungarian	Situation	Kruskal-Wallis	$H = 4.19$ 2 d.f.	$\sim .12$
	Individual Differences	Kruskal-Wallis	$H = 2.07$ 3 d.f.	n.s.
German	Situation	Kruskal-Wallis	$H = 12.26$ 3 d.f.	$< .01$
	Individual Differences	Kruskal-Wallis	$H = 0.86$ 3 d.f.	n.s.
British	Situation	Kruskal-Wallis	$H = 3.47$ 2 d.f.	n.s.
	Individual Differences	Kruskal-Wallis	$H = 1.69$ 2 d.f.	n.s.
French	Situation	Kruskal-Wallis	$H = 6.20$ 2 d.f.	$< .03$
	Individual Differences	Kruskal-Wallis	$H = 1.36$ 2 d.f.	n.s.
Russian	Situation	Kruskal-Wallis	$H = 4.54$ 3 d.f.	.20
	Individual Differences	Mann-Whitney	$U = 3$ $n_1 = 4,$ $n_2 = 4$	.10

increases.[19] There are some indications in the present data that this may also have been the case in 1914: in five of the six nations (France being the exception), the range of perceived hostility among all leaders (including those excluded from Table 10 owing to the absence of data in both periods) was higher during 27 June–28 July than during 29 July–4 August. But it is impossible to determine whether this was the result of a situation that was objectively less ambiguous, more stressful, a combination of both, or some other factor.

Chapter Four

CRISIS COMMUNICATIONS

EDMUND TAYLOR, in describing the events leading up to World War I, concluded that: "Old world bureaucracy was simply snowed under by the blizzard of information that descended upon it. The keenest and most orderly minds could no longer digest and assimilate the raw data that were being fed into them, and in every capital decisions tended to lag behind events, so that each new move on anyone's part was likely to be a false move, adding to the general confusion." [1]

Embedded within this vivid description of political processes during the days immediately preceding the outbreak of war are a number of propositions: that the amount of diplomatic communication increased dramatically during the period between the assassination of Franz Ferdinand and England's declaration of war on Germany; that the sheer volume of messages at some point exceeded the ability of foreign-policy organizations and officials to cope with it; and, perhaps most importantly, that rather than assisting European leaders in the crucial choices they were making, the amount of information with which they were inundated served to inhibit sound policy making. More generally, this suggests that there is some point beyond which additional information impedes decision making.

In this chapter we shall examine these and some related propositions about communication in crisis. Although "communication" in its broad meaning may include a wide variety of behaviours and many channels or media, we are presently using the term in a quite restricted sense. Our analysis is confined to written documents transmitted between governmental officials. We will thus examine the volume of messages sent and received between and within European foreign offices, the pattern of diplomatic communication (who communicates with whom), and the channels by which messages were transmitted. Several hypotheses relating the effects of the deepening crisis to changes in the volume, pattern, and channels of communication will be tested with the 1914 data.

> As stress increases in a crisis, the volume of communication tends to increase.

> As stress increases in a crisis, there is an increasing tendency to rely upon extraordinary or improvised channels of communication.

> As stress increases in a crisis, the proportion of inter-alliance communication will tend to decline.

These hypotheses focus upon the consequences for communication of deepening crisis and we shall bring systematic evidence to bear on them. The problem of communication in crisis can be taken one step further by considering the effects on policy making of being faced with "a blizzard of information." Our data do not provide a conclusive answer to this question, but we shall at least speculate at some length on the reasons why a sudden rise in incoming messages may in itself have contributed to the stressful circumstances in which European leaders tried to cope with the crucial issues of war and peace.

The 1914 communication data differ from those in other chapters in one important respect: *all* documents published in the Austro-Hungarian, British, French, German, and Russian collections were used, including the reports of ambassadors, ministers, and other diplomatic officials to their foreign offices. In all, the 5620 documents totalled almost one and a half million words. There are, nevertheless, some limitations in the data which must be made explicit. The most important of these is that Serbia is virtually excluded from the analysis that follows. Because a collection of documents comparable to those published by the five other nations involved in the crisis has never been made public, we can reconstruct only part of the flow of communications to and from Belgrade from the other five document collections. We have, for example, a record of the messages sent from

London, Paris, St. Petersburg, Berlin, and Vienna to their representatives in Belgrade, as well as the messages from the latter to their respective foreign offices. But we are lacking comparable data on the flow of messages between the Serbian foreign office and its diplomatic representatives abroad. Our record of diplomatic communication in and out of Belgrade thus includes those of the five major European nations, but only a few of those of the Serbian government itself.

A less serious problem arises from the fact that the Austro-Hungarian collection includes only documents written through 31 July 1914. French, British, German, and Russian messages flowing in and out of Vienna between 1 and 4 August are included in our data, but we do not have comparable Austrian documentation for the final four days of the crisis.

Finally, there is the problem discussed in greater detail in Chapter 2—even the most meticulously collected and scrupulously unbiased collection of documents falls short of being comprehensive. There are almost certainly some gaps in the present data, but for the type of quantitative analysis to be undertaken in this chapter any missing evidence is unlikely to affect the results seriously. Consider the possibility that a half-dozen key documents for one nation were suppressed because of what they revealed about that country's policy and some of its leaders. This represents a loss of less than one per cent of any nation's total. When the analysis turns to the *content* of messages the possibility of missing documents poses a potentially more serious problem. But when our concern is with the volume of communication, as in the present chapter, the risks of drawing invalid inferences from the data appear very limited.

Communication Volume

There is substantial anecdotal and systematic evidence that communication tends to increase in crisis situations. A high-ranking American diplomat in Beirut during the Lebanon crisis of 1958 has written: "In a normal month the code room handled between 100,000 and 150,000 words but after the rebellion broke out the traffic quintupled to 700,000 words." [2] One study has shown that cable traffic in the State Department can increase by as much as

fourfold in times of crisis, and another revealed that during the
Cuban missile confrontation communication between the State
Department and its Latin American embassies and consulates
rose sharply.[3]

To test the initial hypothesis that as stress increases in a crisis
situation the volume of diplomatic communication tends to increase, all documents in the Austro-Hungarian, British, French,
German, and Russian collections were classified into five categories.

1. Messages from diplomatic officials stationed abroad (ambassadors, ministers, attachés, consuls, etc.) to their foreign offices.
2. Messages from high-ranking decision makers (heads of state,
prime ministers, foreign ministers, etc.) to their representatives
abroad.
3. Messages sent by statesmen of one nation directly to their counterparts in another nation.
4. Messages received directly from high-ranking decision makers in
other nations.
5. Messages circulated only among one nation's foreign-policy officials.

Two units were used to measure communication volume—the
document and the word. An index of the average number of
words per line in each volume was determined by an exact count
on every fiftieth page. The number of lines in each document
was then counted and multiplied by the index figure. No effort
was made, however, to adjust message volume for linguistic differences, that is, the necessity to use a different number of words
in various languages to express the same idea.[4]

A word of caution concerning the limitations of this type of
analysis may be in order. To communicate (the process of transmitting information) may not be synonymous with "to inform" in
the sense of increasing the receiver's knowledge, although there
is usually some relation between the two. One can only be certain of perfect congruence when there is a total absence of communication. Thus such terms as "volume of communication"
should be understood to refer to the number of signs transmitted
(which is capable of fairly precise measurement) rather than any
measure of change in the receiver's information. Adequate mea-

surement of the latter appears virtually impossible in studies of historical situations.*

The summaries of diplomatic communications in Table 19 and Figures 6-10 reveal that the average daily flow of messages to, from, and within foreign offices rose sharply as the crisis deepened and war approached.† During late June and early July, for instance, the average influx of messages from ambassadors and other diplomatic officials to their foreign offices was approximately four per day. By 30 July this figure had increased over tenfold.

To provide some basis of comparison, the daily volume of diplomatic messages—both incoming and outgoing—with other European nations was measured for a number of periods prior to the crisis. The results are: Russia (4.0), Austria-Hungary (3.5), France (3.8), and Great Britain (2.4).‡ These figures indicate that the diplomatic communications during the few days immediately following the assassination were not appreciably different from a "normal" period. In contrast the volume of messages that entered

---

* "We communicate by means of signs. The amount of information which could be conveyed depends upon (1) the number of signs transmitted and (2) the amount of information per sign.

"To start with the second item, in human communication the referent of a sign is a concept, and a concept takes the physical form of a neural network (or rather, a network of interconnecting networks) within a human brain. *There is at present no way by which we can quantitatively measure the amount of information a particular sign means to a particular person.* A single sign can refer to a concept as simple as that of a nail, or as complex as that of the Roman Empire or the Gold Rush, and it is doubtful if we ever shall be able to measure the amount of information in such concepts. Since the amount of information per message depends on both the number of signs and the amount of information per sign, and we cannot measure the latter, we seem forced to conclude that the information content of a message cannot be measured.

"On the other hand, it is possible to count the number of signs transmitted. It is also possible to compute the number of signs which a given transmission medium can carry. To use a simple example, if with a given margin, style of type, and page size it is possible to average 500 words (signs) per page, then it is possible to transmit 50,000 signs in a 100 page book." Alfred Kuhn, *The Study of Society* (Homewood, Illinois: Irwin-Dorsey, 1963), p. 175 (italics added).

† Tables with communication data on a daily basis may be found in the appendix.

‡ Germany was not included owing to a lack of adequate documentation for periods prior to the 1914 crisis.

TABLE 19
Daily Average Volume of Communication
during Early and Late Periods of the 1914 Crisis

TYPE OF DOCUMENT	AVERAGE NUMBER OF DOCUMENTS PROCESSED PER DAY		
	27 June–28 July	29 July–4 August	% Increase
Officials Abroad to Foreign Office			
Austria-Hungary	18.1	63.7	253
Germany	6.3	33.9	434
France	7.6	45.7	502
Great Britain	5.9	39.7	576
Russia	10.3	34.6	236
TOTAL	48.2	217.6	351
Foreign Office to Officials Abroad			
Austria-Hungary	13.4	44.3	231
Germany	2.7	18.4	585
France	7.8	48.0	515
Great Britain	2.8	17.3	509
Russia	3.6	11.0	206
TOTAL	30.3	139.0	359
Messages within Foreign Office			
Austria-Hungary	6.0	4.0	− 33
Germany	1.7	11.3	580
France	1.8	10.7	492
Great Britain	1.5	8.4	451
Russia	2.0	2.9	45
TOTAL	13.0	37.3	187
Direct Messages Received from Foreign Leaders			
Austria-Hungary	0.2	1.3	755
Germany	0.3	7.0	1935
France	0.3	4.6	1360
Great Britain	0.4	4.6	1026
Russia	0.8	3.0	269
TOTAL	2.0	20.5	925
Direct Messages Sent to Foreign Leaders			
Austria-Hungary	0.5	5.7	1108
Germany	0.2	3.3	1400
France	0.2	1.7	683
Great Britain	0.7	4.4	575
Russia	0.8	2.9	251
TOTAL	2.4	18.0	650

FIGURE 6
Messages from Officials Abroad to Foreign Office

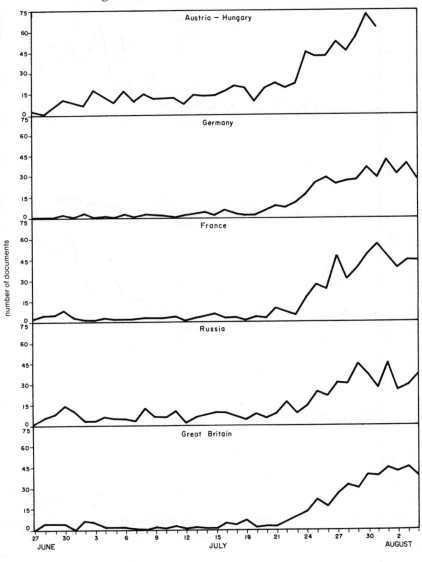

FIGURE 7
Messages from Foreign Office to Officials Abroad

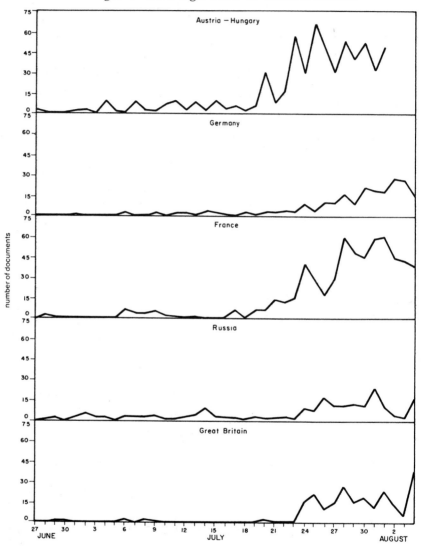

FIGURE 8
Direct Messages to Central Decision Makers Abroad

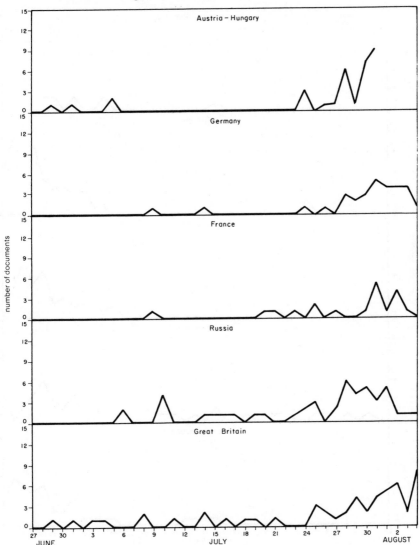

89

FIGURE 9
Direct Messages from Central Decision Makers Abroad

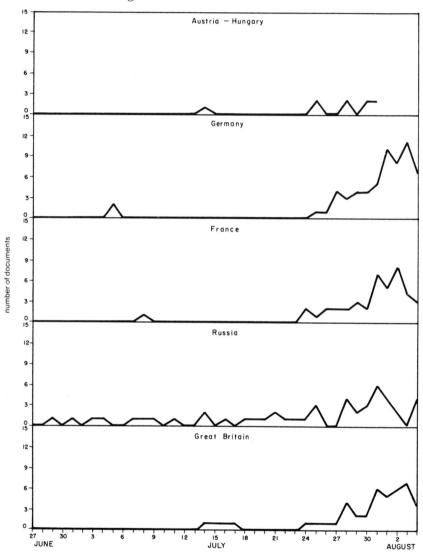

FIGURE 10
Messages within Foreign Office

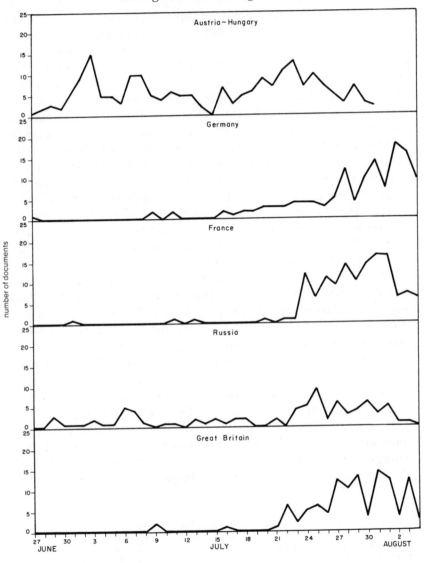

and left foreign offices during late July and early August was clearly far in excess of the norm.

For a more precise test of the hypothesis that as stress increases in a crisis, the amount of diplomatic communication will tend to increase, correlations between stress and message volume were calculated.° The communications data in the previous table were aggregated into two time periods of unequal length, but these correlations were computed on a daily basis. The results are summarized in Table 20. The *gamma* coefficients indicate the degree to which the trend in communications for each country and message type matches daily changes in stress. *Gamma* coefficients have a positive value in every case, indicating that the direction of the relation between stress and communication is as predicted. Also, the strength of the relation is almost uniformly high, but the extent to which this is true appears to depend upon at least three other factors: the degree to which a nation was involved in the early stages of the crisis (centering on the issue of Austro-Hungarian demands upon Serbia), the type of communication, and the unit of measurement.

Of the five major European nations, Austria-Hungary was most deeply involved in the crisis during the days immediately following the assassination. By 28 July Austria-Hungary had severed diplomatic relations with Serbia, had ordered a partial mobilization and was on the point of declaring war on Serbia, and was breaking off its talks with Russia. It is not surprising that Austro-Hungarian message volume was relatively high during the early days of the crisis; starting from this higher base point it increased more moderately than that of the other nations. Owing to its support of Serbia, Russia was also intimately concerned with problems arising out of the assassination and the subsequent Austro-Hungarian demands on the Belgrade government. Initially Russian message volume was also higher than that for the other

---

° Because diplomatic messages for each nation originated in various capitals of Europe, the measure of stress used for Table 20 is the intensity of perceived hostility for *all nations combined*. The alternative of using a separate measure of stress for each nation—as will be done in Chapters 5 and 6—would have resulted in higher *gamma* coefficients in a great majority of cases; for example, all but 9 of the 25 scores reported in the top half of Table 20 would have been higher if the alternative method been employed.

TABLE 20
Strength of Association (Goodman-Kruskal *gamma*)
between Stress and Communication Volume

	Officials Abroad to Foreign Office	Foreign Office to Officials Abroad	Direct Messages to Central Decision Makers Abroad	Direct Messages from Central Decision Makers Abroad	Within Foreign Office
Message Volume Measured by Number of Documents, for					
Austria-Hungary	$.46^b$	$.48^b$	$.67^d$	$.67^b$	.13
Germany	$.66^a$	$.58^a$	$.86^a$	$.81^a$	$.66^a$
Great Britain	$.55^a$	$.64^a$	$.67^a$	$.44^c$	$.72^a$
France	$.50^a$	$.57^a$	$.91^a$	$.55^c$	$.64^a$
Russia	$.49^a$	$.40^c$	$.36^d$	$.48^b$	.20
Message Volume Measured by Number of Words, for					
Austria-Hungary	$.42^b$	$.41^c$	$.58^d$	$.60^b$	.05
Germany	$.54^b$	$.47^b$	$.75^a$	$.70^b$	$.54^a$
Great Britain	$.43^b$	$.49^b$	$.58^c$	$.31^d$	$.67^a$
France	$.42^b$	$.50^b$	$.74^a$	$.49^b$	$.59^a$
Russia	.19	$.35^d$	.23	$.31^d$	.10

[a] $p < .0001$ [b] $p < .001$ [c] $p < .01$ [d] $p < .05$

N (number of days) = 39, except for Austria-Hungary, N = 35

two members of the Triple Entente and it increased more moderately as the crisis approached its climax.

In contrast, until a few days before they were drawn into war, leaders in the other three nations remained relatively unconcerned about the broader implications of the dispute between Austria-Hungary and Serbia. The Balkan situation was first discussed by the British cabinet on the day following delivery of the ultimatum to Serbia, and then only after a bitter debate on the Home Rule issue. Not until five days later was an entire cabinet meeting devoted to international problems, and the European crisis was not debated until 3 August, the day before England declared war on Germany. Much French attention was directed to the sensational trial of Mme. Caillaux, wife of the finance minister, who had killed Gaston Calmette for publishing defamatory materials about her husband. German leaders, especially the kaiser, appear to have remained confident well into the final week of July that the Central Powers could win a major diplomatic triumph—perhaps they could even split the Triple Entente—from the Serbian issue, and that Vienna's demands on Belgrade need not bring Russia, France and, most importantly, Britain into a war against Germany and Austria.

In summary, the three nations that were relatively less concerned with the dispute between Austria-Hungary and Serbia, and yet found themselves in on the brink of world war by the end of July, experienced the most dramatic changes in message volume. On the other hand, there was a more moderate increase in diplomatic communication for the two nations which saw their Balkan interests riding on the future of Serbia almost immediately after the assassination. This finding is consistent with the hypothesis, rather than a deviation from it.

Changes in message volume also appear to depend on the source and destination of the documents. The most consistent increases were in the messages from ambassadors and other diplomatic officials to their various foreign offices. The volume of messages in the other direction—that is, from policy makers in the national capital to their officials abroad—also rose sharply, but less so during the final days of the crisis. This finding is generally consistent with Taylor's thesis that top-ranking policy makers were "snowed under by the blizzard of information" [incoming messages] and that "decisions [outgoing messages] tended to lag behind events."

The differences between message volume within the central decision-making unit during the early and late period of the crisis are in the predicted direction, but the increases were generally smaller. This can perhaps be explained primarily by an increase in face-to-face rather than written communication during the week immediately prior to the outbreak of war. As late as mid-July, some statesmen were not even in their respective capitals. Kaiser Wilhelm was on the royal yacht, Poincaré was visiting Russia, Jagow was on his honeymoon, and many other top officials were away from their respective capitals, necessitating extensive written communication. As the crisis deepened, both the need and the time for written messages decreased and the number of top-level meetings increased.[5]

Finally, the level of change in message volume depends in part on the unit of measurement. The number of diplomatic documents increased more markedly than their total volume when measured by words because messages tended to become shorter during the culminating stages of the crisis.

Although the 1914 data tend to support the first hypothesis, they don't tell us whether the rising rates of communication overtaxed the capabilities of existing channels for international communication. We shall return to this problem later.

Channels of Communication

The normal means of diplomatic communication in 1914 was one in which a nation's ambassador or minister stationed abroad played the central role. Since World War II, summit meetings and other forms of direct communication between heads of government, heads of state, and especially foreign ministers, have often superseded the functions of the ambassador. In contrast, the ambassador was the critical communication link between governments in 1914 (Figure 11). Direct communication between foreign ministers or other top-ranking foreign-policy officials of two nations represented a distinct departure from the usual practice.[6]

According to our second hypothesis, as stress increases, policy makers are likely to bypass normal diplomatic procedures and rely more frequently on improvised or *ad hoc* means of communication. There are at least two reasons why this may happen. As a crisis deepens the usual channels are normally used more often. Figures 6-10 indicated that this was the case in 1914. Thus messages sent directly to foreign leaders will arrive much sooner than if they had been dispatched by the normal diplomatic procedures.

Evidence supporting this hypothesis exists in many other contexts. In his studies of information overload, Miller found that employment of parallel channels is one of the commonly used methods of coping with the problem, especially in complex orga-

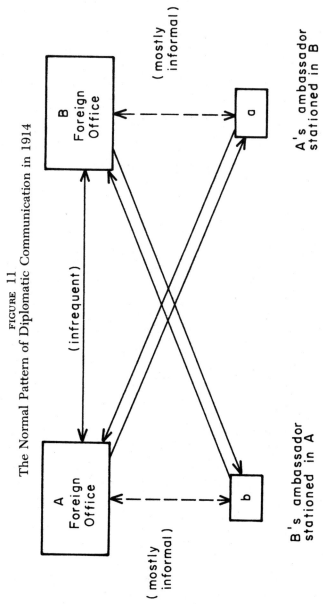

FIGURE 11
The Normal Pattern of Diplomatic Communication in 1914

From Chapter 2 of Robert C. North, *et al.*,
Content Analysis: A Handbook with Applications for the Study of International Crisis
(Evanston, Illinois: Northwestern University Press, 1963), p. 34.

nizations such as groups or bureaucracies.[7] In international politics these channels may take many forms, including direct communication between heads of governments, special emissaries or mediators, and the like. Many of these were used, for example, during the Cuban missile crisis in October 1962. A number of the most important messages were transmitted directly by radio because, as President Kennedy noted after the crisis had passed, normal communications with the Kremlin were "very poor." [*] Special emissaries, including some private citizens, were employed in several instances by both Washington and Moscow. A special advantage of "unofficial" spokesmen is that they may be used in delicate negotiations to float "trial balloons" without seeming to commit the government to a specific course of action; if it becomes advantageous to do so, their efforts may be repudiated as not representing official policy. In Chapter 7 we shall examine Soviet-American communications during the missile confrontation in more detail.

These episodes had their parallel in July 1914, when Albert Ballin, head of the Hamburg-American line, acted as a personal link between London and Berlin. Twenty-five years later Birger Dahlerus, a Swedish businessman, performed a similar function. During the final days of peace in 1939, he was the most active channel of communication between the British and German governments.[8]

The figures reported earlier revealed a high correlation between stress and the volume of direct communication among European leaders. Was this part of a general increase in communication as the crisis deepened, or did the use of direct channels rise at an even faster rate? Table 21 summarizes the proportion of direct messages received and sent by the five nations. The top part of the table, based on the total number of

[*] Columbia Broadcasting System, "A Conversation with President Kennedy," 17 December 1962 (mimeo. transcript), p. 21. For quite different reasons, channels of communication between the United States and North Vietnam have been very poor. In these circumstances, messages between the two governments have been relayed by third and fourth parties ranging from prime ministers and foreign ministers to private citizens of several countries. David Kraslow and Stuart H. Loory, The Secret Search for Peace in Vietnam (New York: Vintage, 1968). See also, Hedrick Smith, "Cambodia Decision: Why President Acted," New York Times, 30 June 1970, pp. 1, 14.

messages received by the foreign offices,* indicates that the number and percentage of all messages arriving directly from another capital more than doubled during the final week of the crisis. The lower half of the table is based on the number of outgoing documents.† Messages sent directly rather than through the normal channels rose by more than a third during the week prior to Britain's entry into the war, and the corresponding percentage of direct messages increased from 7.3% to 11.5%.

TABLE 21
Direct Messages during Early and Late Periods
of the 1914 Crisis: All Nations

Messages Received in Foreign Offices	27 June– 28 July	29 July– 4 August
Total	1606	1406
Direct Messages	65	138
% Direct Messages	4.0%	9.8%

Messages Sent by Foreign Offices	27 June– 28 July	29 July– 4 August
Total	1046	899
Direct Messages	76	103
% Direct Messages	7.3%	11.5%

These figures do not reveal, however, whether there were differences in the use of direct communication among the five major nations in the crisis. For a more detailed analysis we can consider each nation separately as both a sender and a recipient of messages, and examine its method of communication with each of the major powers, as well as with the other European nations combined. Summarizing the data in this manner produces a total of ten communication relationships for each country, plus five for the "other nations" combined.‡ For example, we can consider the

* That is, the data in Figures 6 and 9.

† That is, the data in Figures 7 and 8.

‡ We know how many direct messages originating with foreign offices in Serbia, Belgium, Italy, and other nations were sent to England, France, Russia, Ger-

channels used by English leaders to send messages to France, Russia, Germany, Austria-Hungary, and other nations combined, as well as those used to send messages from these countries to England. Thus there are a total of fifty-five pairs of nations for which we can measure the relative frequency of direct communications. Note that each of these fifty-five pairs is different because the *percentage* of direct communication sent by A to B differs from that of the documents B receives directly from A. Direct messages sent from London to St. Petersburg accounted for 35.0% and 38.9% of all communication from England to Russia during 27 June–28 July and 29 July–4 August. But the same direct messages represented only 22.6% and 17.1% of the documents which Russian leaders received from London during the same periods. The number of direct messages is, of course, the same in both instances. But in the former case we are comparing them to the number of documents sent from the British foreign office to its diplomatic representatives in Russia, whereas in the latter instance the comparison is with the volume of documents from the Russian diplomatic staff in London to the Russian foreign office. Note also that in this example the former case supports our hypothesis whereas the latter one does not.

The relative frequency of direct communication during the early and late periods of the crisis is summarized in Tables 22 and 23. Of the fifty-five pairs of nations described in these tables, direct communication increased during the latter period of the crisis in thirty-seven of them and declined in only thirteen cases. In five instances there were no direct messages exchanged between top-level policy makers—Austria-Hungary neither sent nor received direct messages from either England or France, and France sent no such messages to any nation other than Britain, Russia, and Germany.

When the data are analysed by nation, some clear differences emerge. The flow of direct messages as a percentage of total communication between Berlin and almost every other direct capital increased during the later stages of the crisis. A similar tendency also appears in the case of France and England. Russia and Aus-

many, and Austria-Hungary. But we cannot calculate what proportion of all communications these totals represent. Hence, we have no percentage figures to report for messages sent by "other nations" in Table 23.

TABLE 22
Direct Messages as Percentage of Total Messages Sent
during Early and Late Periods of the Crisis

MESSAGES SENT BY	MESSAGES SENT TO						
	Great Britain	France	Russia	Germany	Austria-Hungary	All Other Nations	Total
Great Britain							
27 June–28 July		17.8	35.0	12.5	0.0	0.0	18.8
29 July–4 August		29.3	38.9	28.9	0.0	0.2	20.4
France							
27 June–28 July	2.2		10.3	0.0	0.0	0.0	2.7
29 July–4 August	8.0		5.3	4.5	0.0	0.0	3.4
Russia							
27 June–28 July	43.7	31.3		20.0	11.1	4.1	18.8
29 July–4 August	27.8	30.0		46.6	0.0	7.7	20.4
Germany							
27 June–28 July	17.7	0.0	10.0		8.6	0.0	7.5
29 July–4 August	20.0	15.4	27.8		13.3	6.0	15.1
Austria-Hungary							
27 June–28 July	3.4	6.5	8.1	8.5		1.1	3.4
29 July–4 August	13.3	9.1	0.0	41.2		0.0	11.3
All Other Nations							
27 June–28 July	0.0	0.9	4.1	0.0	0.5		
29 July–4 August	9.7	5.1	7.7	6.0	0.9		

All figures are percentages

tria-Hungary, on the other hand, used direct means of communication in almost equal proportions during both periods of the crisis. Of the thirteen cases which ran counter to our hypothesis, Russia was involved as the sender or recipient in ten and Austria-Hungary in six of them. As noted earlier, the initial stage of the crisis, centering on the Serbian question, was of more direct concern to Russia and Austria-Hungary than it was to Germany, England, and France. Hence it is not inconsistent with the hypothesis that Austria-Hungary and Russia used direct channels almost as much in the weeks after the assassination as during the days immediately preceding the outbreak of general war.

Communication Within and Between Alliances

Much of the debate between various schools of thought on deterrence centres on the problem of communicating effectively

TABLE 23
Direct Messages as Percentage of Total Messages Received
during Early and Late Periods of the Crisis

MESSAGES RECEIVED BY	MESSAGES SENT FROM						
	Great Britain	France	Russia	Germany	Austria-Hungary	All Other Nations	Total
Great Britain							
27 June–28 July		4.8	28.6	12.0	1.9	0.0	6.5
29 July–4 August		12.7	10.0	10.9	8.3	9.6	10.3
France							
27 June–28 July	13.3		10.3	0.0	5.4	0.9	4.0
29 July–4 August	26.2		16.8	4.0	4.6	5.1	9.1
Russia							
27 June–28 July	22.6	18.7		0.0	6.7	1.6	7.3
29 July–4 August	17.1	7.5		22.2	0.0	4.8	8.0
Germany							
27 June–28 July	3.1	0.0	2.9		8.2	5.3	5.1
29 July–4 August	18.1	6.7	16.7		28.7	13.7	17.1
Austria-Hungary							
27 June–28 July	0.0	0.0	2.2	3.1		0.5	0.9
29 July–4 August	0.0	0.0	0.0	9.4		0.9	2.1

All figures are percentages

with adversaries, especially under crisis conditions. How can one nation's leaders convince those of potential enemies of their commitment to certain central goals, and that they have and will use the capabilities necessary to achieve those ends? How can they, at the same time, convey sufficient reassurance that a pre-emptive attack is not imminent, thereby reducing the adversary's incentives for striking first? These and similar questions take on added significance because it is generally recognized that it is easier to communicate with trusting friends than with suspicious enemies.

As a crisis deepens the need for clear communication between potential enemies thus becomes more urgent. At the same time it is likely to become more difficult to maintain unimpeded *means* of transmitting information and the *will* to continue discussions and negotiations, both of which are necessary (but not sufficient) conditions for conveying one's messages with clarity to adversaries. It is less likely that difficulties in communication between allies will arise to a similar extent. Moreover, during the latter stages of the crisis we might expect certain types of discussions with allies to increase. As war becomes more probable, more attention might be given to the problems of clarifying and coordinating military plans, especially within an alliance in which such plans were only sketchily worked out. Hence the hypothesis that as the severity of a crisis deepens, the proportion of messages directed to members of the opposing alliance will decline.

Table 24 reveals some support for the hypothesis. During the first month after the assassination, about one-third (31.9%) of all international communications involved partners in the opposing coalition. During the last week prior to the outbreak of general war, on the other hand, messages across alliance lines accounted for just over one-quarter (26.4%) of the total. For all messages,

TABLE 24
Communication with Members of the Opposing Alliance
during the Early and Late Periods of the 1914 Crisis

		27 June– 28 July	29 July– 4 August
Austria- Hungary	Total Messages Inter-alliance Messages % Inter-alliance Messages	1027 349 34.0%	345 91 26.4%
Germany	Total Messages Inter-alliance Messages % Inter-alliance Messages	307 119 38.8%	438 174 39.7%
France	Total Messages Inter-alliance Messages % Inter-alliance Messages	510 171 33.5%	700 160 22.9%
Great Britain	Total Messages Inter-alliance Messages % Inter-alliance Messages	313 107 34.2%	462 126 27.3%
Russia	Total Messages Inter-alliance Messages % Inter-alliance Messages	496 101 20.4%	360 58 16.1%
All Nations	Total Messages Inter-alliance Messages % Inter-alliance Messages	2653 847 31.9%	2305 609 26.4%

rising stress was moderately associated with declining inter-alliance communication ($gamma = .27$, N = 39, p = .02).

The data for Austria-Hungary, Great Britain, France, and Russia are consistent with the hypothesis, although in the latter case the most striking finding is the very limited communication between St. Petersburg and nations of the Dual Alliance at any time during the entire period. There is also one marked exception to the general trend: during the final days of the crisis the proportion of German communication with members of the Triple Entente increased slightly.°

Finally, we get a more detailed insight into patterns of communication by considering the source and destination of each message to and from the five major European capitals. Table 25 reveals that despite the overall tendency for the proportion of inter-alliance communication to decline as war approached, this was not true in all instances. The most apparent exceptions are the decline of communication between Austria and Germany during the culminating days of the crisis and the concomitant increase in the number of messages between London and Berlin. One possible explanation in the former instance might have been that contingency plans between Vienna and Berlin, long-time allies, had been well formulated and required little elaboration. Historical records reveal, however, that this was not the case; on the contrary, military coordination within the Dual Alliance had been rather casual for a number of years.[9] The increased communication between Great Britain and Germany probably reflected the lack of British concern with the crisis during its initial stages, as well as Germany's lingering hopes that London could be detached from the Entente.

° For purposes of this discussion the following types of messages were classified as communications across alliance lines:

FOR	MESSAGES EXCHANGED WITH
Austria-Hungary	France, Great Britain, Russia, Serbia
Germany	France, Great Britain, Russia, Serbia
France	Austria-Hungary, Germany
Great Britain	Austria-Hungary, Germany
Russia	Austria-Hungary, Germany

TABLE 25
Changes in the Frequency of Communication
between the Early and Late Periods of the Crisis

Communi- cations of	INTRA-ALLIANCE COMMUNICATION			INTER-ALLIANCE COMMUNICATION		
	To Foreign Office from	From Foreign Office to	Change	To Foreign Office from	From Foreign Office to	Change
Austria- Hungary	Germany		−	Great Britain		−
		Germany	−		Great Britain	−
				France		−
					France	−
				Russia		−
					Russia	−
Germany	Austria- Hungary		−	Great Britain		+
		Austria- Hungary	−		Great Britain	+
				France		+
					France	+
				Russia		−
					Russia	+
Great Britain	France		+	Austria- Hungary		−
		France	+		Austria- Hungary	−
	Russia		−	Germany		+
		Russia	−		Germany	+
France	Great Britain		+	Austria- Hungary		−
		Great Britain	+		Austria- Hungary	NC
	Russia		+	Germany		NC
		Russia	+		Germany	NC
Russia	Great Britain		−	Austria- Hungary		−
		Great Britain	−		Austria- Hungary	−
	France		+	Germany		−
		France	+		Germany	NC

Key: + Increased communication during late (29 July–4 August) period
  − Decreased communication during late period
  NC No change from early (27 June–28 July) to late period

The Consequences of Communication Overload

Information and communication are crucial aspects of individual and organizational decision making. The effects of insufficient communication have received the greatest share of attention, and there has been less concern for the consequences of too much communication. As indicated in Chapter 1, evidence on this point has been derived mostly from the laboratory rather than from historical studies, but it does suggest that communication overload may significantly affect decision processes.

To this point we have found that the three hypotheses relating deepening crisis to the volume, channels, and pattern of communication have generally been supported by the 1914 data. But some interesting questions on the *consequences* of these changes in communication remain unanswered. We began by suggesting that too much communication may hamper decision making as much as insufficient communication, an assumption for which experimental evidence exists.[10] Although there is also strong evidence that channel capacity is inversely related to the size of the system, we know comparatively little about *what magnitude of communication constitutes overload* at complex levels such as the foreign-policy organizations in the various capitals of Europe during the 1914 crisis.° Compounding this difficulty is the fact that organizations and individuals both differ in their capacity to process incoming information.

One indicator of communication overload might be delay in transmission of messages, such as happened in many instances in 1914. For example, the kaiser did not receive a copy of the Serbian reply to the ultimatum until 27 July, two days after it had been submitted to Austria-Hungary, and then it was received through the Norddeutsch news agency.[11] This was largely the result of decisions in Berlin and Vienna not to alarm Wilhelm, rather than of any overload which hampered the transmission of messages. Thus, of the many instances of delay in communication, some were the consequence of deliberate actions.† In other cases, however, it is evident that the volume of

---

° "It appears that channel capacities *per channel* are less the larger the system. This is a regular, hierarchical difference, proceeding from a maximum of several hundred impulses (or bits) per second at the level of the neurone, to perhaps 200 at the organ system, to about 30 for the individual, to a good deal less for the group and the social institution, although these last values are less certain." Miller, "Information Input Overload and Psychopathology," 699.

† The French also complained of interrupted telegraphic service with Vienna (26 July) and Berlin (31 July) prior to the outbreak of war: "The resumé of the Serbian response to the Austrian note reached us twenty hours late, telegrams seemingly stopped in Austria." France, #98. "Germany has broken all international telegraph and telephone communications." Great Britain, #364.

diplomatic correspondence was severely taxing, if not exceeding the ability of existing channels to keep up with the message flow. By 2 August, telegraphic service between Berlin and London had become so poor that German leaders were led to believe that the British had cut the cables. Tirpitz viewed this seriously enough to ask Jagow whether Britain and Germany were at war. Inquiries produced a telegram from Grey, sent in the clear, explaining that "the delay has been due to extraordinary congestion." [12]

A crude index which may indicate the presence of communication overload is suggested by Taylor's generalization that during the summer of 1914 decision makers were unable to respond to the "blizzard" of incoming messages. We can measure the relation between the number of incoming and outgoing messages for each foreign office by the following formula,

$$\text{Index} = \frac{\text{Number of messages received}}{\text{Number of messages received} + \text{number of messages sent}}$$

The index value will vary between 1.00 when messages are being received and none are being sent out, to 0.00 when the reverse situation is true, or when all communication ceases. A figure of 0.50 indicates that at any time the number of incoming and outgoing messages is the same.

The index for each nation is presented in Figure 12.° Despite some differences among the five nations the pattern is, in one respect, roughly the same for all of them. During the initial stages of the period under consideration, the proportion of incoming messages was very high for all five nations because diplomatic representatives dispatched numerous reports relating to

---

° As shown before, the volume of communication during the early days of the crisis was very low. In Figure 12 the data are aggregated into twelve periods of unequal length so that the total number of messages—the denominator in our index—is sufficiently high in all cases to provide a stable measure of the relation between incoming and outgoing messages.

This index assumes that each incoming message is equally likely to require a response. It might reasonably be argued that the need for a reply from the foreign office increases as the severity of the crisis deepens. If this is the case it would add greater significance to the high index values during late July and early August.

FIGURE 12
The Proportion of Incoming Messages to the Total Message Volume

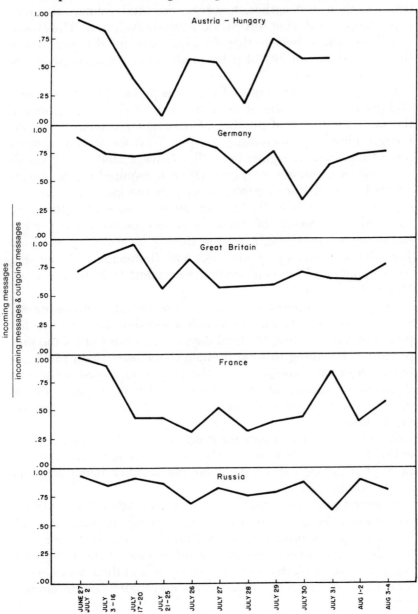

the assassination and its likely consequences to their foreign offices. As indicated earlier, however, the total volume of diplomatic messages during this period was relatively low. Thus there is little reason to believe that the high index for this period was the result of an inability of policy makers to cope with the inflow of communications.

During the middle stages of the crisis period there was a general decline in the ratio of incoming to total documents, despite the fact that the total number of messages received at various foreign offices was increasing sharply. Thus for at least a short period top-level foreign-policy officials were able to cope with the flood of incoming messages. Often it required extraordinary efforts to do so. For example, on 30 July the kaiser and his foreign-policy officials in Berlin sent out more messages than they received. But many of these were composed during what amounted to an all-night session during the evening of 29–30 July. Between 10:15 p.m. and 2:55 a.m. Bethmann-Hollweg sent six telegrams to Vienna alone in a vain effort to restrain Austro-Hungarian leaders.[13]

Clearly it is impossible for prime ministers, foreign ministers, and their advisers to maintain such a schedule for an extended period of time. During the final days of the crisis period the proportion of incoming to total messages increased again in all nations. This fact, combined with the greatly expanded volume of diplomatic communication, does suggest that the capacity of foreign offices to cope with incoming information was being severely taxed.

In one respect the results for Russia stand out. Throughout the entire five and a half weeks the volume of messages arriving in St. Petersburg exceeded by far the number being sent out by the foreign office.

A second problem is that we have not considered whether the increasing volume of diplomatic correspondence may have affected the policy processes and decisions in 1914. Is there reason to believe that a suddenly increasing volume of incoming messages is a source of stress on organizations and their members, at least for some kinds of organizations and under certain circumstances?

At this point the discussion becomes frankly speculative. Such anecdotal and secondary evidence as Edmund Taylor's generalization quoted at the beginning of this chapter is hardly sufficient to demonstrate that, for instance, communication overload hampered policy making in European foreign offices. Nor is it satisfactory to postulate that sharply rising message volume *invariably* has an adverse effect on decision making. The *type of organization, message content,* the ability to *anticipate* changes in communication volume, and the *time* available for response may heighten or mitigate such consequences.

The consequences of increased communication are unlikely to be the same for all organizations. We can classify them according to the nature of the services they provide (essential or non-essential) and according to the absence or presence of other firms that may furnish similar services (monopoly or non-monopoly). These distinctions permit us to identify four types of organizations:

	Monopoly	*Non-monopoly*
Essential services	A	B
Non-essential services	C	D

Let's consider how the effects of communication overload is likely to vary among them.

Communication overload is least likely to induce severe stress in type D organization. A cosmetics manufacturer faced with more incoming messages—for example, orders for its products—than it can process may adopt many strategies for coping with the situation. The firm may refuse to fill them, withdraw a given item from production, give priority to orders from preferred customers, or allocate its products on some sort of quota system. These are but a few of the rather broad range of socially and organizationally sanctioned responses to the situation. Given the wide latitude of strategies of coping with the problem, communication overload is not likely to create severe stress in type D organizations.

The means for dealing with the problem may be somewhat more restricted for type C than for type D organizations, but even sharp increases in incoming messages are unlikely to create serious difficulties. For example, as a special service to collectors, many mints produce and distribute sets of coins made with special highly polished dies ("proof sets"). A sudden rise in orders over the past few years have been met by a number of strategies: raising the price of coins; limiting the number of coin sets that may be ordered; reducing the period during which orders are accepted; or fixing production at a certain level, queuing orders, filling them until supplies are exhausted, and returning all others. Given the non-essential nature of the services provided and the limited clientele, the United States Mint was even able to suspend production of proof coins as a way of coping with burgeoning demand.

Type B organizations usually have less latitude for dealing with communication overload. An urban hospital or bank rarely enjoys a local monopoly on the services it provides, but the nature of its functions is such that even temporarily closing down or limiting responses to incoming communications runs counter to both organizational norms and those of the society in which it operates. For example, a bank that offered a free-cheque service in order to attract more customers was faced with an unexpected and unmanageable rush of new depositors. Bank officials were unable to develop a strategy for meeting the situation. Screening applicants to eliminate all but large depositors was neither practical nor conducive to good will. Closing the bank would have been disastrous to future operations and might even have caused another and more disastrous type of communication overload— demands for withdrawal from nervous depositors. Ultimately a federal agency was forced to take over the bank's operations. In this case the organization was simply unable to develop internal means of coping with a flood of incoming communication.[14] It seems reasonable to suppose that in this and similar cases a high degree of stress is generated within the organization.

Finally, organizations which have a monopoly on some essential service (type A) are least likely to have latitude in dealing with communication overload. Utilities (whether publicly or privately owned), police, fire, and public health agencies are at

times faced with dramatic increases in incoming communication
—for example, in disasters such as earthquakes or hurricanes. Either rigid adherence to a "first come, first served" policy or any
deviation from that approach—deciding that some claims for service take priority over others—is likely to create internal tensions
as well as conflict between the organization and its clientele.
Strategies such as temporarily ceasing to accept any new messages while the backlog is being reduced, or complete withdrawal from the situation, are unthinkable options. Similarly, foreign-policy decisions are an essential service from which no
government can escape, short of abdicating all responsibilities for
governing. The difficulty may be compounded by bureaucratic
rules which require that elaborate procedures be followed in responding to incoming messages. A State Department desk officer
recently complained that he sometimes needed as many as twen-
ty-nine clearances before sending a routine cable to the American embassy in a small nation.[15]

To summarize the argument to this point, then, it appears that
an overload of incoming information is likely to create the sever-
est stress for type A organizations followed in order by those of
types B, C, and D. Within this typology, it is clear that foreign
offices are of type A. If our reasoning is generally valid, we may
therefore assume that the greatly increased flow of messages into
foreign offices in Vienna, Berlin, St. Petersburg, Paris, and London during the final stages of the 1914 crisis was not only a response to the increasing severity of the situation, but also probably contributed to the stress within these organizations.

In addition to organizational factors we can relate the
consequences of communication overload to the content of the
incoming communication, the degree to which the sudden influx
of messages can be anticipated, and the time within which a response must be drawn up.

There are several ways in which the *content* of incoming messages may be related to stress. Messages of a routine nature may
create little, if any, difficulty. A sudden influx of applications for
passports or driver's licenses might result in periods of heavy
workload at the clerical level, but not throughout the organization. Moreover, as long as responses to incoming messages require only the application of previously established routines, expe-

dients such as hiring temporary clerical assistance may be used. But should the increase in incoming messages also require development of new rules for responding, all parts of the organization, including top-level decision makers, are likely to be engaged. It is almost axiomatic that messages during a major international crisis will require continued attention from those at the top of the foreign-policy organization.

There is a second aspect of increased message inflow that is likely to create stress in a crisis. As the amount of threatening information—diplomatic warnings, ultimata, news of military preparations by opponents, and the like—increases, tensions among those receiving the messages is likely to increase, irrespective of the type of organization. We would expect this result, for instance, if the cosmetics firm used to illustrate type D organizations were faced with a sudden influx of messages which threatened its survival: cease-and-desist orders from the Food and Drug Administration relating to impurities in the firm's major products, legal threats arising from a suit for patent infringement, streams of letters from consumers and retailers complaining about the quality of the cosmetics, and threats of a proxy fight from dissident stockholders.

Many European leaders appear to have been agonizingly slow to appreciate that they were on the brink of war. Nevertheless, when the danger was recognized, the likely consequences of a general European war were often perceived with acute prescience. At almost the same moment that Moltke wrote telling Bethmann-Hollweg that a general war would "annihilate for decades the civilization of almost all Europe," the British foreign minister was warning the German ambassador, Lichnowsky, "If war breaks out, it will be the greatest catastrophe that the world has ever seen." [16] A flood of diplomatic reports, the contents of which made it increasingly certain that the catastrophe would take place, could hardly have failed to produce high tensions.

When increased communication inflow can be *anticipated*, it is often possible to take certain steps which reduce stress on the organization. Post offices can be certain that the volume of mail will rise sharply during the weeks prior to Christmas. Temporary mail carriers are hired on a seasonal basis to permit the permanent staff to carry out other duties related to handling the increased communication load. This strategy is only possible because the tasks involved are simple ones which involve only the mechanical application of routine decision rules at the lowest levels of the organization.

The situation with respect to increased communication during the 1914 crisis was quite the opposite. Neither the event which initiated the crisis—the assassination—nor the rapid escalation of a local crisis into general war was widely anticipated. Equally important, the nature of messages flowing into the various foreign offices was such that they required more than routine responses from lower-ranking members of foreign-office staffs. For these reasons it seems reasonable to assume that a sudden unexpected increase in messages of the gravest urgency tended to generate stress within the foreign offices of the nations involved in the crisis.

The *time available for response* is also an important factor in coping with communication overload.[17] If there is no imperative to respond one-for-one to messages as fast as they are received, such strategies as queuing and setting priorities in the queue may prove quite sufficient, even in the case of organizations with a monopoly on essential services. Tax-collection agencies or various licensing bureaus can handle sudden and massive increases in communication at certain times of the year not only because these situations can be anticipated, but also because incoming messages can be queued and responses delayed within reasonable limits. For example, tax returns can be audited for errors or refund cheques sent out months after the returns are filed without serious repercussions.

Again it is clear that extended time for responses was not available in 1914, especially during the culminating stages of the crisis. More important, there is also strong evidence (to be presented in the next chapter) that European leaders felt themselves to be under increasing pressure of time as war approached.

When we apply these ideas to a situation such as the 1914 crisis, there is therefore reason to believe that the sudden and greatly expanded volume of diplomatic messages into foreign offices in London, Paris, St. Petersburg, Berlin, and Vienna tended to increase stress. Such organizations have a monopoly of foreign-policy decisions and provide an essential service. Hence, stress-reducing strategies such as ignoring the communications, letting other agencies cope with the problem, or withdrawing could not have been considered. Moreover, the nature of these communications posed increasingly severe burdens of decision upon these to whom they were addressed. The strategy of permitting persons at the lowest levels of the organization to respond by applying routine decision rules was clearly not feasible. Thus the burden of coping with incoming messages fell upon the small number of top-level policy makers in each nation. Because the situation was unanticipated the strategy of expanding staffs could not be employed. In any case, there is evidence from other situations that one response to crisis is to *reduce* rather than enlarge the relevant decision group.[18] Finally, such strategies as queuing messages and delaying responses were not sanctioned by the situation. Some of the most important messages, such as the ultimatum delivered to Serbia, contained rigid deadlines. And, as we shall demonstrate later, the decision makers themselves felt that the imperatives of the situation gave them little time for responding at leisure.

In summary, our data have demonstrated that as the 1914 crisis deepened and war approached, message volume increased dramatically. We have also developed a line of reasoning—but certainly not demonstrated conclusively—that a sharp influx of communication probably increased the stress within foreign offices in the various European capitals. Owing to the conjunction of several factors—the nature of foreign-policy organizations and of the incoming messages, the lack of anticipation, and the limited time for response—there were relatively few ways of escaping stress-inducing consequences. Or, to put it somewhat differently, socially sanctioned means of resolving any difficulties arising from communication overload were few indeed.

There remains the most difficult problem of tracing out the impact of communication on policy making. The point that more information does not automatically give rise to either more *useful* information or more informed decisions has been summarized effectively by Dinerstein.

Masses of information and misinformation are collected. The analyst spends much of his time sifting and the really important items are often lost in the mass of trivia. By contrast the ambassador of the

Spanish king to the court of James I was on intimate terms with the latter, had a keen idea of what was relevant to his royal master and had to select data carefully if only because he had to write his dispatches by hand. Modern intelligence collection, by comparison, is mindless. Masses of information are collected, much of it secret which automatically reduces the number of outsiders who can volunteer to help sort the material. To separate the wheat from the chaff is almost impossible and the memoirs of intelligence operations in World War II are replete with instances of the most significant intelligence being ignored or dismissed.[19]

In this respect 1914 was a historical midpoint, without vast intelligence agencies such as the CIA, but with means of communication and bureaucratic foreign offices that were unknown to James I and his contemporaries. Other questions can also be raised. How are statesmen affected by being inundated with incoming messages? How is the information processed by foreign offices? Which information is used and which is discarded? A survey of experimental findings has identified a number of strategies for coping with the problem: omission, error, queuing, filtering, cutting categories of discrimination, employing multiple channels, and escape.[20] It has also been shown that there is little difference among them when information input is moderate; as the volume of communication rises, however, omissions and filtering increase the most sharply. An example of filtering and omission has been vividly described by a high-ranking colleague of former Secretary of State Dulles.

I remember at staff meetings, we would start out briskly with Mr. Dulles making some pronouncements on maybe one little piece of some foreign problem. Then the various Assistant Secretaries and the various divisions of the Department would begin reporting on maybe the week's developments in Berlin, Egypt, Israel, Indonesia, China, in Greece, or wherever it was. And with each added problem—and there were problems by the hundreds every hour of the day—Mr. Dulles would seem to be more bewildered and seem to be willing to pay less attention to any of these numerous problems which were pressing on everyone around the State Department. He kind of shrugged them off to maybe devote himself to some particular case.[21]

Only the most fragmentary evidence on this point can be adduced from the 1914 data. Employment of multiple channels during the latter stages of the crisis through more frequent direct communication between decision makers has already been noted. There is, in addition, evidence of selective filtering of incoming information. Kaiser Wilhelm tended to dismiss the consistently accurate reports of his ambassador in London regarding British intentions as more utter nonsense from "that old goat." [22] On the other hand the reports of the German ambassador in St. Petersburg, which supported the "preferred view" that Russia was bluffing in its announced policy of supporting Serbia, were accepted quite uncritically. During the most intense period of the crisis Wilhelm virtually ignored all signals that England would join its allies if either Russia or France became involved in war with Germany. In one of three similar telegrams that he dispatched on 25 July, Lichnowsky, the German ambassador in London, warned Berlin that if France were drawn into war, "England would [not] dare to remain disinterested." [23] On the other hand, the kaiser was ready to accept at face value a second-hand (and very misleading) report from the German naval attaché stating that King George had assured Prince Henry of Prussia that England would remain out of the war.[24] Despite the shaky foundations on which his hopes for British neutrality rested, Wilhelm rejected all information to the contrary. To suggestions that he temper his optimism he replied, "I have the word of a king, and that is sufficient for me." [25]

Similarly, on 30 July the kaiser read two articles published the previous day in the English *Daily Chronicle* which criticized British involvement in the crisis. The articles charged, among other things, that the crisis was the result of Serbian and Russian intrigues, that France and Britain would be dragged into war merely to support Russian ambitions, and that Winston Churchill's demands for mobilization of the fleet was "an outburst of meddlesome Chauvinism." Wilhelm responded by such notations on the margin as "Yes," "Right," "Bravo," "Excellent," and "So these are the voices of public opinion that drove Grey to threaten Lichnowsky! Why, this is the very opposite! He was either bluffing or lying outright!" [26] Thus, two unauthoritative articles which supported the kaiser's hopes and expectations that Britain would remain neutral were accepted quite uncritically, whereas Grey's warnings, as reported accurately by Lichnowsky, were dismissed.

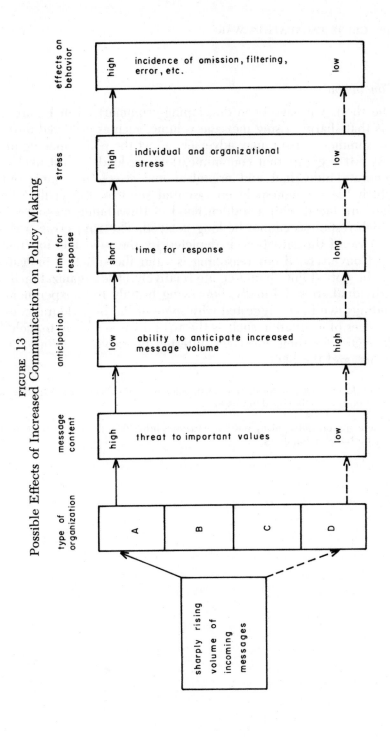

FIGURE 13
Possible Effects of Increased Communication on Policy Making

Conclusion

The thesis we have been developing—summarized in Figure 13 —is that sharply rising message volume, such as occurred during the summer of 1914, may adversely affect the policy-making process.* It suggests that communication overload is most likely to generate individual and organizational stress in organizations which have a monopoly on essential services, especially when they are faced with a sudden flood of threatening messages for which responses cannot be long delayed. The 1914 crisis, a classic case of this situation, is depicted by the solid line in Figure 13. Conversely, if our reasoning is valid the situation indicated by the dotted line should create relatively little organizational or individual stress.† Finally, borrowing heavily from experimental findings, we have suggested why some of the behavioural consequences of a situation such as the 1914 crisis are likely to include disregard for some messages, filtering of incoming information, errors, and the like.

* Note that the second, third, and fourth columns of this diagram incorporate the definition of crisis described in Chapter 1.

† There are, of course, many possible situations other than the two extreme examples illustrated in Figure 13.

Chapter Five

CRISIS, TIME PRESSURE,
AND POLICY MAKING

Introduction

NEARLY EVERY DISCUSSION of the effects of modern technology sooner or later touches upon a point that has almost become a cliché—virtually every facet of our existence has been affected by a continually shrinking time dimension. Instantaneous communication and travel at speeds faster than sound are but two of the more familiar manifestations of this phenomenon. Certainly international politics have been vitally affected. The policy-making process in all nations—whether democratic or authoritarian—share at least one important characteristic: in crisis situations, leaders have been denied the luxury of decision making in leisure. Technology has provided the capacity of responding with weapons of almost incalculable speed of delivery, thus often cutting available decision time to almost nothing. At the same time the potency of these weapons has created one of the cruel paradoxes of the nuclear age—the very decisions which should be made with the greatest deliberation, because of their potentially awesome consequences, may have to be made under the most urgent pressure of time.

To those conditioned to the presence of these vast arsenals of nuclear weapons which can be delivered to any spot in the world within hours, the relevance of time pressures in pre-1945 crises may seem remote. Indeed, were our analysis confined to the state of military technology in the early years of the twentieth century, we would be unlikely to look to this factor as an explanation for the rapid escalation of a local incident into a cataclysmic world war. Recall that in 1914 cavalry units moved not in tanks but on horseback—as did their predecessors half a millennium earlier—and airplanes were considered to be curiosities rather than potent weapons of war. We may thus be tempted to look back to the international system of 1914 and assume, with more than a touch of nostalgia and envy, that European leaders of that era must have been mercifully free of the intense pressures of time which characterize our own age.

But would this assumption prove valid if we try to picture the situation as it appeared to European leaders in 1914? In this chapter we will consider this question in greater detail. Did European leaders feel increased time pressure as the crisis deepened? If so, how did this affect the nature of policy decisions in Vienna, Berlin, London, Paris, and St. Petersburg, and—more importantly—the interactions between them?

In discussions of crisis, time pressure has usually been treated in one of three ways. It is sometimes considered as one of the *defining characteristics* of crisis. That is, a situation is not considered a crisis unless decision time is short. Perceived time pressure has also been considered as one of the *consequences* of the stresses which accompany a crisis. It has been suggested, for example, that the higher the stress in a crisis situation, the shorter the perceived time necessary for the enemy to deliver a punishing blow. A corollary hypothesis states that as crisis-induced stress increases, the net rewards for early action are calculated to be much higher than the net benefits of delaying action.[1] Finally, considerable attention has been directed to time pressure as a factor which affects both the *processes* by which policy decisions are made, and the *nature of the resulting policies*. Propositions of this type include the following examples.

The greater the time pressure, the more vigorous the search for alternatives.[2]

As time pressure is pushed to the limit, the search for alternatives becomes less fruitful.[3]

The shorter the decision time, the fewer are the number of significantly differentiated alternatives which will be considered.[4]

The greater the urgency with which a decision must be made, the greater the likelihood of converting a false alarm into war itself.[5]

Selective perception is most acute where time is shortest.[6]

The experimental studies reviewed in Chapter 1 shed further light on the close relation between stress, decision time, and performance of complex tasks. To recapitulate very briefly, the evidence indicates that some stress is a necessary impetus to motivate action, but that increasing it beyond a certain point tends to reduce the quality of performance. Stress and time are closely related. Short decision time tends to increase stress; conversely, the ability to judge time is impaired in situations of high tension. Further, when persons have little time relative to the tasks in which they are engaged, performance becomes more erratic, there is a greater tendency to rely upon stereotyped images, and the ability to estimate more than a single outcome for each alternative course of action is impaired.

One way of linking these and other propositions about crisis and time pressure is presented in Figure 14. The primary linkages (A-B, B-C, B-D) require little comment. The initial proposition (A-B) is that as crisis-induced stress increases, concern for decision time will become more acute. Among the hypothesized consequences of perceived time pressure are tendencies to act more quickly (E-C) and less effectively (B-D). Time pressure also increases selectivity of perception. During international crises this is likely to manifest itself in several ways. Because judgment of time may become impaired, more attention is likely to be paid to those aspects of the adversary's military capabilities which facilitate a sudden attack (B-E), rather than to factors which may constrain such action. The result may be a significant overestimation of the adversary's mobility, efficiency, freedom of action, and ability to deliver a crippling surprise attack, thereby magnifying any existing pressures to act quickly (E-C). There may also be a greater tendency to focus on the immediate rather than the more distant future (B-F) in considering the possible consequences of one's actions, further increasing the tendency for quick action (F-C). Actions based almost exclusively on short-run calculations, to the exclusion of long-range considerations, are more likely to be less effective (F-D). Finally time pressure creates incentives

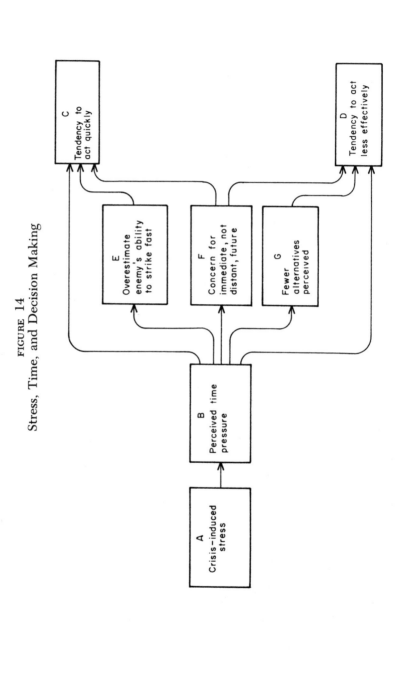

FIGURE 14
Stress, Time, and Decision Making

for seeking alternative means of resolving the crisis. It is also likely to make that search less creative and productive (B-G), again reducing the likelihood that an effective response will be found (G-D).*

Assuming that Figure 14 accurately depicts some tendencies of decision-making in crisis situations,† the resulting policies will probably be ineffective if the desired goal is to attain limited objectives without recourse to war. These actions are likely to be precisely of the type which confirm the suspicions of the other side that they, too, are under severe time pressure. Thus, unless means are found to break through this process, escalation of crisis situations into open conflict is a probable outcome.

Figure 14 is *not* intended to suggest the deterministic view that these consequences must automatically follow when decisions are made in a crisis; if this were the case, a far greater number of international crises would soon result in war. Rather, it suggests that these consequences are more probable during crises than in other situations; that conscious efforts to expand decision time are required to prevent rapid escalation; and that when crises do get out of control it may be precisely because neither side was successful in conveying to the other that they need not act in haste to avoid catastrophe.‡

Time Pressure and Escalation in 1914

To examine the effects of deepening crisis on perceptions of time pressure, all the data derived from documents written by top-ranking foreign-policy officials were recoded. The resulting 167

* For a detailed discussion of perceived alternatives during the 1914 crisis, see Chapter 6.

† The contrary thesis that short decision time may improve the quality of decision making appears in Harold L. Wilensky, *Organizational Intelligence: Knowledge and Policy in Government and Industry* (New York: Basic Books, 1967), pp. 76–81. Wilensky bases his argument on the Korean decision in 1950 and the missile crisis of 1962 (situations marked by time pressure) and the decision to reunite Korea late in 1950 and the Bay of Pigs invasion (both of which evolved over some time and resulted in disasters).

‡ For a further elaboration of this point, see the discussion of the Cuban missile crisis in Chapter 7, and the consideration of policy implications in the final chapter.

statements in which there was a reference to time as a factor in policy decisions are classified according to date and nation in Table 26. Statements of concern about decision time increased steadily (except in the case of Austria-Hungary), not only in absolute frequency,* but even in relation to the total number of policy themes.

When these themes are further classified according to the stated reason for time pressure, they reveal the very close relation to the major diplomatic and military developments during the crisis (Table 27).

During the earliest period—the three and a half weeks ending on 20 July—approximately two-thirds of the references to time focused on the desirability or necessity of early action by Austria-Hungary against Serbia. Count Alexander Hoyos, for example, wrote on 7 July that "from a military standpoint . . . it would be much more favorable to start the war now than later since the balance of power would weigh against us in the future." The view that time was working against the Dual Monarchy was supported by General Conrad, Austro-Hungarian chief-of-staff: "In the years 1908–1909 it would have been a game with open cards," he said. "In 1912–1913 the chances were in our favour. Now it is a sheer gamble (ein va-banque spiel)."[7] Hoyos's fear that "through a policy of delay and weakness, we at a later moment, endanger this unflinching support of the German Empire,"[8] was not wholly without foundation. Germany was exerting considerable pressure on its ally not to postpone a showdown until a less clearly defined future. Gottlieb von Jagow, German foreign minister, wrote on 15 July: "We are concerned at present with the pre-eminent political question, perhaps the last opportunity of giving the Greater-Serbia menace its death blow under comparatively favorable circumstances."[9]

In contrast, the view in London, Paris, and St. Petersburg was one of relative unconcern. Certainly there is no evidence that leaders in the capitals of the Entente nations felt themselves under any pressure of time to react to this latest episode of instability in the Balkans.

Time perceptions from 21 July through 28 July focused pre-

* Note that after 31 July, frequency scores are based on only four nations; the Austro-Hungarian collection includes documents only through the end of July.

TABLE 26
Frequency of Time Perceptions

| Period | Total Themes | Time Perceptions in Documents of | | | | | | % Themes with Time Perceptions | Daily Average Time Perceptions |
		Austria-Hungary	Germany	Great Britain	France	Russia	TOTAL		
27 June–20 July	1031	13	9	0	0	0	22	2.1	0.9
21–28 July	1658	3	11	18	13	8	53	3.2	6.6
29 July–2 August	1910	0	35	12	13	3	63	3.3	12.6
3–4 August	479	0	14	12	3	0	29	6.1	14.5
27 June–4 August	5078	16	69	42	29	11	167	3.3	4.3

dominantly (55%) on the necessity of delaying the course of events in the Balkans in the hope of averting war, or at least containing it within a local area. Once the content of the Austrian ultimatum became known, the short forty-eight hour time limit within which the Serbian government had to draft a reply became an immediate subject of concern. Some European officials recognized that the conflict in the Balkans might well engulf all Europe if existing alliance commitments were honoured.

Whereas the German and Austro-Hungarian leaders had frequently expressed the desirability of moving swiftly against Serbia, those in London, Paris, St. Petersburg, and Belgrade were

TABLE 27
Time Perceptions by Type (All Nations)

Period	A	B	C	D	E	TOTAL
27 June–20 July	15	1	0	2	4	22
21–28 July	11	29	10	2	1	53
29 July–2 August	1	8	29	16	9	63
3–4 August	0	0	2	22	5	29
27 June–4 August	27	38	41	42	19	167

Codes for relevance of time
A–As a factor in Austro-Hungarian action toward Serbia
B–As a factor in localization of conflict between Austria-Hungary and Serbia
C–As a factor in mobilization
D–As a factor in political commitments
E–Other

especially concerned with the necessity to gain the time which might be used to work out a settlement of Vienna's demands on Serbia by means other than war. Although these leaders were far from united on the details of policy, the single common theme in their proposals was the fear that precipitate action could only lead to war. Typical of diplomatic messages during this period were the following assertions by Serbian, Russian, French, and British leaders, respectively.

It is neither possible to accept the Austrian note nor to refuse it; rather time must be won at any price.[10]

It is impossible for the powers in the short time remaining to undertake anything useful toward the settlement of the complications which have arisen. Therefore we would deem it necessary in order to avoid innumerable consequences undesired by all, to which the conduct of Austria can lead, that above all the deadline given Serbia for reply be extended.[11]

However, the time flies, for if the Austrian army crosses the frontier, it will be very difficult to stem the crisis.[12]

The immediate danger was that in a few hours Austria might march into Servia and Russian Slav opinion demand that Russia should march to help Servia; it would be very desirable to get Austria not to precipitate military action and so to gain more time.[13]

By 29 July it was apparent that war between Austria-Hungary and Serbia could not be prevented. At the same time, it was increasingly evident that a chain reaction was in danger of being set off. Russia was on the verge of mobilization. Although the intent in St. Petersburg was merely to deter Austria from crushing Serbia, the Russian mobilization was the act which brought the local conflict centering on Serbia irreversibly into the centre of the European alliance system.

As late as 1 August many European leaders continued to express the belief that if time permitted the concert powers to be reconvened, general war might be avoided. The British foreign minister wrote, for example: "I still believe that if only a little respite in time can be gained before any Great Power begins war it might be possible to secure peace." [14] By this time, however, the pressure of time had taken a different meaning for many decision makers. A major concern (46% of all time perceptions from 29 July to 2 August) was that one's nation should not be caught unprepared for the war which might break out.

As they perceived the situation, leaders in the major capitals of Europe found themselves in a terrible dilemma. It was widely recognized that more time would be required if a general European war were to be averted; above all, a moratorium on military operations was necessary. On 1 August King George V wrote of his efforts "to find some solution which permits in any case the adjournment of active military operations and the granting of time to the powers to discuss among themselves calmly." [15] It was equally evident that military preparations could become the justification for similar actions by others. The German ambassador in St. Petersburg, for example, warned the Russian foreign minister that "the danger of every preparatory military measure lay in the counter-measures of the other side." [16]

But increasingly these considerations were overshadowed by the fear that if a potential adversary gained a head start in mobilizing its military power, the results would be disastrous. As early as 24 July, the French minister of war, apprehensive about the outcome of the crisis in the Balkans, asserted that for France "first military precautions could not be delayed." [17] Although no *official* mobilization orders except those of Austria-Hungary and Serbia were issued until 29 July, there were increasing rumours and suspicions of under-cover preparations. Such suspicions were not wholly without foundation. On 25 July the Russian government decided to set into motion all the preparations preliminary to mobilization. Despite a badly divided cabinet, even the British were undertaking a number of important military preparations. Winston Churchill, for example, mobilized the British navy contrary to a decision of the cabinet.

At the Cabinet [meeting of 1 August] I demanded the immediate calling out of the Fleet Reserves and the completion of our naval preparations. . . . However, I did not succeed in procuring their assent. . . . I found the Prime Minister upstairs in his drawing room: with him were Sir Edward Grey, Lord Haldane and Lord Crewe; there may have been other Ministers. I said that I intended instantly to mobilise the Fleet notwithstanding the Cabinet decision, and that I would take full personal responsibility to the Cabinet the next morning. The Prime Minister, who felt himself bound to the Cabinet, said not a single word, but it was clear from his look that he was quite content. . . . I went back to the Admiralty and gave forthwith the order to mobilise. We had no legal authority for calling up the Naval Reserves, as no proclamation had been submitted to His Majesty in view of the Cabinet decision, but we were quite sure that the Fleet men would unquestioningly obey the summons.[18]

In the early hours of the morning of 30 July, the kaiser wrote on the margin of a message from the tsar: "The Czar—as is openly admitted by him here—instituted 'mil [itary] measures which have <u>now come into force</u>' against Austria and us and as a matter of fact five days ago. Thus it is almost a week ahead of us. And these measures are for a defense against Austria, which is in no way attacking him!!! I can not agree to any more mediation, since the Czar who requested it has at the same time secretly mobilized behind my back. It is only a maneuver, in order to hold us back and to increase the start they have already got. My work is at an end!" [19] Later the kaiser added: "In view of the colossal war preparations of Russia now discovered, this is all too late, I fear. Begin! Now!" [20]

On 25 July German Chancellor Bethmann-Hollweg had urged the kaiser to consider the provocative implications of military deployment: "As the previous reports from Your Majesty's Ambassador at London make it plain that for the present, at least, Sir E. Grey is not considering direct participation by England in a possible European war, and is trying to work for the localization of the Austro-Hungarian–Serbian conflict as far as may be most feasible, I venture most humbly to advise that Your Majesty order no premature return of the Fleet." [21] At a conference in Potsdam two days later, there was general agreement with the chancellor's view that peace would prevail; as a consequence no military orders were issued. But by 30 July Bethmann-Hollweg was concerned primarily with the disadvantages of delay: "The military preparations of our neighbors, especially in the east, will force us to a speedy decision, unless we do not wish to expose ourselves to the danger of surprise." [22]

As late as 30 July René Viviani, French premier, urged Russia to take no provocative measures. "But in the same interest of general peace, and given that a conversation is under way between the less involved Powers, I think that it would be advisable, in the measures of precaution and defense to which Russia thinks it ought to proceed, for it not to take immediately any action which would offer Germany a pretext for a total or partial mobilization of its forces." [23] The previous day Russia had ordered—and then cancelled—a general mobilization. The fourteen corps actually mobilized totalled 800,000 men, including 500,000 regulars. The Russian intent was to deter the Austro-Hungarian attack on Serbia. Later it was decided in St. Petersburg that a partial mobilization of the four southern military districts would be clearly directed against Austria-Hungary only.

Hence, there would be no misunderstanding of Russian intentions, especially in Berlin. But the Russians reversed their decision once again on 30 July in favour of general mobilization, German warnings notwithstanding. This general mobilization included an additional 4,000,000 men—or a total of 4,800,000 men called to arms. "In these conditions," according to Sazonov, "Russia can only hasten its armaments and face the imminence of war and that it counts upon the assistance of its ally France; Russia considers it desirable that England join Russia and France without losing time." [24]

In response to what was perceived as a mounting threat against its eastern frontiers, the German Empire proclaimed a "state of threatening danger of war" on 31 July and dispatched a twelve-hour ultimatum to Russia demanding a cessation of military preparations along the border. Berlin then ordered mobilization on 1 August. The seven German armies participating in the Schlieffen plan totalled 1,700,000 men. Eastern front units amounted to 314,500 men, and additional Landwehr and Landsturm units brought the German total to approximately 4,000,000 men. The stated reason for the German mobilization was: "We could not sit back quietly and wait to see whether a more common-sense view would gain the upper hand at Petersburg, while at the same time the Russian mobilization was proceeding at such speed, that, if the worst came, we should be left completely outstripped in a military sense." [25]

The French government ordered general mobilization simultaneously with Germany, on 1 August. General Joffre had argued that "if the state of tension continues, and if the Germans, under the cover of diplomatic conversations continue the application of their mobilization, which they are carrying out by avoiding the pronunciation of the word, it is absolutely necessary that the government know that from this evening on, any delay of twenty-four hours applied to the calling up of reserves and to the sending of the telegram ordering covering troops will result in a backward movement of our troops, that is to say an initial abandonment of a part of our territory, either 15 or 20 kilometers every day of delay." [26] He added: "It can thus be said that by 4 August, even with an order for mobilization, the German army

will be entirely mobilized, already realizing an advance over ours
of 48 hours and perhaps of three days." [27]

Although official British mobilization of 420,000 men and three
fleets of the navy was delayed until 2 August, many officials in
London had advocated such action considerably earlier. Winston
Churchill, first lord of the admiralty, was perhaps the most ener-
getic proponent of early military preparations. "My own part in
these events was a very simple one. It was first of all to make
sure that the diplomatic situation did not get ahead of the naval
situation, and that the Grand Fleet should be in its War Station
before Germany could know whether or not we should be in the
war, and therefore if possible before we have decided
ourselves." [28] On 31 July, Arthur Nicolson had advocated immediate military preparations: "It seems to me most essential, whatever our future course may be in regard to intervention, that we
should at once give orders for mobilization of the army. It is use-
less to shut our eyes to the fact that possibly within the next 24
hours Germany will be moving across the French frontier—and if
public opinion, at present so bewildered and partially informed,
is ready in event of German invasion of France to stand by the
latter, if we are not mobilized our aid would be too late. Mobilization is a precautionary and not a provocative measure—and to
my mind essential." [29] Three days later he added: "We ought to
mobilize today so that our expeditionary force may be on its way
during the next week. Should we waver now we shall rue the day
later." [30]

Thus, ten days after the small-scale mobilizations by Serbia
and Austria-Hungary on 25 July each of the major European
countries had ordered a general mobilization. The armies totalling less than 400,000 men called to fight a limited war had grown
to nearly twelve million men. When each mobilization was ordered it was defended as a necessary reaction to a previous decision within the other coalition. And with each mobilization came
assurances that it was a defensive measure, although a decision
to mobilize was commonly regarded in 1914 as tantamount to an
act of war. In the rush to mobilize no one wanted to be beaten to
the draw, even though there was sometimes an awareness of the
logical end of military measures and countermeasures; each mo-

bilization acted as a stimulus that elicited a reflex-like response. Decision makers in each capital cited the similar actions of adversaries, coupled with the pressure of time, as the reason for mobilization.

In some cases, the escalation of military actions and counteractions was sustained almost by accident, or by the failure to perceive the effects of one's own acts. The mobilization of the Russian Baltic fleet is a good example. "On 25 July, when the Tsar looked over the minutes and resolutions of the Council of Ministers of the 24th, he not only approved them by adding 'agreed,' but, where it was the question of mobilizing the districts of Kiev, Moscow, Odessa and Kazan and the Black Sea fleet, he inserted in his own hand 'and Baltic' without any of his Ministers drawing his attention to the fact that the mobilization of the Baltic fleet constituted an act of hostility toward Germany." [31] Although the Russian Baltic fleet was no match for the powerful German navy, the kaiser apparently felt genuinely threatened. In response to Bethmann-Hollweg's plea that the German fleet be left in Norway, he wrote: "There is a Russian Fleet! In the Baltic there are now five Russian torpedo boat flotillas engaged in practice cruises, which as a whole or in part can be at the Belts within sixteen hours and close them. Port Arthur should be a lesson! My Fleet has orders to sail for Kiel, and to Kiel it is going to sail!" [32]

During the hours immediately preceding England's declaration of war on Germany, leaders in both coalitions became increasingly concerned (76% of all time perceptions 3–4 August) that their allies honour their commitments immediately. For example, the Russian foreign minister wrote on 29 July: "It would be extremely desirable that also England would agree with France without losing time, since this is the only manner in which it will succeed in preventing a dangerous disruption of the European balance of power." [33] A week later Jagow wired the German ambassador in Vienna: "Please urgently advocate there that Austria-Hungary make declarations of war at once on France, Russia and England." [34]

An even greater tone of urgency is clear in the messages concerning members of the opposing alliance. Three days prior to England's entry into the war, Kaiser Wilhelm wrote: "England must absolutely show her colors! Immediately! One way or another!"[35] The pressure of time is similarly evident in many of the other messages exchanged in the final hours prior to the outbreak of war.

Germany to France (31 July):
Please ask the French Government if it intends to remain neutral in a Russo-German war. Answer must be given within eighteen hours. Telegraph immediately hour at which the inquiry is made. Utmost haste is necessary.[36]

England to Germany (31 July):
A similar request [respect of neutrality of Belgium] is being addressed to German Government. It is important to have an early answer.[37]

Germany to Russia (1 August):
Immediate, affirmative, clear and unmistakable answer from your Government is the only way to avoid endless misery.[38]

England to Germany (4 August):
In these circumstances, and in view of the fact that Germany declined to give the same assurance respecting Belgium as France gave last week in reply to our request made simultaneously at Berlin and Paris, we must repeat that request, and ask that a satisfactory reply to it and to my telegram No. 266 of this morning be received here by 12 o'clock tonight.[39]

Nations without formal alliance commitments did not escape intense—although not always successful—pressure from Berlin and Vienna for immediate political alignment and military support. Although Bulgaria and Turkey joined the Central Powers, Italy and Greece were notably successful in evading commitment. The kaiser's note regarding the latter is indicative of the time pressure exerted from Berlin: "Tell Athens that I have made an alliance with Bulgaria and Turkey for the war against Russia and will treat Greece as an enemy in case she does not join us at once."[40]

This inquiry into time pressures associated with the 1914 crisis supports, at least anecdotally, the propositions in Figure 14. Concern for time increased as the crisis deepened, and it is also clear that time pressures were related to the central rather than peripheral issues in the crisis. When there was a conflict between the need to delay action in order to seek non-military means of resolving the crisis and the perceived needs of military prepared- ness, the latter consideration prevailed, in large part because so many officials throughout Europe felt that the costs of falling be- hind the adversary's timetable would be catastrophic. Many of the crucial decisions during the crisis were undertaken in great haste, and the processes by which they were made were at times highly erratic. Two examples are the Russian mobilization and Germany's efforts to influence Austro-Hungarian policy during the final days of July.° The initial Russian decision for a general mobilization was followed in short order by an order for only a partial call-up of forces, and then by another reversal to the orig- inal decision. In Germany's case, when it became clear that the conflict between Serbia and Austria-Hungary might lead to a general European war, a series of highly contradictory messages was dispatched from Berlin to Vienna. Demands for restraint in some of them were offset by a telegram from Moltke stating that Austria-Hungary should immediately mobilize against Russia, and that Germany would soon follow suit.

Stress and Time Pressure

We can also use the time perception data to test several of the propositions in Figure 14 more systematically. The first hypothe- sis is: *as stress increases in a crisis situation, time will be per- ceived as an increasingly salient factor in decision making.*†

As a measure of the independent variable—the level of crisis- induced stress—we shall again use the data on perceptions of hostility. Recall that in order to obtain a measure which is free from the effects of message volume, *intensity* of perceived hostil- ity is used to index stress.

The relation between the index of stress and frequency of time perceptions for all nations is depicted in Figure 15. There are

---

° These episodes are further described in Chapter 6.

† Short decision time was cited earlier as a defining attribute of crisis. This hy- pothesis relates *changes* in perceived time pressure to changing levels of stress; thus the hypothesis is not merely a circular argument which restates the defini- tion.

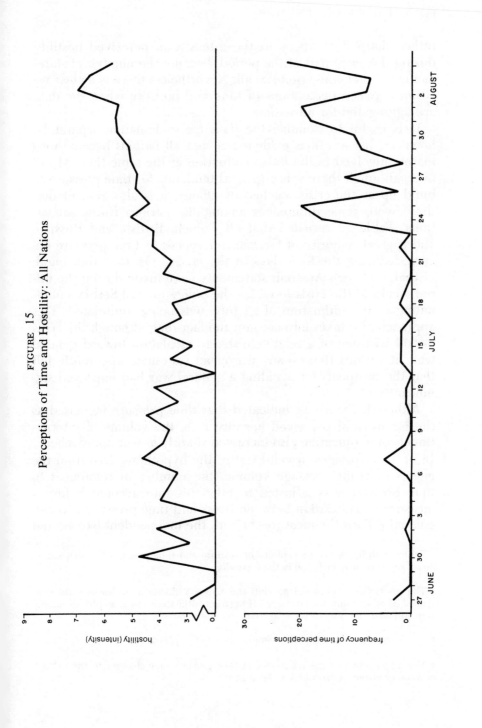

FIGURE 15
Perceptions of Time and Hostility: All Nations

rather sharp fluctuations in the intensity of perceived hostility during the early part of the period, because the number of statements was generally quite small. Nevertheless there is a clear relation between perceptions of time and hostility when the data are aggregated for all nations.

It is useful to examine the data for each nation separately, however, because it is evident that not all nations became intimately involved in the Balkan situation at the same time. Moreover, although there was a general tendency for time pressure to build up as the crisis reached its climax, it is also evident that there were some differences among the various European nations. Table 26 revealed that all French, British, and Russian, and a great majority of German references to time pressure occurred during the final days of the crisis.* On the other hand, virtually all such Austrian statements were made during the initial weeks of the crisis in which the policy toward Serbia, culminating in the ultimatum of 23 July, was being formulated. This approach also takes into account the fact that, although the crisis period was one of a relatively steady escalation toward general war, at various times many European statesmen apparently felt that the prospects for avoiding a general war had improved significantly.†

Although Figure 15 indicated that time pressure increased as the intensity of perceived hostility rose, the volume of international communication also increased sharply as war approached.‡ In order to perform a valid test of the hypothesis, free from the effects of rising message volume, the number of references to time pressure was adjusted to take this into account before a measure of association between stress and time pressure was calculated.§ Thus the measures of both the independent (stress) and

---

* Tables with figures on perceptions of hostility and time pressure for each nation on a daily basis may be found in the appendix.

† The reactions of Winston Churchill and Kaiser Wilhelm upon learning the content of Serbia's reply to the Austro-Hungarian ultimatum are examples of temporary optimism that war could be averted. See p. 57 above.

‡ See the data on international communication in Chapter 4.

§ The adustment of time references to take into account changes in the volume of communication is described in the appendix.

dependent variables (time pressure) are free from the effects of increasing diplomatic communication during the later stages of the crisis period.

The summary in Table 28 supports the hypothesis that perceptions of time increased with rising stress.° For each nation the relation between stress and time is in the predicted direction, and in only one case is the association between these variables a weak one. The results also indicate rather substantial differences in this respect between Austria-Hungary on the one hand, and Germany and the three members of the Triple Entente on the other. The reasons for this difference are apparent in Table 25. During the early days of the crisis, when a world war still

TABLE 28
Strength of Association (Goodman-Kruskal *gamma*)
between Stress and Perceptions of Time

	N °	Gamma	P
Austria-Hungary	35	.16	n.s.
Germany	31	.33	.04
Great Britain	29	.61	.003
France	28	.68	.0004
Russia	38	.82	.0006

° Number of days on which documents written by top-level foreign-policy leaders.

seemed only a remote possibility—and the level of stress, as indexed by perceptions of international hostility, was relatively low —officials in Vienna, and to a lesser extent in Berlin, nevertheless felt that time was of great importance in dealing with the Serbian questions. In contrast, it was not until much later, when the possibility that the local dispute might bring the two great European alliance systems directly into the conflict was widely recognized, that evidence of time pressure appeared in British, French, and Russian documents.

One reason for these differences may be that our measure of

° N for each country is different because on some days there were no documents written by the officials included in this analysis. These days were disregarded for purposes of calculating the correlations in order not to inflate *gamma* artificially.

the independent variable is less useful for Austria-Hungary than for the other nations because it indexes only international sources of stress, not those that are domestically generated. Internal problems raised grave doubts about the ability of the multinational Dual Monarchy to survive in its existing form. Domestic tensions were bound to be magnified as a result of the assassination because the existence of Serbia was widely seen as a threat to the stability of Austria-Hungary. Also, some German leaders felt that liberal and socialist groups threatened basic policies such as the development of a first-class navy. Thus an index which took into account domestic as well as international sources of threat might have revealed that officials in Vienna were in fact under considerable stress during the early stages of the crisis.*

Finally, there is also evidence that after a nation had been drawn into the war time pressure dropped sharply. It appears that after being faced with the problems of the prewar crisis, those of waging war actually provided some relief from time pressure. For example, by 29 July Austria-Hungary had broken diplomatic relations and declared war on Serbia, and started shelling Belgrade with gunboats cruising on the Danube. Austro-Hungarian documents from that date forward contain no assertions of time pressure. Similarly, by 2 August France and Russia were both at war with Germany, and after that date their diplomatic messages are almost free of evidence of time pressure. Indeed, during 3 and 4 August the major question that remained to be answered was whether Great Britain would be drawn into the war against Germany. The data for that forty-eight hour period reveal that perception of time pressure were almost wholly confined to leaders in London and Berlin.

A second hypothesis concerning perceptions of time which can be tested with these data is: *as stress increases in a crisis situation, decision makers will become increasingly concerned with the immediate rather than the distant future.*†

* For other evidence of stress generated by domestic considerations see the various accounts of the Cuban missile crisis, which occurred during the 1962 Congressional campaign. Robert Kennedy has written that the president expected to be impeached if he were unable to have the Soviet missiles removed from Cuba. Robert F. Kennedy, "Thirteen Days: The Story About How the World Almost Ended," *McCalls*, November 1968, p. 152.

† Expressions of concern for the immediate future were those which considered only the situation at hand and developments within that context (for example, the

The data in Table 29 lend support to this hypothesis. Of the 167 statements in which time was perceived to be a factor in decision making, only 8 reveal a concern for the distant future—for example, the ultimate outcome of various diplomatic and military actions, the effects of the Balkan conflict on European stability, the possible consequences of general European war, and the like. The overwhelming majority of time perceptions focused on such themes as the immediate requirements of the situation created by one or another event. Moreover, as indicated in Table 29, the few statements of concern for the more distant future all occurred during the first month after the assassination.

TABLE 29

Perceptions of the Immediate and Distant Future during Early and Late Periods of the 1914 Crisis

	27 June–28 July	29 July–4 August
Perceptions of		
Immediate Future	67	92
Distant Future	8	0

$\emptyset = .25$ $p < .002$

The 1914 data indicate that stress and perceptions of time as a factor in decision making are associated. They do not, however, reveal the direction of the relation. Is stress the antecedent condition which is followed by perceptions of time pressure? Or, conversely, does stress follow as a consequence of time pressure? Recall that each of these explanations found some support in experimental studies reviewed in Chapter 1, and both of them are at least intuitively plausible.

In an effort to test these alternative interpretations, *gamma* coefficients were recalculated with one-day time lags, first for the measure of time pressure, then for the index of stress. The results, summarized in Table 30, are inconclusive. Compared to the find-

likely responses of one or another country to an event). Expressions of concern for the distant future were those which considered the future beyond the context of the immediate crisis (for example, that a particular policy would ultimately lead to better Anglo-German relations, or the destruction of European civilization, or the decline of Austro-Hungarian status in a postcrisis European system, etc.). For additional examples, see the appendix.

TABLE 30
Test of Two Interpretations of Relationship
between Stress and Perceptions of Time

Direction of Relationship between Stress and Perceptions of Time			
Antecedent Condition	Subsequent Condition	Test	Results
Stress	Perceptions of time pressure	Compare index of stress on day n with measure of time pressure on day $n+1$, stress on day $n+1$ with time pressure on day $n+2$, and so on through the entire crisis period. Accept interpretation if correlations higher than those reported in Table 28.	Austria-Hungary .25 (+) ° Germany .27 (−) Great Britain .43 (−) France .65 (−) Russia .63 (−)
Perceptions of time pressure	Stress	Compare index of time pressure on day n with measure of stress on day $n+1$, time pressure on day $n+1$ with stress on day $n+2$, and so on through the entire crisis period. Accept interpretation if correlations higher than those reported in Table 28.	Austria-Hungary .22 (+) Germany .25 (−) Great Britain .54 (−) France .67 (−) Russia .68 (−)

° Correlation coefficient higher (+) or lower (−) than in Table 28.

ings reported in Table 28, the time-lag correlations are lower in eight out of ten cases.

Conclusion

In this chapter we have continued our examination of the effects of stress on foreign-policy decisions in a crisis. The evidence indicated that time pressures—especially those arising out of immediate rather than long-range considerations—increased sharply during the most intense stages of the crisis. Furthermore, time pressure appears to have been a central factor in the decisions which led to a general European war in 1914.

What lessons can be drawn from the results? Do they have any relevance for policy in an age in which weapons systems have only the faintest resemblance to those existing in 1914? An analysis of European military technology and doctrines would reveal, for example, that objectively time was of incalculably less importance than in the present nuclear age. In contrast to the ability of the Soviet Union and United States to strike each other in a matter of minutes, estimates of the time required for Austria-Hungary to field a full army ranged from three to four weeks. The necessity of harvesting summer crops was a factor in the military calculations of all the continental countries. Russia's ability to mount a rapid offensive against Germany could be discounted; indeed, the entire Schlieffen plan was predicated on the assumption that Russia's lack of speed would permit German strength to be massed on the western front during the early weeks of the war. It is thus far from evident that there was a distinct military advantage to be gained by striking first or, conversely, that a delay of a day or two in mobilizing would have resulted in catastrophic consequences.

Yet the "reality" as defined by European leaders was quite different. In the situation of high tensions the decision makers of 1914 *perceived* that time was of crucial importance—and they *acted* on that assumption. During the final stages of the crisis, foreign-policy officials increasingly perceived that their enemies were capable of delivering a sudden punishing blow. In doing so they attributed to their adversaries a flexibility and speed of military operations which they knew was impossible for their own forces. As a consequence, the penalties for delaying immediate military action were perceived as increasingly high. Or, to use the language of deterrence theory, national leaders in each coalition perceived that those of the other alliance were able and willing to launch a decisive first strike, and thus they hastened their own preparations. Hence, the entire European concert system—which was assumed to act as a stabilizing influence—became instead a "runaway system."

A closely related question, one with clear relevance for contemporary security policy, concerns the deployment of weapons that need not be used in the first instance because they are not vulnerable to an enemy first strike. In current military jargon, these are weapons that provide their owners with the "capacity to delay response." Would possession of such weapons and adherence to second-strike military doctrines have materially altered the outcome in 1914? Obviously we can only speculate. If there is any lesson to be learned from the 1914 crisis, however, it is that possession of weapons systems which can withstand a first strike may be a necessary condition for successful (i.e. peaceful) deterrence, but it is not sufficient. We shall return to this point in a discussion of weapons systems, strategic doctrines, and crisis management in the concluding chapter.

Chapter Six

POLICY OPTIONS
IN AN INTERNATIONAL CRISIS

SINCE THE FRANCO-PRUSSIAN WAR in 1870, European leaders had faced periodic crises in the Balkans and elsewhere. But in each case they had successfully employed international conferences, mediation, and other means to avert war between the major powers. Why, then, were they unable to find alternatives to general war in 1914? This problem raises a number of related questions about policy making during the crisis period. What alternative means of resolving the crisis were perceived? How did leaders in Vienna, Berlin, St. Petersburg, London, and Paris assess the policy options open to themselves, their allies, and nations in the opposing alliance? What happened to the range of perceived alternatives as stress increased during the crisis? How did military planning affect the options open to foreign-policy officials? The answers to these and similar questions are central to an understanding of events during the summer of 1914; they are of equally great importance for crisis management in an age of nuclear weapons and intercontinental delivery systems.

In the first chapter we made a number of general observations about crisis, stress, and policy options. The main points can be summarized very briefly. Crisis was defined as an unanticipated situation of high threat to important values and short decision time. In these circumstances policy making is rarely a process of selecting from a neatly delineated set of alternatives; rather, it is usually concerned with seeking out and perhaps even creating options. Thus the need for creativity probably increases as a crisis becomes more severe, but considerable evidence was adduced to suggest that the stress accompanying intense crises will in fact reduce the options considered.

Secondly, crises offer few if any really attractive alternatives. The choice is often that of identifying and selecting the least of several evils rather than the best benefits.

Finally, decisions are made not only on the basis of choices perceived open to oneself; they may also depend on the alternatives perceived available to the other party. The problem of manipulating alternatives is central to strategies of crisis management. One may attempt at every step to reduce the likelihood that either party will find itself in the position that escalation is perceived as the only available option, or the least undesirable one. This approach was pursued with skill by President Kennedy during the Cuban missile crisis.*

At the other extreme, it may be advantageous to adopt the strategy of "burning bridges" by manoeuvring oneself into "a position in which one no longer has an effective choice over how he shall behave or respond," in order to make the outcome "depend solely on the other party's choice." [1] At least some subordinate Soviet officials tried to give the impression during the early days of the 1962 missile crisis that they had lost control of events, implying that only an American backdown could avert World War III. At a reception held on 23 October 1962, the day following President Kennedy's public announcement that Russian missiles had been discovered in Cuba, Lieutenant-General V. A. Dubovik asserted that, "Our ships will sail through. And if it is decreed that these men must die, they will obey their orders and stay on course, or be sunk." The Soviet ambassador refused to refute these statements because, "He [Dubovik] is a military man; I am not. He is the one who knows what the Navy is going to do, not I." [2]

Aside from considerations of strategic advantage, rigid military plans may also impose very real constraints on policy options, a point to which we shall return later. However, there is also reason to believe that crises tend to create dissonances which in turn reduce perceived options. The line of reasoning developed

---

* For a further discussion, see Chapter 7.

in Chapter 1 suggests that there may be a tendency to absolve oneself and one's allies from responsibility for the situation by denying the existence of alternatives to the chosen policies. This may be reinforced by persuading oneself that only the adversaries have the freedom to take deadlock-breaking actions.

This discussion suggests several hypotheses about the manner in which policy makers are likely to perceive alternatives during a crisis. The first two compare the range of options open to oneself, allies, and adversaries.

In a crisis situation decision makers will tend to perceive the range of their own alternatives to be more restricted than those of their adversaries.

In a crisis situation decision makers will tend to perceive their allies' range of alternatives to be more restricted than those of their adversaries.

A second pair of hypotheses relates perceived policy options to the level of stress.

As stress increases decision makers will tend to perceive the range of alternatives open to themselves as becoming narrower.

As stress increases decision makers will tend to perceive the range of alternatives open to their adversaries as expanding.

Perceptions of Alternatives

For the purpose of testing hypotheses relating to perceived alternatives, the documents were recoded. This process yielded 505 statements of perceived alternatives. These were classified as perceptions of "choice," "necessity," or "closed," according to the following definitions.*

The "necessity" category includes all statements indicating that the author sees only one possible course of action in a given situation.

---

* Intercoder reliability for this coding was 0.87.

The "closed" category includes all statements indicating that some course of action is not possible.

The "choice" category includes all statements in which the actor perceives that more than one course of action is open.

Figure 16 indicates for each day in the crisis period the kinds of alternatives British, French, German, Austro-Hungarian, and Russian leaders saw for their own nations. Similar data for allies and nations in the opposing alliance are presented in Figures 17 and 18.

The same data are presented on a nation-by-nation basis in Tables 31–33. The time periods into which the figures are grouped correspond roughly to four stages during the 1914 crisis.° During the initial weeks following the assassination, leaders in Vienna came to an agreement on the demands to be made on Serbia and received German support for a vigorous policy. The week of 21–28 July included presentation of the ultimatum to Serbia and the break of diplomatic relations between Belgrade and Vienna. It was during this period that the possibility of the Balkan dispute giving rise to a European crisis was generally recognized. The next five days—29 July through 2 August—began with the outbreak of war between Austria-Hungary and Serbia and ended with the start of hostilities on the western front, as Germany invaded Luxembourg. In the intervening days, marked by mobilizations throughout Europe, Germany and Russia had also declared war upon each other. The final period ended at midnight 4 August with the British entry into the war against Germany.

Tables 31–33 also reveal interesting differences in the extent to which statesmen took into account the policies of nations other than their own. More than one-half of the French (59%) and British (52%) statements relating to policy options are concerned with other countries. In contrast, only about one-third of the Russian (35%) and German (29%) statements are about either allies or enemies, and those of Austro-Hungarian leaders reveal a virtual absence of attention to any other nation. This suggests that policy deliberations in Vienna were carried on with little consideration for the broader European implications of Austrian diplomacy.

° Tables for the data on a daily basis may be found in the appendix.

FIGURE 16

Perceptions of Alternatives: Own Alternatives (All Nations)

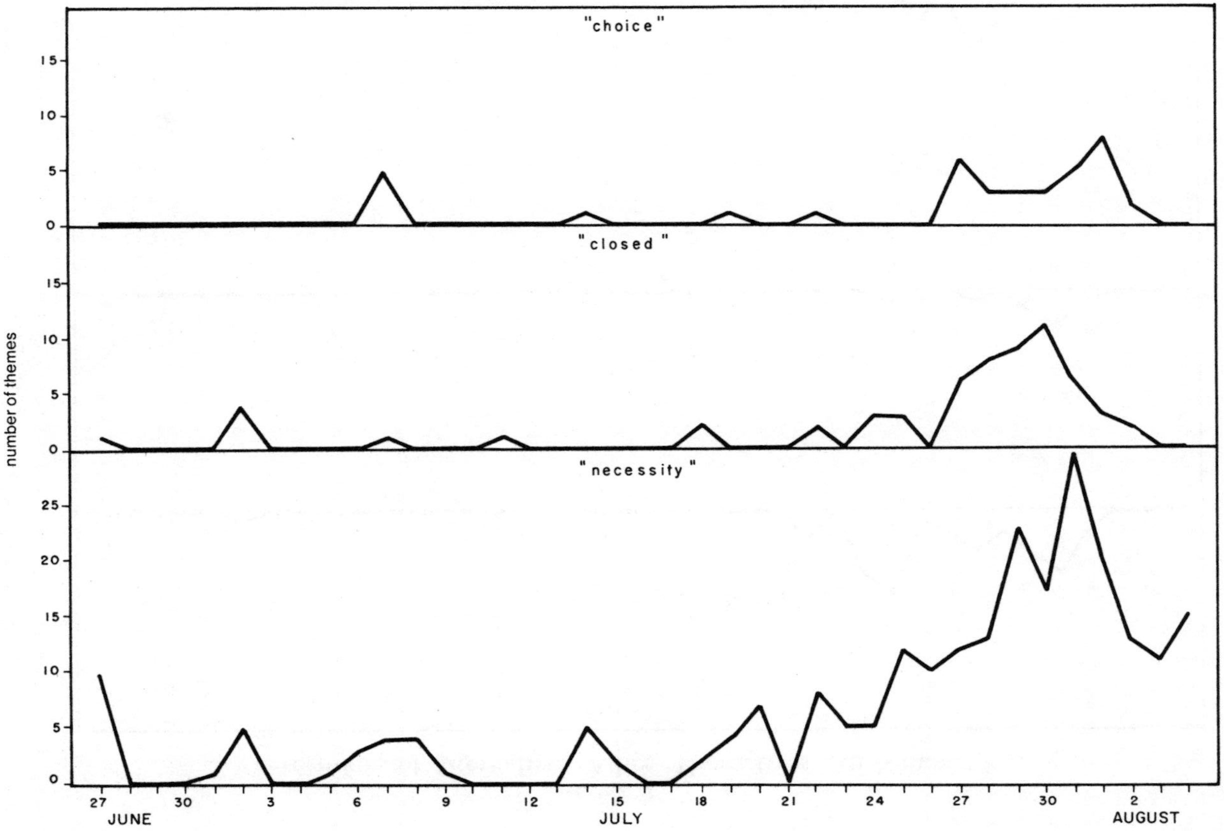

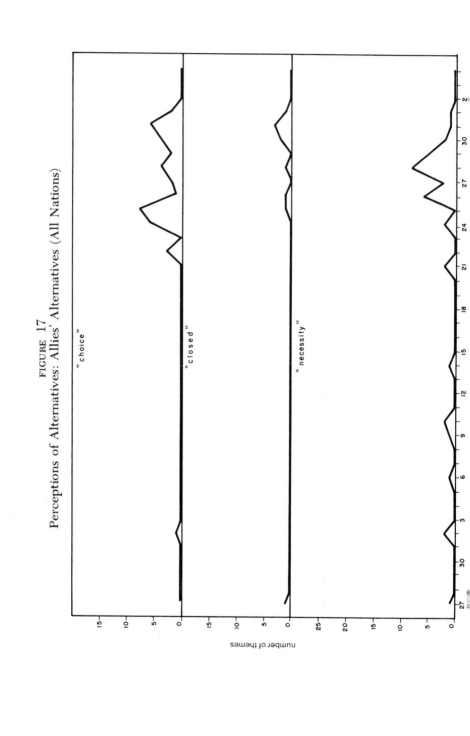

FIGURE 17

Perceptions of Alternatives: Allies' Alternatives (All Nations)

FIGURE 18

Perceptions of Alternatives: Enemies' Alternatives (All Nations)

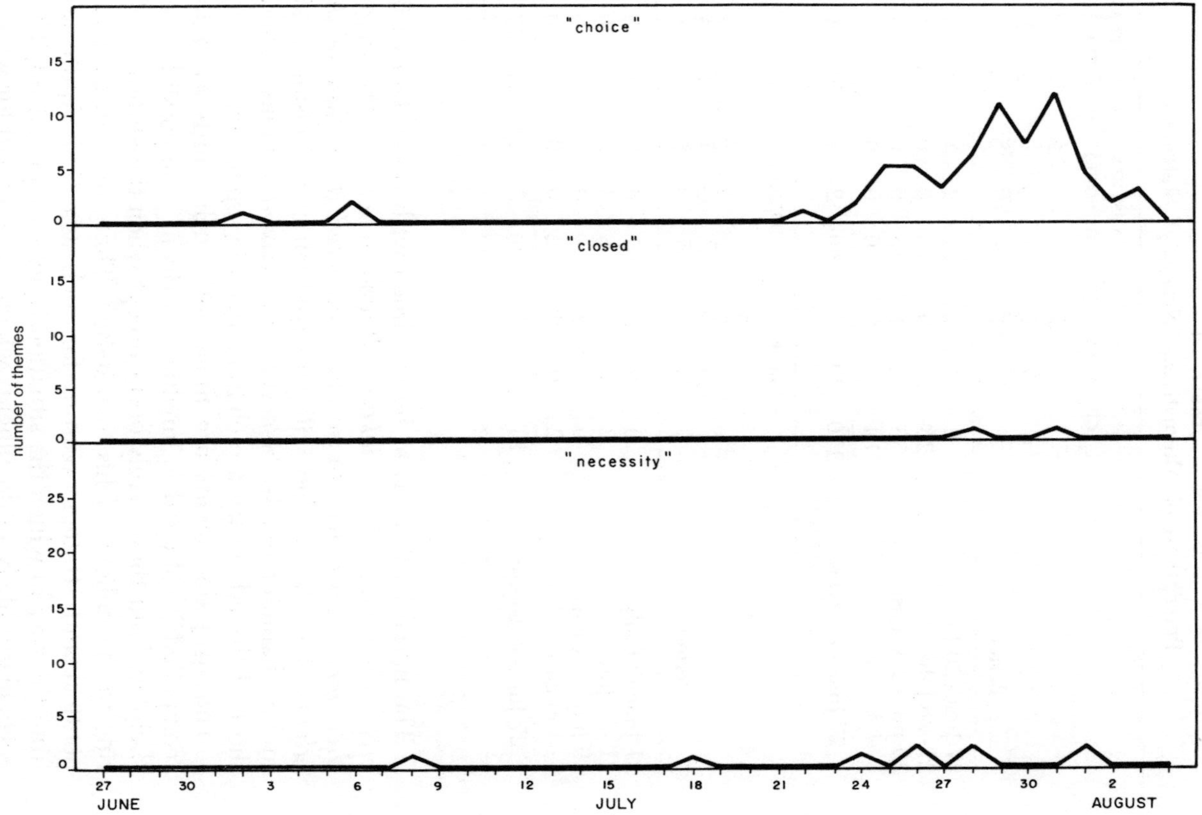

TABLE 31
Perceptions of Alternatives: "Necessity" Statements

Period	GERMANY own	allies	enemies	AUSTRIA-HUNGARY own	allies	enemies	GREAT BRITAIN own	allies	enemies
27 June–20 July	9	5	1	37	2	1	2	1	0
21–28 July	26	13	0	25	0	0	4	2	2
29 July–2 August	56	2	1	18	0	0	11	5	0
3–4 August	19	0	0	0	0	0	3	0	0
27 June–4 August	110	20	2	80	2	1	20	8	2

Period	FRANCE own	allies	enemies	RUSSIA own	allies	enemies	ALL NATIONS own	allies	enemies
27 June–20 July	0	0	0	1	0	0	49	8	2
21–28 July	2	2	2	8	3	1	65	20	5
29 July–2 August	9	2	0	9	0	1	103	9	2
3–4 August	2	0	0	2	0	0	26	0	0
27 June–4 August	13	4	2	20	3	2	243	37	9

The initial hypothesis to be examined with these data is: *in a crisis situation, decision makers will tend to perceive the range of their own alternatives to be more restricted than those of their adversaries.* That is, they will perceive their own decision making to be characterized by *necessity* and *closed* options, whereas those of the adversary are characterized by *open* choices. The 1914 documents are filled with such words as "must," "compelled," "obliged," "unable," "driven," "impossible," and "helpless," but these rarely occur except when the author is referring to the policies of his own nation. There may, of course, be political and strategic reasons for such assertions, quite aside from the way in which the situation is actually perceived. This is particularly likely in documents which are intended for wide circulation among officials in allied or enemy countries. On the other hand, the most "private" documents—those intended only

TABLE 32
Perceptions of Alternatives: "Closed" Option Statements

Period	GERMANY own	allies	enemies	AUSTRIA-HUNGARY own	allies	enemies	GREAT BRITAIN own	allies	enemies
27 June–20 July	7	0	0	2	1	0	0	0	0
21–28 July	4	1	0	4	0	0	9	0	0
29 July–2 August	9	1	0	1	0	0	14	2	0
3–4 August	0	0	0	0	0	0	0	0	0
27 June–4 August	20	2	0	7	1	0	23	2	0

Period	FRANCE own	allies	enemies	RUSSIA own	allies	enemies	ALL NATIONS own	allies	enemies
27 June–20 July	0	0	0	0	0	0	9	1	0
21–28 July	3	0	1	2	2	0	22	3	1
29 July–2 August	2	2	1	5	1	0	31	6	1
3–4 August	0	0	0	0	0	0	0	0	0
27 June–4 August	5	2	2	7	3	0	62	10	2

for circulation within the various foreign offices—do not differ
materially from the entire set of documents in respect to the findings reported here. The clearest evidence in support of this assertion is to be found in the kaiser's marginal notations and in the
various minutes of Eyre Crowe, assistant under-secretary of state
in the British foreign office.

Even a cursory survey of the diplomatic documents reveals
that, with the exception of Austria-Hungary, European leaders
consistently perceived fewer options open to themselves than to
their adversaries. In at least one respect even the data for Austria-Hungary are similar to those of the other nations. In an overwhelming majority of references to alternatives, the decision
makers in Vienna perceived themselves to be acting out of necessity and facing closed options rather than open choice. There are,
however, only two statements regarding the alternatives of ene-

TABLE 33
Perceptions of Alternatives: "Choice" Statements

Period	GERMANY			AUSTRIA-HUNGARY			GREAT BRITAIN		
	own	allies	enemies	own	allies	enemies	own	allies	enemies
27 June–20 July	0	0	2	7	1	1	0	0	0
21–28 July	2	4	6	3	0	0	0	11	8
29 July–2 August	8	3	17	3	0	0	7	10	13
3–4 August	0	0	0	0	0	0	0	0	0
27 June–4 August	10	7	25	13	1	1	7	21	21

Period	FRANCE			RUSSIA			ALL NATIONS		
	own	allies	enemies	own	allies	enemies	own	allies	enemies
27 June–20 July	0	0	0	0	0	0	7	1	3
21–28 July	0	5	6	5	4	2	10	24	22
29 July–2 August	1	1	6	2	0	1	21	14	37
3–4 August	0	0	0	0	0	3	0	0	3
27 June–4 August	1	6	12	7	4	6	38	39	65

mies, and none are perceptions of choice. This finding is not altogether surprising. Of the nations involved in the events of 1914,
the Austrians most consciously pursued a policy which would
leave the adversary as few options as possible. Count Alexander
Hoyos, who had stated on 7 July that "the situation cannot be
improved through diplomatic success," added that "how the conflict should begin is a matter of detail, and if in the opinion of the
Hungarian government a surprise attack is not proper then another way should be found." [3] Only during the earliest phases of
the crisis did Austro-Hungarian leaders—notably Istvan Tisza—
acknowledge the existence of a number of ways to deal with Belgrade. Soon the policy of punishing Serbia was followed with a
single-mindedness and consistency not evident in the British policy of seeking a mediated solution; nor in the German policy of
trying simultaneously to preserve the "dignity and honour" of her

ally and to win for Germany a significant diplomatic victory by splitting the Triple Entente, while at the same time avoiding a general war from which a number of leaders in Berlin felt Germany was inadequately prepared militarily or economically; ° nor in the Russian policy which, like that of Germany, sought to support the prestige of a weaker ally without provoking a world war.

The other nations also perceived few acceptable alternatives open to themselves in regard to the events in the Balkans. Edward Grey, who took the most active role in seeking mediation, wrote on 24 July: "We can do nothing for moderation unless Germany is prepared *pari passu* to do the same." [4] Until the final hours of the crisis, leaders in Berlin were opposed to mediation of the local conflict, in part because previous conferences called to settle international crises (for example, Algeciras in 1906) had, in the eyes of the kaiser and others, denied them the diplomatic victories to which they were entitled. According to Bethmann-Hollweg, "We cannot mediate in the conflict between Austria and Serbia but possibly later between Austria and Russia." [5] Nor were the Russians inclined to mediation because, in the words of Sazonov, "We have assumed from the beginning a posture which we cannot change." [6]

But the same leaders who expressed varying degrees of inabil-

---

° The mixed evidence on this point probably reflects a lack of consensus in 1914 among knowledgeable Germans. In their famous memorandum of December 1912, Ludendorff and Moltke asserted that "it is just as impossible for Germany to try and compete with Russia as a land power as it is for her to attempt to catch up with England as a sea power." They went on to point out that owing to the dubious quality of Berlin's allies, the military burden in any conflict with the Triple Entente would fall on Germany. In May 1914, Moltke continued to assess the military balance in a pessimistic vein. Later Admiral Tirpitz wrote: "It [the German government] was convinced from the very beginning that we should not win . . . that government itself was most deeply convinced of its helplessness." Alfred von Tirpitz, *My Memoirs* (London: Hurst and Blackett, 1919), p. 272. And just before the outbreak of the war Kaiser Wilhelm wrote of the prospect that Germany would be "bled to death."

It is, of course, possible that Moltke, like virtually all military leaders, was merely trying to develop a case for expanding military expenditures; that Tirpitz was writing to justify German policy in 1914; and that the kaiser was merely reacting emotionally to the sudden spectre of Britain's entry into the war. But it is equally plausible to assume that although many Germans were confident of winning a diplomatic victory or a limited war at the expense of the Triple Entente, many also had real (and as it turned out, justified) doubts about German prospects in a general European war—at least in 1914.

ity to cope with the situation in the Balkans tended to perceive more freedom of action for members of the opposing alliance. After the outbreak of war between Serbia and Austria-Hungary, for example, Grey wrote: "I urged that the German Government should suggest any method by which the influence of the four Powers [Germany, Italy, France, Britain] could be used together to prevent war between Austria and Russia. France agreed, Italy agreed. The whole idea of mediation or mediating influence was ready to be put into operation by any method that Germany could suggest if mine was not acceptable. In fact, mediation was ready to come into operation by any method that Germany thought possible if only Germany would 'press the button' in the interests of peace." [7]

The tendency to perceive one's own alternatives to be more restricted than those of the adversary is also evident in the reaction to the events leading up to general war. On 28 July Nicholas II had warned that, "I forsee that I will succumb very soon to the pressure put upon me and will be compelled to take extreme measures which will lead to war." [8] Three days later, in the course of his desperate last minute correspondence with the kaiser, the tsar asserted: "It is technically impossible to stop our military preparations which were obligatory owing to Austria's mobilization." [9]

The reaction of German decision makers to the series of events leading up to mobilization and war was almost identical. On the one hand they repeatedly asserted that *they* had no choice but to take vigorous military measures against the threat to the east.[*] On the other hand, they credited Russia with complete freedom to take the actions necessary to prevent war.[†] And Wilhelm, like the tsar, finally asserted that he had lost control of his own mili-

---

[*] "Then I must mobilize too! . . . He [Nicholas] expressly stated in his first telegram that he would be presumably forced to take measures that would lead to a European war. Thus he takes the responsibility upon himself." *Ibid.*, #399.

"Responsibility for the safety of my Empire forces preventative measures of defense upon me." *Ibid.*, #480.

[†] "I therefore suggest that it would be quite possible for Russia to remain a spectator of the Austro-Serbian conflict without involving Europe in the most horrible war she ever witnessed." *Ibid.*, #359.

"The responsibility for the disaster which is now threatening the whole civilized world will not be laid at my door. In this moment it still lies in your [Nicholas] power to avert it." *Ibid.*, #480.

tary and that only the actions of the adversary could stop further escalation: "On technical grounds my mobilization which had already been proclaimed this afternoon must proceed against two fronts, east and west as prepared. This cannot be countermanded because I am sorry your [George V] telegram came so late. But if France offers me neutrality which must be guaranteed by the British fleet and army I shall of course refrain from attacking France and employ my troops elsewhere." [10]

The same theme of a single option open to oneself, coupled with perceptions that the initiative for peace rested with the enemy, is evident in the French and Austrian statements regarding their own mobilizations.[11] During the last week only the British consistently stated that they were able to act with some degree of freedom. Owing in part to a badly divided Cabinet, to estimates of public apathy, and to strong pressure from the business community for neutrality, Grey asserted repeatedly that British "hands were free." [12] Statements such as these explain, in part, the kaiser's violent reaction to Grey's telegram of 29 July, in which the British foreign minister had warned that "there would be no question of our intervening if Germany was not involved, or even if France was not involved. But we know very well that if the issue did become such that we thought British interests required us to intervene, we must intervene at once, and the decision would have to be very rapid." [13] Upon reading this, Wilhelm wrote: "The net has been suddenly thrown over our head, and England sneeringly reaps the most brilliant success of her persistently prosecuted purely anti-German world policy." [14]

An increasing sense of helplessness and resignation to the irresistible course of events is evident in many of the documents. On the day of the Serbian reply to the Austro-Hungarian ultimatum, Paul Cambon stated that he saw "no way of halting the march of events." [15] In contrast to Edward Grey, who maintained the hope that the European powers would find a way to prevent a general war, Arthur Nicolson asserted on 29 July: "I am of the opinion that the resources of diplomacy are, for the present, exhausted." [16] At the same time, in St. Petersburg Sazonov wrote of the "inevitability of war" [17] while in Berlin, the kaiser, in one of the most vitriolic of his marginal notes, concluded that "we have proved ourselves helpless." [18]

To students of strategy the assertions of the kaiser, the tsar, and others that they were helpless once they had set their military machines into motion may appear to be a "real life" application of the tactics of *commitment*, "a device to leave the last clear chance to decide the outcome with the other party, in a manner that he fully appreciates; it is to relinquish further initiative, having rigged the incentives so that the other party must choose in one's favor." [19] The behaviour of military leaders in St. Petersburg and Berlin proved, however, that neither monarch was merely bluffing. After Sazonov and General Tatischev had browbeaten the vacillating Nicholas into ordering general mobilization, the former called General Ianuschkevitch and said: "Now you can smash the telephone. Give yours orders, General, and then—disappear for the rest of the day." In Berlin, Moltke effectively undermined the belated German effort to restrain Austria-Hungary by wiring: "Stand firm to Russian mobilization. Austria-Hungary must be preserved. Mobilize at once against Russia. Germany will mobilize." In Vienna Conrad von Hotzendorf insured himself against any second thoughts Francis Joseph might have had by ordering mobilization one day ahead of schedule.[20]

Significantly contributing to the belief that options were severely restricted was the rigidity of the various mobilization plans.[21] Austria-Hungary and Russia had more than one plan for mobilization, but once any one of them was set in motion it was impossible to change to another. The Russians could order either a general mobilization against both Germany and Austria-Hungary, or a partial one directed only at the latter. But, as Russian generals were to argue vehemently during the crucial days at the end of July, a partial mobilization would preclude a general one for months to come, leaving Russia completely at the mercy of Germany. According to General Dobrorolski, "The whole plan of mobilization is worked out ahead to its end in all its detail. When the moment has been chosen, one has only to press the button, and the whole state begins to function automatically with the precision of a clock's mechanism. . . . Once the moment has been fixed, everything is settled; there is no going back; it determines mechanically the beginning of war." [22] Although Austria-Hungary also had a number of different military plans, the condition of her army served as a constraint. One of the proposals to confine the Balkan dispute to a local area was the "Halt in Belgrade" plan. But this proposal broke down because the Austrian army was not even in a condition to occupy Belgrade.

The other two continental powers—France and Germany—each had but a single plan for calling up their armed forces and, in the case of Germany, political leaders were ill-informed about the rigidity of mobilization and war plans. The kaiser's last minute attempt to reverse the Schlieffen plan—to attack only in the east—shattered Moltke, who replied: "That is impossible, Your Majesty. An army of a million cannot be improvised. It would be nothing but a rabble of undisciplined armed men, without a commissariat. . . . It is utterly impossible to advance except according to plan; strong in the west, weak in the east." [23]

Finally, all the mobilization plans existed only on paper: except for the Russo-Japanese war, no major European power had mobilized since 1878. This fact rendered the plans all the more rigid and made military leaders responsible for carrying them out less likely to accept any last-minute modifications. It may also have added to the widely believed dictum that one did not mobilize for any purpose other than war.

The options perceived by each nation's leaders for themselves and their enemies are summarized in Tables 34 and 35. In every instance the proportion of open choices relative to all options was seen as higher for adversaries than for oneself. With the exception of Austria-Hungary, whose documents are characterized by an absence of much attention to other countries, the findings indicate strong support for the hypothesis that in a crisis situation decision makers will tend to view their own options as more restricted than those of their adversaries.*

According to the second hypothesis relating stress to percep-

---

* The $\emptyset$ coefficient—sometimes called the "fourfold point correlation"—measures the degree of association or correlation between two sets of attributes. In Tables 34, 35, and 36, the two attributes are the type of option (choice, necessity, closed) and nation (own, allied, enemy). $\emptyset$ reaches a maximum score of 1.00 when the association between attributes is perfect; for example if, in Table 34, all 120 German perceptions of their own options had been in the "necessity" category, and all 27 enemy alternatives had been in the "choice" category. $\emptyset$ is closely related to the chi-square statistic, which was used to calculate the one-tailed probabilities in Tables 34, 35, and 36. For a further description of $\emptyset$, see William L. Hays, *Statistics for Psychologists* (New York: Holt, Rinehart & Winston), 1963, pp. 604–606.

TABLE 34
Perceptions of Own and Enemies' Alternatives

	GERMANY			
	Own Alternatives		Enemies' Alternatives	
Choice	10	(8.3%)	25	(92.6%)
Necessity	110	(91.7%)	2	(7.4%)

$$\emptyset = .77 \qquad p < .0001$$

	AUSTRIA-HUNGARY			
	Own Alternatives		Enemies' Alternatives	
Choice	13	(14.0%)	1	(50.0%)
Necessity	80	(86.0%)	1	(50.0%)

$$\emptyset = \text{not meaningful}$$

	GREAT BRITAIN			
	Own Alternatives		Enemies' Alternatives	
Choice	7	(25.9%)	21	(91.3%)
Necessity	20	(74.1%)	2	(8.7%)

$$\emptyset = .66 \qquad p < .001$$

	FRANCE			
	Own Alternatives		Enemies' Alternatives	
Choice	1	(7.1%)	12	(85.7%)
Necessity	13	(92.9%)	2	(14.3%)

$$\emptyset = .79 \qquad p. < .001$$

	RUSSIA			
	Own Alternatives		Enemies' Alternatives	
Choice	7	(25.9%)	6	(75.0%)
Necessity	20	(74.1%)	2	(25.0%)

$$\emptyset = .43 \qquad p = .02$$

	ALL NATIONS			
	Own Alternatives		Enemies' Alternatives	
Choice	38	(13.5%)	65	(87.8%)
Necessity	243	(86.5%)	9	(12.2%)

$$\emptyset = .67 \qquad p < .0001$$

TABLE 35
Perceptions of Own and Enemies' Alternatives

	GERMANY			
	Own Alternatives		Enemies' Alternatives	
Choice	10	(33.3%)	25	(100.0%)
Closed	20	(66.7%)	0	(0.0%)

$\emptyset = .69$ p < .001

	AUSTRIA-HUNGARY			
	Own Alternatives		Enemies' Alternatives	
Choice	13	(65.0%)	1	(100.0%)
Closed	7	(35.0%)	0	(0.0%)

$\emptyset$ = not meaningful

	GREAT BRITAIN			
	Own Alternatives		Enemies' Alternatives	
Choice	7	(23.3%)	21	(100.0%)
Closed	23	(76.7%)	0	(0.0%)

$\emptyset = .76$ p < .001

	FRANCE			
	Own Alternatives		Enemies' Alternatives	
Choice	1	(16.7%)	12	(85.7%)
Closed	5	(83.3%)	2	(14.3%)

$\emptyset = .66$ p = .01

	RUSSIA			
	Own Alternatives		Enemies' Alternatives	
Choice	7	(50.0%)	6	(100.0%)
Closed	7	(50.0%)	0	(0.0%)

$\emptyset = .48$ p = .04

	ALL NATIONS			
	Own Alternatives		Enemies' Alternatives	
Choice	38	(38.0%)	65	(97.0%)
Closed	62	(62.0%)	2	(3.0%)

$\emptyset = .59$ p < .0001

tions of alternatives, *in a crisis situation, decision makers will tend to perceive their allies' range of alternatives to be more restricted than those of their adversaries.* Just as European leaders tended to perceive fewer alternatives open to themselves than to their adversaries, so they regarded their allies as being in a similar position vis-à-vis their enemies. On the one hand, German documents are replete with explanations that Austria was pursuing the *only* policy open to her and thus Germany could not play a moderating role in Vienna,° although merely four months earlier Wilhelm had stated that if Vienna gets into a war against the Slavs through "great stupidity," it would "leave us [Germany] quite cold."²⁴ On the other hand, the kaiser appealed to England, apparently convinced that the latter could perform the very role which he felt was impossible for Germany—restraining the most belligerent member of the coalition. "Instead of making proposals for conferences, His Majesty the King should order France and Russia, frankly and plainly, at one and the same time —they were HIS ALLIES—to DESIST at once from the mobilization, remain NEUTRAL and await Austria's proposals, which I should immediately transmit as soon as I was informed of them. . . . I could do nothing more DIRECT; it was for him to take hold now and prove the honesty of English love of peace." † The assumption of British freedom to determine the policy of her allies, coupled with restrictions on German policy, is nowhere as clear as in one of the kaiser's marginal notes: "He [Grey] knows perfectly well, that if he were to say one single serious sharp warning word at Paris and Petersburg, and were to warn them to remain neutral, both would become quiet at once. But he takes care not to speak the word, and threatens us instead! Common

---

° "Thus, there remains nothing for the Austro-Hungarian Government to do, unless it is willing to make the final sacrifice of its status as a Great Power, but to enforce its demands by the use of heavy pressure, or, if need be, by taking military measures." Germany, #423.

† Germany, #474. "Instead of mediation, a serious word to Petersburg and Paris, to the effect that England would not help them would quiet the situation at once." *Ibid.,* #368. "If Grey wanted <u>really</u> to <u>preserve</u> peace he need only, as Prince Henry suggested on 20th July intimate to the two <u>allies</u> France and Russia—<u>not</u> to <u>mobilize</u> but to wait, until the pourparlers which I was directing had succeeded or otherwise between Vienna and Russia." *Ibid.,* #720.

cur! England alone bears the responsibility for peace and war, and not we any longer." [25]

This approach to the problem of allies was not confined to Berlin. Adducing arguments that were strikingly similar to those used by the kaiser, British leaders denied their ability or willingness to dictate a policy of moderation in Paris or St. Petersburg. Nicolson wrote on 29 July: "I do not think that Berlin quite understands that Russia cannot and will not stand quietly by while Austria administers a severe chastisement to Servia. She does not consider that Servia deserves it, and she could not, in view of that feeling and of her position in the Slav world, consent to it." [26] Grey assessed the requirements of his French ally in similar terms: "France did not wish to join in the war that seemed about to break out, but she was obliged to join in it, because of her alliance." [27] However, he believed that Germany could constrain the cause of her ally: "But none of us could influence Austria in this direction unless Germany would propose and participate in such action in Vienna." °

The result was that only when mobilization and other actions had gone too far to be stopped were some attempts made to restrain the militant members of each alliance. More typical was the advice of Sir Eyre Crowe, who had written on 25 July: "The moment has passed when it might have been possible to enlist French support in an effort to hold back Russia. It is clear that France and Russia are decided to accept the challenge thrown to them. Whatever we may think of the merits of the Austrian charges against Serbia, France and Russia, consider that these are the pretext, and that the bigger cause of Triple Alliance versus Triple Entente is definitely engaged. I think it would be impolitic, not to say dangerous, for England to attempt to convert this opinion, or to endeavour to obscure the plain issue, by any representation at St. Petersburg and Paris." [28] This became the position adopted by Grey.

Similarly, a last-minute German attempt to hold Austria in

° Great Britain, #99. On 28 July Nicholas had appealed to his counterpart in Berlin: "To try and avoid such a calamity as a European war, I beg you in the name of our old friendship to do what you can to stop your allies from going too far." Russia, #170.

check failed. At 2:55 a.m., 30 July, Bethmann-Hollweg concluded a telegram to Vienna: "Under these circumstances we must urgently and impressively suggest to the consideration of the Vienna Cabinet that acceptance of mediation on the mentioned honorable conditions. The responsibility for the consequences that would otherwise follow would be an uncommonly heavy one both for Austria and for us." [29] Five minutes later, another telegram from Berlin warned Vienna: "We are, of course, ready to fulfil the obligations of our alliance, but must refuse to allow ourselves to be drawn wantonly into a world conflagration by Vienna, without having any regard paid to our counsel." [30] However, this coincided with Moltke's wire to Vienna urging immediate mobilization against Russia.[31] Thus there appears to be some truth in the assessment that "he [Grey] allowed Britain to be towed in Russia's wake in exactly the same way that Germany permitted itself to be dragged after Austria. Neither nation had the least idea that the other was not in the driver's seat. Thus Europe lurched and jolted toward war." °

Because there were relatively few statements about allies' alternatives, the figures in Table 36 distinguish only between assertions of open choice on the one hand, and "closed" and "necessity" statements on the other. In every case allies were perceived to have a lower proportion of open choices than those of enemies. But the data for Austria-Hungary are too limited to be very meaningful, and those for France and Russia provide only moderate support for the hypothesis that the range of alternatives for allies was perceived as narrower than that of enemy nations.

The first two hypotheses have involved comparison of policy options available to one's own nation, allies, and enemies. We shall now examine the effects of increasing stress on the range of policy options. The next hypothesis to be tested with these data is that *as stress increases, decision makers will tend to perceive*

° Cowles, *The Kaiser*, p. 322. For a different interpretation, see Fritz Fischer, *Germany's Aims in the First World War* (New York: W. W. Norton, 1968), pp. 3–92. Fischer's thesis is that policy for the Dual Alliance was formulated in Berlin rather than in Vienna, and that the war was the direct outcome of a deliberate policy pursued by German leaders, especially Bethmann-Hollweg. He ascribed last minute German efforts to stop the escalation toward war as a calculated plan to make Russia seem the aggressor, rather than as a genuine attempt to avert war.

TABLE 36
Perceptions of Allies' and Enemies' Alternatives

| | GERMANY | | | |
	Allies' Alternatives		Enemies' Alternatives	
Choice	7	(24.1%)	25	(92.6%)
Necessity and Closed	22	(75.9%)	2	(7.4%)
	$\emptyset = .69$	p<.001		

| | AUSTRIA-HUNGARY | | | |
	Allies' Alternatives		Enemies' Alternatives	
Choice	1	(25.0%)	1	(50.0%)
Necessity and Closed	3	(75.0%)	1	(50.0%)
	$\emptyset =$ not meaningful			

| | GREAT BRITAIN | | | |
	Allies' Alternatives		Enemies' Alternatives	
Choice	21	(67.7%)	21	(91.3%)
Necessity and Closed	10	(32.3%)	2	(8.7%)
	$\emptyset = .33$	p=.01		

| | FRANCE | | | |
	Allies' Alternatives		Enemies' Alternatives	
Choice	6	(50.0%)	12	(75.0%)
Necessity and Closed	6	(50.0%)	4	(25.0%)
	$\emptyset = .26$	p=.15		

| | RUSSIA | | | |
	Allies' Alternatives		Enemies' Alternatives	
Choice	4	(40.0%)	6	(75.0%)
Necessity and Closed	6	(60.0%)	2	(25.0%)
	$\emptyset = .35$	p=.16		

| | ALL NATIONS | | | |
	Allies' Alternatives		Enemies' Alternatives	
Choice	39	(45.3%)	65	(85.5%)
Necessity and Closed	47	(54.7%)	11	(14.5%)
	$\emptyset = .42$	p<.001		

the range of alternatives open to themselves as becoming narrower.

If the hypothesis is correct, the number of statements of action based on "necessity" and "closed" should increase in the latter days of the crisis. The total number of documents from which the perceptions of alternatives were drawn, however, also increased as war became more imminent. In order to perform a valid test of the hypothesis, "necessity" and "closed" statements were adjusted for message volume for each day.°

When the data are grouped into four periods (Table 37), they reveal an overall pattern in which the proportion of "choice" statements remained relatively steady until the climactic days of the crisis. But when the number of "necessity" and "closed" perceptions relative to message volume is compared to the level of stress on a *daily basis* (Table 38), the hypothesis receives substantial support. For each country the relation between stress and narrowing alternatives is in the predicted direction, and the strength of association ranges from moderate to very high.

According to the second hypothesis relating crisis-induced stress to perceived alternatives, *as stress increases decision makers are likely to perceive an expanding range of alternatives open to their adversaries.*

Table 39 reveals that as general war approached, there was a tendency to believe that the enemy had more rather than fewer options. If only assertions about open choices are considered (Table 40), we find that there was also a steady increase in the proportion of them that are viewed as resting with the enemies.

When the relation between stress and perceptions of enemy alternatives † is examined on a *daily basis* (Table 41), the hypothesis also receives substantial support. For all nations increasing stress was associated with the belief that the adversaries' options were increasing, but in the case of Russia the relation was a very weak one. Moreover, there were not enough Austro-Hungarian

---

° The adjustment to take into account changes in the volume of communication is described in the appendix, which also provides tables revealing the distribution of perceived alternatives for self, allies, and enemies by nation and date.

† Adjusted for message volume in the same way as for earlier hypotheses. For details, see the appendix.

TABLE 37

Degree of Choice in Perceptions of Own Alternatives

Period	GERMANY		AUSTRIA-HUNGARY		GREAT BRITAIN		FRANCE		RUSSIA		ALL NATIONS	
	N°	% Choice	N°	% Choice	N°	% Choice	N°	% Choice	N°	% Choice	N°	% Choice
27 June–20 July	16	0	46	15	2	0	0	0	1	0	65	11
21–28 July	32	6	32	9	13	31	5	0	15	33	97	10
29 July–2 August	73	11	22	14	32	22	12	8	16	13	155	13
3–4 August	19	0	0	0	3	0	2	0	2	0	26	0
27 June–4 August	140	7	100	13	50	14	19	5	34	21	343	11

° Total perceptions of alternatives (necessity + closed + choice).

TABLE 38

Strength of Association (Goodman-Kruskal *gamma*)
between Stress and Perceptions of Own
Alternatives Narrowing

	N	*Gamma*	P
Germany	31	.37	.01
Austria-Hungary	35	.41	.006
Great Britain	29	.48	.006
France	28	.75	.0001
Russia	38	.60	.0004

TABLE 39
Degree of Choice in Perceptions of Enemies' Alternatives

Period	GERMANY N°	GERMANY % Choice	AUSTRIA-HUNGARY N°	AUSTRIA-HUNGARY % Choice	GREAT BRITAIN N°	GREAT BRITAIN % Choice	FRANCE N°	FRANCE % Choice	RUSSIA N°	RUSSIA % Choice	ALL NATIONS N°	ALL NATIONS % Choice
27 June–20 July	3	67	2	50	0	0	0	0	0	0	5	60
21–28 July	6	100	0	0	9	67	10	80	3	67	28	78
29 July–2 August	18	94	0	0	7	86	13	100	2	50	40	92
3–4 August	0	0	0	0	0	0	0	0	3	100	3	100
27 June–4 August	27	93	2	50	16	75	23	91	8	75	76	86

° Total perceptions of alternatives (necessity + closed + choice).

TABLE 40
Enemy Percentage of All Open Choices

Period	GERMANY N°	GERMANY %+	AUSTRIA-HUNGARY N°	AUSTRIA-HUNGARY %+	GREAT BRITAIN N°	GREAT BRITAIN %+	FRANCE N°	FRANCE %+	RUSSIA N°	RUSSIA %+	ALL NATIONS N°	ALL NATIONS %+
27 June–20 July	2	100	9	11	0	0	0	0	0	0	11	27
21–28 July	12	50	3	0	19	42	11	55	11	18	56	39
29 July–2 August	28	61	3	0	30	43	8	75	3	33	72	51
3–4 August	0	0	0	0	0	0	0	0	3	100	3	100
27 June–4 August	42	60	15	7	49	43	19	63	17	35	142	46

° Total perceptions of open choices (own + allies + enemies).
+ Percentage of all open choices which are perceived to rest with enemies.

TABLE 41
Strength of Association (Goodman-Kruskal *gamma*)
between Rising Stress and Perceptions
of Enemies' Alternatives as Expanding

	N	Gamma	P
Germany	31	.56	.004
Austria-Hungary	35	.68	.0002
Great Britain	29	.54	.005
France	28	.45	.10
Russia	38	.11	n.s.

or Russian statements about the opponents' options to make the findings for these two countries very meaningful.

Conclusion

It is not very useful or instructive to ask why European leaders did not consider *all* the ways in which they might have been able to avert, or at least localize, a war during the summer of 1914. Some options were unacceptable for what were perceived to be reasons of the most urgent national interest. Nevertheless other possibilities for avoiding a general war seem obvious to those who examine the events of 1914 after the fact. But it is now commonly accepted that decision making is rarely "objectively rational," if by that we mean that the process includes identifying all possible policy options, from which the best one is chosen.[32] This criterion is poor because we can point to overlooked options in virtually any policy decision, not only those that are made under crisis conditions.

But even if we reject the standards of perfect rationality or those established with the benefit of 20-20 hindsight, the evidence from the 1914 crisis gives rise to some sobering thoughts about decisions under conditions of crisis-induced stress. Most European leaders tended to view their own freedom of choice and that of their allies as severely restricted.° At the same time

---

° Stress, fatigue, time pressure, communication overload, and other aspects of the crisis appear to have contributed to a constriction of perceived policy options. But we cannot attribute all decisions to human failing under intense pressure. The rigidity of military plans, for instance, was a "real" rather than an imagined reason for a sense of reduced policy options during the final stages of the crisis.

they generally believed that in order to slow down or reverse the escalation it remained only for leaders in the other alliance to take some "reasonable" steps. The failure of adversaries to do so only confirmed the suspicion that their intentions were aggressive. The belief that decision making for one's adversaries requires only the exercise of free will appears to be a rather general one—witness the popularity of this view among radical groups of both left and right. Certainly the 1914 documents are virtually devoid of any empathy for the dilemmas of opposing leaders. Nor do they reveal any extensive consideration of the ways in which one might open up new options for the adversary —or at least keep from restricting them. This followed logically from the belief that the enemy was free to take the necessary steps to bring events under control. Finally, the evidence indicated that these tendencies became more pronounced as the crisis deepened.

Yet, because all crises do not go to war, we can assume that the decision processes which appear to have been so prevalent in 1914 are neither inescapable nor beyond the possibility of human control. For this reason it is useful to examine the Cuban missile crisis of 1962 in light of the questions we have considered in this and the preceding chapters.

Chapter Seven

DECISION MAKING IN A CRISIS
THAT DIDN'T GO TO WAR
OCTOBER 1962 [1]

Introduction

A SINGLE U-2 American surveillance plane took off on 14 October 1962, for a reconnaissance flight over Cuba. Immediately upon returning its high altitude cameras were unloaded. After intensive study of the developed films, intelligence analysts uncovered unmistakable evidence of two medium-range ballistic missile (MRBM) sites in areas previously photographed and found to be empty. Overflights three days later confirmed these reports and revealed nine sites—thirty-six launch positions—six for the 1,100 mile MRBM and three for 2,200 mile intermediate-range ballistic missiles (IRBM) in various states of readiness.

Although discovery of the missile launching sites in Cuba was a surprise, not least of all to American intelligence services, the general background of Soviet-American relations against which the Cuban crisis was set was reminiscent of the worst days of the cold war. Even the surface appearances of easing tension between Moscow and Washington, which characterized the periods around the summit conference of 1955 and the Eisenhower-Khrushchev meetings in 1959, had been buried under more recent events: the downing of an American U-2 over the Soviet Union in the spring of 1960, followed immediately by the collapse of the Paris summit conference; continued nuclear testing of bombs in the high megaton range; periodic crises over Berlin, followed by the erection of the Berlin Wall in 1961; and the threat of a new Soviet effort against West Berlin immediately following the American congressional elections in November 1962.

For several years, moreover, the issue of Cuba had served to increase Soviet-American tensions. John Kennedy had won the presidency in 1960 after a campaign in which he had accused the Eisenhower administration of taking insufficient steps against the Castro regime. Soon after coming to office, the new president permitted the Central Intelligence Agency to continue a project aimed at overthrowing Castro through American support for an invasion of Cuba by an assortment of anti-Castro exile groups. That inept plan, predicated in part on the assumption that masses of Cubans would welcome and assist the invasion force, was an almost complete disaster for American foreign policy. Aside from the cost to the moral position of the United States, the Bay of Pigs episode convinced Cubans who might have entertained doubts on that score that the United States would indeed seek to overthrow the new regime there. It probably also led Soviet Premier Khrushchev to believe that the American president was both reckless in using force and lacking in courage to use resources sufficient to ensure success in foreign-policy undertakings.

For a short period after the Bay of Pigs fiasco, Berlin, Laos, and other issues partially eclipsed Cuba as the focal point of Soviet-American conflict. By the summer of 1962, however, rumours of unusual Soviet activities in Cuba were heard with increasing frequency. In August official American sources reported that a large number of Soviet ships had arrived in Cuba, bringing with them military equipment and technical personnel, but in quantities thought to be insufficient to provide Cuba with any offensive capabilities.

When campaigning for the congressional elections of 1962 began, President Kennedy found himself the target of increasingly vocal demands that he end his "do nothing" policy toward Castro. Senator Homer Capehart charged that, "He [President Kennedy] said to Mr. Khrushchev you go ahead and do whatever you want to in Cuba, you arm in any way you wish, and do anything you want to. We'll do nothing about it." [2] Capehart demanded an immediate invasion of Cuba, an option which the president ruled out on 29 August. He did, however, order increased surveillance of Soviet military activities in Cuba.

On 2 September the USSR announced that it had agreed to supply further arms and technical specialists to Cuba in order to meet the threat from the "aggressive imperialist quarters." Following further attacks on the administration by Senators Strom Thurmond and Kenneth Keating, the latter the most persistent critic of administration policy toward Cuba, President Kennedy pledged that the United States would act against any aggression from Cuba. He also asked Congress for standby authority to call up 150,000 National Guardsmen and Reservists for one year, but this was on the expectation of another Berlin crisis in the near future.

Throughout September and early October campaign discussions about American policy toward Cuba generated considerable public debate. In answer to Republican charges of a "do nothing" policy and demands for a quarantine (Richard Nixon), blockade (Senators Karl Mundt, Hugh Scott, and Keating), or invasion (Senators Barry Goldwater and Thurmond), Democrats countered with charges that "hot-blooded and hot-headed extremists" were urging rash and unwarranted action (Chester Bowles) and that, in any case, the origin of the problem was the failure of President Eisenhower to enforce the Monroe-Doctrine (Harry S Truman). By mid-October the Republican national chairman declared that the "irresolution" of the Kennedy administration on Cuba was the "dominant issue of the 1962 campaign." On the basis of a poll of newspaper editors and members of Congress, the non-partisan *Congressional Quarterly* confirmed that Cuba was indeed the most important election issue. When the president arrived in Chicago on a campaign tour in mid-October, one "welcoming" sign asked for "Less Profile—More Courage." [3]

Charges and countercharges on Cuba were not confined to the domestic political scene. In response to President Kennedy's warning against aggression from Cuba, the Soviet Union asserted on 11 September that any attack on Cuba or on Soviet ships bound for Cuba might bring on nuclear war. The statement added that arms being sent to Cuba were purely defensive. Foreign Minister Gromyko repeated the warning before the United Nations, and soon thereafter he privately assured President Kennedy (who by that time already possessed photographic evidence to the contrary) that no weapons with offensive capabilities were being sent to Cuba by the USSR. Meanwhile, the House and Senate had approved, by votes of 384-7 and 87-1 respectively, a resolution sanctioning the use of force, if necessary, to defend the hemisphere against Cuban aggression.

Despite various rumours and claims about what was going on in Cuba, "hard" evidence about Soviet military activity was lacking. The most vocal critics of the Kennedy administration were unwilling to reveal their sources of information, making it impossible for intelligence experts to check their accuracy. For some time, every Soviet ship heading for Cuba had been photographed and the entire island was covered by aerial reconnaissance flights twice a month. Additionally, on 29 August periodic U-2 flights over Cuba were ordered by the president, whose approval was required for each such mission. Photographs taken on the first flight revealed the presence of surface-to-air antiaircraft missiles (SAMs), Komar torpedo boats armed with short-range rockets for coastal defence, and an increase in Soviet military personnel. A week later it was also discovered that MIG-21 fighters were stationed in Cuba.

Owing to bad weather conditions, no further photographs of military installations were available until the flights of 26 and 29 September and 5 and 7 October. These flights produced no evidence of equipment or construction indicating the presence of offensive missiles. Moreover, knowledgeable observers of Soviet foreign policy, including most members of the intelligence community, were convinced that Premier Khrushchev would not risk placing offensive missiles in an outpost so far removed geographically from the Soviet Union.[4]

It was against this background of already high international tensions that President Kennedy met his most intimate advisers in the cabinet room of the White House at 11:45 a.m., 16 October, to consider the problem of Soviet missile sites in Cuba. Initially meeting with the president were: Dean Rusk, George Ball, Edwin Martin, Alexis Johnson, Llewellyn Thompson, and Charles Bohlen of the State Department; Robert McNamara, Roswell Gilpatrick, Paul Nitze, and Maxwell Taylor of the Defense Department; Marshall Carter of the CIA; and Robert Kennedy,

Douglas Dillon, McGeorge Bundy, and Theodore Sorensen. During later meetings they were joined from time to time by John McCone, Lyndon Johnson, Kenneth O'Donnell, Dean Acheson, Adlai Stevenson, Robert Lovett, and Donald Wilson.[5] Recalling the sombre atmosphere in which this and subsequent meetings took place, Attorney-General Robert Kennedy stated: "We all agreed in the end that if the Russians were ready to go to nuclear war over Cuba, they were ready to go to nuclear war, and that was that. So we might as well have the showdown then as six months later." [6]

The initial phase of the crisis—a period of some 150 hours ending at 4:00 p.m., Monday 22 October—was confined to the almost around-the-clock meetings and discussions among the president and his advisers. In order to avoid arousing Soviet suspicions that their missile sites had been discovered, however, the president's previously arranged schedule of campaign speeches, meetings with visiting dignitaries, and the like was allowed to remain unchanged.

The "international phase" of the missile crisis began when President Kennedy addressed the nation (and the world) on 22 October:

Within the past week unmistakable evidence has established the fact that a series of offensive missile sites is now in preparation on that imprisoned island [Cuba]. The purpose of these bases can be none other than to provide a nuclear strike capability against the Western Hemisphere.

Additional sites not yet completed appear to be designed for intermediate-range ballistic missiles capable . . . of striking most of the major cities in the Western Hemisphere.

This urgent transformation of Cuba into an important strategic base—by the presence of these large, long-range, and clearly offensive weapons of mass destruction—constitutes an explicit threat to the peace and security of all the Americas.

In response the United States would, according to the president: impose a "strict quarantine" around Cuba to halt the offensive Soviet build-up; continue and increase the close surveillance of Cuba; answer any nuclear missile attack launched from Cuba against any nation in the Western hemisphere with "a full retaliatory response upon the Soviet Union"; reinforce the naval base at Guantanamo; call for a meeting of the Organization of American States to invoke the Rio Treaty; and call for an emergency meeting of the United Nations. At the same time he stated that additional military forces had been alerted for "any eventuality." In accordance with the Joint Congressional Resolution passed three weeks earlier, the president signed an executive order on 23 October mobilizing reserves.[7]

In its initial response the Soviet government denied the offensive character of its weapons in Cuba, condemned the quarantine as "piracy," and warned that Soviet ships would not honour it. Warsaw Pact forces were also placed on alert.

Although the issue was immediately brought before the United Nations and the Organization of American States, the events of 22–24 October pointed to a possibly violent showdown in the Atlantic, in Cuba, or perhaps in other areas of the world. President Kennedy apparently expected some form of retaliation in Berlin. In his 22 October address he specifically warned the Soviet Union against any such move: "Any hostile move anywhere in the world against the safety and freedom of the people to whom we are committed—including in particular the brave people of West Berlin—will be met by whatever action is needed."

The quarantine went into effect at 10 a.m. on 24 October with 16 destroyers, 3 cruisers, 1 aircraft carrier, 6 utility ships, and 150 other vessels in reserve.° At that time a fleet of 25 Soviet ships nearing Cuba was expected to test the American policy within hours. They had recently been joined by Russian submarines. An American businessman visiting Moscow was told by Premier Khrushchev on 24 October that "as the Soviet vessels were not armed the United States could undoubtedly stop one or two or more but then he, Chairman Khrushchev, would give instructions to the Soviet submarines to sink the American vessels." [8]

Although the Soviet premier dispatched a letter to Bertrand Russell calling for a summit conference, statements from Moscow and Washington gave no evidence that either side would retreat. The next day rumours of an American attack or invasion of Cuba

---

° Theodore C. Sorensen, *Kennedy* (New York: Harper & Row, 1965), p. 708. On the advice of Ambassador Stevenson, the blockade was postponed one day in order to give the Organization of American States an opportunity to sanction it. Henry M. Pachter, *Collision Course: The Cuban Missile Crisis and Coexistence* (New York: Praeger, 1963).

were strengthened when Representative Hale Boggs (who was not, however, speaking for the administration) stated: "If these missiles are not dismantled, the United States has the power to destroy them, and I assure you that this will be done." At the same time American intelligence sources revealed that work on the missile sites was proceeding at full speed.

The first real break in the chain of events leading to an apparently imminent confrontation came on 25 October when twelve Soviet vessels turned back in mid-Atlantic. It was at this point that Secretary of State Dean Rusk remarked, "We're eyeball to eyeball, and I think the other fellow just blinked." [9] Shortly thereafter the first Soviet ship to reach the patrol area—the tanker *Bucharest*—was allowed to proceed to Cuba without boarding and search.

By the following day the crisis appeared to be receding slightly from its most dangerous level. The Soviet-chartered freighter, *Marucla* (ironically a former American Liberty ship now under Lebanese registry), was searched without incident and, when no contraband was discovered, allowed to proceed to Cuba. In answer to an appeal from Secretary-General U Thant, Soviet Premier Khrushchev had agreed to keep Soviet ships away from the patrol area for the time being. President Kennedy's reply to the secretary-general stated that he would try to avoid any direct confrontation at sea "in the next few days." At the same time, however, the White House issued a statement which said: "The development of ballistic missile sites in Cuba continues at a rapid pace. . . . The activity at these sites apparently is directed at achieving a full operational capability as soon as possible." The State Department added that "further action would be justified" if work on the missile sites continued. Photographic evidence revealed that such work was continuing at an increased rate and that the missile sites would be operational in five days.

The "bargaining phase" of the crisis opened in the evening of 26 October.* A secret letter from Premier Khrushchev acknowl-

---

* It was also on 26 October that "Mr. X" (Aleksandr S. Fomin), head of Soviet Intelligence in the United States, approached John Scali of ABC News with essentially the same terms for a détente. This episode has been described in more detail in ABC News, "John Scali, A.B.C. News," 13 August 1964, mimeo. transcript.

edged the presence of Soviet missiles in Cuba for the first time.°
He is reported to have argued they were defensive in nature but
that he understood the president's feelings about them. Embedded within the long, emotional, and rambling letter there appeared to be a proposal that if the United States pledged not to
invade Cuba the missiles would no longer be needed and would,
therefore, be withdrawn under UN inspection. A second message
from Moscow, dispatched twelve hours later, proposed a trade of
Soviet missiles in Cuba for NATO missile bases in Turkey; the
United Nations Security Council was to verify fulfilment of both
operations, contingent upon the approval of the Cuban and
Turkish governments.

In his reply to Khrushchev's secret letter of Friday evening,
the president all but ignored the later proposal to trade bases in
Turkey for those in Cuba. Ironically, he had ordered American
missiles to be withdrawn from the Turkish bases many months
earlier but the order had not been carried out. At the attorney
general's suggestion, the president simply interpreted Premier
Khrushchev's letter as a bid for an acceptable settlement—as if
the message regarding bases in Turkey had never been received.†

As I read your letter, the key elements of your proposals—which
seem generally acceptable as I understand them—are as follows:
   1) You would agree to remove these weapons systems from Cuba
under appropriate United Nations observation and supervision; and
undertake, with suitable safeguards, to halt the further introduction of
such weapons systems into Cuba.
   2) We, on our part, would agree—upon the establishment of adequate arrangements through the United Nations to ensure the carrying out and continuation of these commitments—(a) to remove

° This is the only written communication between the United States and the Soviet Union during the crisis period which has not been made public. The letter is
paraphrased in Elie Abel, *The Missile Crisis* (Philadelphia: J. B. Lippincott,
1966), pp. 179–183.

† Pachter develops the thesis that the message linking Turkey with Cuba was
written prior to the secret note from Khrushchev, but that difficulties in communication caused them to be received in reverse order. The validity of this interpretation, which would absolve the Soviet premier from the charge of trying to
raise the ante during a nuclear poker game, cannot be determined from the available sources. *Collision Course*, p. 68.

promptly the quarantine measures now in effect and (b) to give assurance against an invasion of Cuba.

He added, however, that

the first ingredient, let me emphasize, . . . is the cessation of work on missile sites in Cuba and measures to render such weapons inoperable, under effective international guarantees. The continuation of this threat, or a prolonging of this discussion concerning Cuba by linking these problems to the broader questions of European and world security, would surely lead to an intensification of the Cuban crisis and a grave risk to the peace of the world.

In responding to Khrushchev's proposal to trade missile bases in Turkey for those in Cuba, a White House statement rejected that offer:

Several inconsistent and conflicting proposals have been made by the U.S.S.R. within the last 24 hours, including the one just made public in Moscow. . . . The first imperative must be to deal with this immediate threat, under which no sensible negotiation can proceed.

Despite the sense of relief that warfare on the high seas had been avoided and the fact that negotiations on a formula to end the crisis had been initiated, there were several indications that events were rapidly moving toward an even more dangerous phase.

On 27 October an American U-2 reconnaissance plane had been shot down over Cuba, and several other planes had been fired upon. The Defense Department warned that measures would be taken to "insure that such missions are effective and protected." At the same time it announced that twenty-four troop-carrier squadrons—14,000 men—were being recalled to active duty. Continued construction on the missile sites, which, it was believed, would become operational by the following Tuesday, caused even more concern than attacks on the U-2s. It was generally agreed that the danger of nuclear war was never more acute than on that Saturday.[10] Another meeting at the White House was scheduled on Sunday; top item on the agenda was selection of a strategy to remove the missile sites before they became operational. That evening the attorney-general and the secretary of state met with Soviet Ambassador Dobrynin to convey personally the determination of the president to have the missile bases removed, by American action if the Soviets did not agree to do so within the next day. In addition to delivering this ultimatum, Kennedy and Rusk suggested that accord on several matters, including withdrawal of American missiles in Turkey, could follow—but only after the present crisis was resolved.*

On Sunday morning (28 October), however, Radio Moscow stated that the Soviet premier would shortly make an important announcement. The message was broadcast in the clear to shortcut the time required by normal channels of communication. Premier Khrushchev declared:

I regard with great understanding your concern and the concern of the United States people in connection with the fact that the weapons you describe as offensive are formidable indeed. . . . The Soviet Government, in addition to earlier instruction on the discontinuation of further work on weapons construction sites, has given a new order to dismantle the arms which you describe as offensive, and to crate and return them to the Soviet Union.

The statement made no reference to the withdrawal of American missiles from Turkey.

In reply, President Kennedy issued a statement welcoming Premier Khrushchev's "statesmanlike decision." He added that the Cuban blockade would be removed as soon as the United Nations had taken "necessary measures," and further, that the United States would not invade Cuba. Kennedy said that he attached great importance to a rapid settlement of the Cuban crisis, because "developments were approaching a point where events could have become unmanageable."

Although Khrushchev stated that the Soviet Union was prepared to reach an agreement on United Nations verification of the dismantling operation in Cuba, Fidel Castro announced on the same day that Cuba would not accept the Kennedy-Khrushchev agreement unless the United States accepted a series of

* Kennedy, "Thirteen Days," p. 170. The importance of the ultimatum delivered to Ambassador Dobrynin by the attorney-general is confirmed by Premier Khrushchev's account of the missile crisis. *Khrushchev Remembers* (Boston: Little, Brown & Co., 1970).

further conditions, including the abandonment of the naval base at Guantanamo. But the critical phases of the Soviet-American confrontation seemed to be over. Despite the inability to carry out on-site inspection, photographic surveillance of Cuba confirmed that the missile sites were being dismantled. The quarantine was lifted on 21 November, at which time the Pentagon announced that the missiles had indeed left Cuba aboard Soviet ships.

Decision Making During the Missile Crisis

The 1914 and Cuban situations were similar in a number of respects and differed in others. For present purposes the similarity of primary interest is that both situations conform to the definition of crisis used here. Despite widespread rumours of Soviet missile installations in Cuba, photographic evidence of their presence was a surprise to virtually all officials in Washington, including the president; the rate of construction on the missile sites made it evident that any decision to prevent their completion could not be long delayed; and almost all who joined the American decision group interpreted the Soviet move as a serious threat to national security.* As one participant in these discussions puts it: "Everyone round the table recognized that we were in a major crisis. We didn't know, that day, if the country would come through it with Washington intact." [11]

By these criteria the Cuban missile episode was also a crisis for Soviet leaders. They clearly had not anticipated premature American discovery of the missile sites and, although this is pure conjecture, it is reasonable to assume that they were surprised by the American response to the Cuban missiles. Direct evidence on the extent to which time pressure and perceptions of threat were felt in the Kremlin during the week of 22–28 October is not available, but certainly Soviet messages indicate the presence of these factors.

The most significant difference between these two events is

---

* The one notable exception appears to have been Secretary of Defense Robert McNamara, whose initial reaction was: "A missile is a missile. It makes no great difference whether you are killed by a missile fired from the Soviet Union or from Cuba." Quoted in Abel, *Missile Crisis*, p. 51.

that the 1914 crisis led to a world war whereas the Cuban confrontation was resolved without recourse to violence. Stated somewhat differently, the situation which confronted national leaders in the two crises shared a number of attributes (surprise, high threat, short decision time), but the decisions they made led to significantly different results: peaceful settlement as opposed to a world war.

The question then naturally arises: "How can we account for the different outcomes?" In an attempt to explore this question, the remainder of this chapter examines several aspects of the decision-making process in 1962, with special attention to time pressure, the search for and definition of alternative courses of action, and the patterns of communication. The purpose is to develop the basis for comparison with the findings in the previous three chapters.

Whereas the 1914 data are relatively complete, permitting systematic quantitative analyses of several hypotheses, primary documentation for the Cuban crisis is limited to the formal communications between Soviet and American leaders during the week following President Kennedy's disclosure of the presence of missiles in Cuba. Notably lacking are documents from the week of 16–22 October, during which the initial American decisions regarding Cuba were made. For this crucial period we are therefore forced to rely on the numerous memoirs and journalistic accounts of these deliberations. Moreover, the 1914 data reveal something of the decision processes in all the major capitals of Europe, but we are lacking all except the most fragmentary and inferential information on Soviet decision making during the Cuban crisis.[12] For this reason only some of the hypotheses tested with the 1914 data can be re-examined in the Cuban crisis, and then impressionistically rather than exhaustively.

PERCEPTIONS OF TIME PRESSURE

Several sources of time pressure impinged on the president and his advisers during the missile crisis. Initially there was the need to formulate a policy before the Soviets were alerted by the stepped-up U-2 flights to the fact that their launching installations had been discovered. Conversely, once developments in

Cuba become public knowledge, there would be no further time for deliberation and debate on the proper response.

The overriding concern throughout the period was the knowledge that construction on the missile sites was continuing at a rapid pace. The first photographic evidence of construction activities in Cuba indicated that they would be operational within a week to ten days. This expectation clearly fixed a deadline on policy deliberations. American officials were aware that their task would become immeasurably more difficult once construction on the launching sites was completed: "For all of us knew that, once the missile sites under construction become operational, and capable of responding to any apparent threat or command with a nuclear volley, the President's options would be dramatically changed." [13] Thus, the situation did not compel a reflex-like response—at least as it was defined by the president. But in relation to the task at hand, decision time was indeed short.[14] In view of the awesome implications of the situation, it is hardly surprising that all accounts of decision making during the Cuban crisis—especially that of Robert Kennedy—are replete with indications of time pressure.

Despite the sense of urgency created by these deadlines, the president and his advisers sought to reduce the probability that either side would respond by a "spasm reaction." Efforts were made to delay taking overt actions as long as the situation permitted, and to weigh alternative courses of action by the criterion: does this response lengthen rather than reduce the time available for considering other options? Equally important, discussions in Washington revealed a sensitivity for the time pressures under which the adversary was operating. There was a concern that Premier Khrushchev should not be rushed into an irrevocable decision; it was agreed among members of the decision group that "we should slow down the escalation of the crisis to give Khrushchev time to consider his next move." [15] An interesting example of a tactic designed to increase Soviet decision time emerges from the president's management of the naval quarantine. He ordered American ships to delay intercepting Soviet vessels until the last possible moment, *and had the order transmitted in the clear.*[16] The Soviets, who were certain to intercept the message, would at least know that they had time in which to decide how to react to the blockade. This ploy also revealed a sophisticated understanding of the social psychology of communication; a message from a distrusted source is more likely to be believed if the recipient must use his own efforts to obtain the information. Similarly, the Soviet decision, on 25 October, to slow down the westward progress of their ships in mid-Atlantic, can be interpreted as an effort to lengthen decision time.

A content analysis of the messages exchanged between Moscow and Washington during the crisis reveals the relation between perceived time pressure and developments during the week of 22–28 October (Figure 19). Soviet and American documents indicate that the incidence of references to time reached a peak at about the time that the Russian ships heading for Cuba turned back, thereby reducing the probability of a naval conflict in the Atlantic. That this was true slightly earlier for the Soviet Union than for the United States is perhaps explained by the fact that Soviet leaders were aware of their decision not to challenge the blockade before it was apparent in Washington. References to time pressure rose again as it became increasingly evident that steps beyond a blockade might be taken by the United States to ensure removal of the missiles. After the agreement to dismantle and remove the missile sites in exchange for a pledge against invading Cuba, references to time pressures declined in both Soviet and American documents.

A comparison of the 1914 and 1962 crises points to the importance of a subjective rather than an objective definition of decision time. Objectively time was of incalculably greater importance in 1962 than in 1914: the period between a decision to use force and execution of military acts is far shorter in an age of intercontinental ballistic missiles capable of reaching any target on earth in a matter of minutes. Hence, Soviet and American leaders in 1962 were no less aware of time pressures and of the potential costs of delaying action than were their counterparts in 1914. But they also perceived the dangers of acting in haste and they were successful in mitigating the most severe dangers attending such pressures. They resisted the pressures for premature decisions and, perhaps even more important, they took a number of actions which avoided putting their adversaries in a position of having to respond in haste. Such efforts to prolong decision time

FIGURE 19

The Relation between Perceived Time Pressure and
Developments during the Missile Crisis

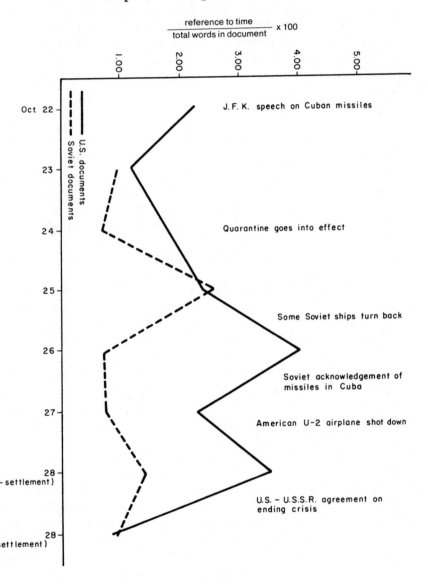

$$\frac{\text{reference to time}}{\text{total words in document}} \times 100$$

U.S. documents

Soviet documents

Oct. 22 — J.F.K. speech on Cuban missiles

23 —

24 — Quarantine goes into effect

25 —

Some Soviet ships turn back

26 —

Soviet acknowledgement of
missiles in Cuba

27 — American U-2 airplane shot down

28 —
(pre-settlement)

U.S. - U.S.S.R. agreement on
ending crisis

28 —
(post-settlement)

within the limits established by the situation were instrumental in the ultimate resolution of the crisis by means short of war. President Kennedy himself later acknowledged that the ability to delay a decision after receipt of the photographic evidence of missile sites was crucial to the *content* of American policy: "If we had had to act on Wednesday [17 October], in the first 24 hours, I don't think probably we would have chosen as prudently as we finally did, the quarantine against the use of offensive weapons." [17]

POLICY OPTIONS

During the Cuban missile crisis, the search for alternatives was intimately related to time pressures; in the words of Arthur Schlesinger, "The deadline defined the strategy." [18] Pressures of time notwithstanding, American policy makers made efforts to prevent premature foreclosure of options. Despite widely circulated rumours that offensive missiles were being deployed in Cuba, the Kennedy administration had resisted taking action until photographic evidence of launching sites became available on 15 October. McGeorge Bundy recalled that upon receiving the first news of the photographic evidence, "his [President Kennedy's] first reaction was that we must make sure, and were we making sure? and would there be evidence on which he could decide that this was in fact really the case." [19] As late as 18 October, a series of alternatives was being considered pending more accurate information, and while the decision to institute a blockade was being hammered out, open discussion of the alternatives was encouraged. The president recalled that "though at the beginning there was a much sharper division . . . this was very valuable, because the people involved had particular responsibilities of their own." [20] Another participant in the crisis decision group asserted that President Kennedy, aware that discussion of alternatives in the National Security Council would be more frank in his absence, encouraged the group to hold preliminary meetings without him.[21] Thus the eventual decision was reached by relatively open and frank discussions. Group decision making does not ensure the emergence of sound policy, of course, but it does limit the probability of a decision performing a personality-oriented function.[22] We shall return to this point in Chapter 8 when we assess Dean Acheson's charge that these "uninhibited" and "leaderless" meetings were "a waste of time" as well as a serious dereliction of constitutional responsibilities.[23]

Six alternative responses emerged from the initial discussions between the president's advisers. The United States could: do nothing; rely on diplomatic pressure against the Soviet Union; attempt to split Castro from the Soviets; initiate a blockade of Cuba; undertake an air strike against military targets in Cuba; or launch an invasion to overthrow the Castro government. The choice soon narrowed down to the blockade and the air strike.

Initially the option of a sudden air strike against the missile sites had strong support among most of the conferees, including that of the president. But after numerous discussions and much shifting of positions the blockade emerged with a majority in the decision group. An informal vote is reported to have revealed an 11-6 majority in favour of the blockade.[24] The naval quarantine appeared to offer a reasonable prospect for inducing Soviet withdrawal of the offensive missiles, while minimizing the probability of provoking a violent Soviet response. According to Kennedy, the decision to impose a naval blockade was based on the reasoning that "the course we finally adopted had the advantage of permitting other steps, if this one was unsuccessful. In other words, we were starting, in a sense, at a minimum place." [25]

The concern of the president and his advisers with maintaining a number of options was based, at least in part, on an explicit distinction between threats and acts. The use of threats had become a more or less accepted tool of international politics in the nearly two decades of cold warring. The United States and the Soviet Union had, on the other hand, carefully abstained from direct violent action against each other. The desire to avoid killing Soviet troops thus weighed heavily against an air strike on Cuba. The blockade shifted the immediate burden of decision concerning the use of violence to Premier Khrushchev and, should the blockade have proved unsuccessful, it did not preclude later employment of a "much more massive action." [26] By adopting that strategy no irrevocable decisions on the use of violence had been made, and multiple options remained for possible future actions by the United States. Equally important, Soviet leaders were given the time and the opportunity to assess their own choices. Thus, unlike several of the key foreign-policy officials in the 1914 crisis, those in October 1962 seemed to perceive a close relation between their own actions and the options of their adversaries. Theodore Sorensen described the deliberations as follows: "We discussed what the Soviet reaction would be to any possible move by the United States, what our reaction with them would have to be to that Soviet reaction, and so on, trying to follow each of those roads to their ultimate conclusion."[27]

American decision makers also displayed a sensitivity for the position and perspective of the adversary, trying to ensure that a number of options other than total war or total surrender were available to Soviet leaders: an important advantage of the blockade over other strategies was that it appeared to avoid placing Soviet leaders in that situation. An air strike on the missile bases or invasion of the island would have left Soviet leaders only the alternatives of capitulating to the United States or of counterattacking. In that case, the latter might have seemed the less distasteful course. A blockade, on the other hand, gave the Soviet government a choice between turning back the weapon-bearing ships or running the blockade. Even the latter course would have left the United States with an option other than sinking the Soviet ships—disabling their rudders.[28] Thus the decision of whether or not to escalate was thrown back to the Kremlin, for a few days at least, and under circumstances which made it unlikely that recourse to violence would improve the Soviet bargaining position.

In selecting the initial step of a blockade around Cuba, the president and his colleagues chose to reject the advice of the military. Throughout the crisis—and even after the Soviet agreement to withdraw the missiles—the Joint Chiefs of Staff continued to press for a military attack on the grounds that the Soviet Union would do nothing in response, or, should that premise prove incorrect, war would be in the American national interest. One member of the Joint Chiefs even suggested a *nuclear* attack on the grounds that the Soviets would use such weapons if they were attacking the United States.[29]

The blockade of Cuba, which went into effect on 24 October, did not end consideration of alternative American strategies. By

26 October it seemed clear that, Khrushchev's earlier threats to the contrary notwithstanding, Soviet ships would not challenge the blockade. Despite the advent of negotiations, however, the situation was still extremely dangerous because it was far from certain that the Soviet missiles would be removed from Cuba; indeed, there was ample evidence of an accelerated pace of construction on the launching sites in Cuba which, it was then believed, would be completed by 30 October. Again the question of next steps to be taken in case the blockade proved insufficient to force withdrawal of all offensive missiles confronted American leaders. Among the options considered were: tightening the blockade to include all commodities other than food and medicine; increased low-level flights over Cuba for purposes of reconnaissance and harassment; action within Cuba; an air strike; and an invasion. These were the alternatives which, had the crisis not been settled by the Kennedy-Khrushchev agreement of 28 October, were to have been considered at what would have been "the most serious meeting ever to take place at the White House." [30] Just before that meeting was to have started, Premier Khrushchev agreed to withdraw all offensive missiles from Cuba in exchange for President Kennedy's pledge not to invade Cuba.

PATTERNS OF COMMUNICATION

Limited access to Soviet and American documents during the missile crisis precludes a complete analysis of patterns of communication. Nevertheless, some comparisons are possible. Perhaps the most striking similarity in the 1914 and Cuban crises was the use of improvised channels of communication to convey diplomatic messages. For instance, even before discovery of the missiles was made public on 22 October, President Kennedy relied on a special emissary, former Secretary of State Dean Acheson, rather than on the State Department and diplomats stationed in Europe, to inform General de Gaulle and NATO leaders of the situation in Cuba.

More important to the ultimate resolution of the crisis was the use of *ad hoc* methods of communicating American intentions to the Soviets during the week of 22–28 October. As the president himself noted after the crisis had passed, normal channels of communication with the Kremlin were "very poor."[31] A minimum of four hours was required to transmit a formal message between the White House and the Kremlin.[32] Or, to put this figure into proper perspective, it would have taken almost ten times as long to send a message to the opposing nation's leader as to deliver a salvo of nuclear-armed missiles into his heartland.

Some extraordinary means were devised in an effort to overcome this problem. Reference has already been made to an important message affirming American desires to slow down escalation of the crisis which was sent to patrolling ships in the clear rather than in code. Upon intercepting the message the Soviets would presumably attach greater credence to its contents than had Washington simply informed the Soviet ambassador of American intentions.[33] Later, Premier Khrushchev announced acceptance of President Kennedy's formula for settlement of the crisis by a public broadcast in order to shortcut the time required to encode, transmit, and decode messages through the normal diplomatic channels.

Several private citizens were also used to transmit important messages during the missile crisis. On the day that the blockade went into effect, Premier Khrushchev summoned a visiting American businessman, William Knox of Westinghouse International, to the Kremlin for a meeting which lasted three hours. Knox, a former neighbour of Secretary of State Dean Rusk, was certain to relay to Washington the Soviet premier's message—the key points of which were an admission that offensive missiles were in Cuba and that they would be used against the United States if need be—to Washington.

Two days late John Scali, diplomatic correspondent for American Broadcasting Company, received an urgent request for a meeting from Aleksandr S. Fomin, the top KGB operative in the Soviet Embassy. At a nearby restaurant Fomin asked whether the State Department would be interested in a settlement based on Soviet withdrawl of the missiles, a Cuban promise to accept no such weapons in the future, and an American pledge not to invade Cuba. Scali conveyed the message to Dean Rusk and later that evening he met again with Fomin to assure him of American interest in the formula. This response was immediately cabled to

Moscow. That the crisis was settled on essentially these terms testifies to the importance of the Scali-Fomin meetings.

Later, according to Scali, Fomin suggested that "in order to benefit from this near disaster from now on Secretary Rusk should meet three times a day with the Russian Ambassador so that they could avoid future crises and what he called future misunderstandings." [34] The important role played by both the Kennedy-Khrushchev and Scali-Fomin negotiations in the resolution of the crisis led directly to establishment of the White House-Kremlin "hot line." The first use during crisis of this channel of communication came during the Arab-Israeli war of 1967 to prevent any misunderstanding between Moscow and Washington which might have led to a direct Soviet-American confrontation in the Middle East. Thus one means to escape the limits of ordinary channels of communication in crisis has been institutionalized.

Although there were certain similarities in method of communication during the 1914 and 1962 crises, responses to information about adversaries—whether in the form of written communications or policy actions—differed rather sharply in the two situations. During the missile crisis there was a tendency to perceive rather accurately the nature of the opponent's actions and the intentions behind them. Forty-two Soviet and sixty-two American actions were coded on an escalation—de-escalation scale, with the following results for the period 22 October–2 November.

	US Actions	Soviet Actions
Escalation	29	24
De-escalation	19	12
Neither	14	6

Figures 20 and 21 reveal how each nation's actions changed during the course of the crisis as well as the adversary's perceptions of them. There was a close correspondence between Soviet actions and American perceptions of the USSR. The relation is less

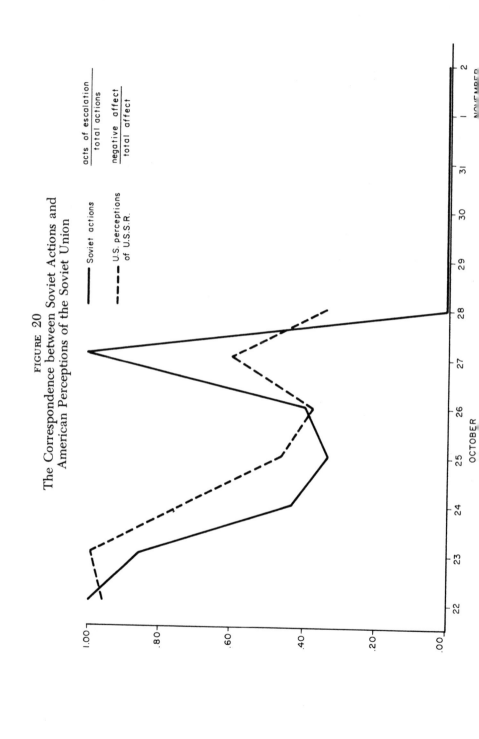

FIGURE 20

The Correspondence between Soviet Actions and
American Perceptions of the Soviet Union

——— Soviet actions

––––– U.S. perceptions
of U.S.S.R.

$\dfrac{\text{acts of escalation}}{\text{total actions}}$

$\dfrac{\text{negative affect}}{\text{total affect}}$

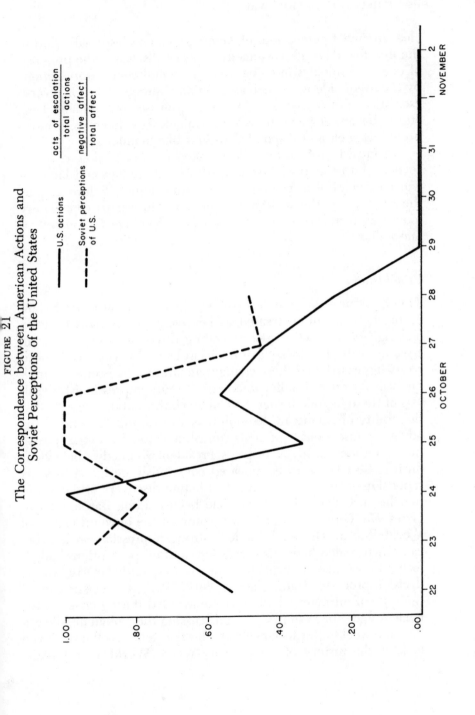

FIGURE 21
The Correspondence between American Actions and
Soviet Perceptions of the United States

clear in Soviet perceptions of American actions, especially during the first few days after Kennedy's speech disclosing the presence of offensive missiles in Cuba. But in general conciliatory actions by the other side were seen as genuine efforts to delay or reverse escalation, rather than as tricks to be dismissed out of hand. Thus efforts by either party to avert a violent showdown were interpreted as such and responded to in a like manner.

In contrast, the various efforts taken in 1914 to slow down or reverse the escalation, first toward a local conflict and later toward a general European war, met with complete failure. In part the reason was the widespread tendency to regard conciliatory moves as insincere efforts to gain an advantage for oneself or one's allies.

Conclusion

Time pressure, the search for alternatives, and patterns of communication are often treated as key elements in crisis decision making. As revealed in the preceding three chapters, data from 1914 indicate that these factors did in fact vary as crisis-induced stress increased, and these changes apparently had serious consequences for critical policy decisions. A more impressionistic analysis of these factors during the Cuban confrontation suggests that the ability of American decision makers to mitigate some of the adverse consequences of crisis contributed to its eventual peaceful resolution. In many respects President Kennedy's behaviour during the Cuban crisis appeared consciously designed to avert repetition of the 1914 disaster. Just before discovery of the Soviet missiles in Cuba the president had been reading Barbara Tuchman's *The Guns of August,* an account of the opening month of World War I. The book made a strong impression on him because it revealed how miscalculations and misperceptions had affected the course of events in 1914. He frequently referred to the decision processes leading up to World War I as a classic case of the type of mistakes which must be avoided during crises in the nuclear age. For example, when discussing the Cuban missile crisis some weeks after its conclusion, he asserted: "Well now, if you look at the history of this century where World War I really

came through a series of misjudgments of the intentions of others
. . . it's very difficult to always make judgments here about what
the effect will be of our decisions on other countries." [35] Yet the
ability of American and Soviet leaders to avoid a nuclear Arma-
geddon in October 1962 is not an assurance that even great skill
in crisis management will always yield a peaceful solution. As
President Kennedy said some months later, referring to the missile crisis, "You can't have too many of those." *

Comparison of these crises sheds light on some aspects of decision making in high-stress situations, but some other interesting
questions remain. We have concentrated our attention on the nature of the situation without considering how the consequences
of crisis may also be affected by organizational, personal, or other
intervening factors. Several possible further observations may be
made, although the evidence permits only speculation rather
than any definite answers.

From a *systemic* perspective we can point to several plausible
explanations. Perhaps nuclear capabilities, and the recognition in
both Washington and Moscow that their use would entail destruction without parallel in history, served as a constraint
against undue provocation of the adversary. But, although we
have now been able to avoid nuclear war for a quarter of a century, only the most optimistic would assert that nuclear terror is
a perfect guarantee for peaceful solution of crises. Some analysts
have suggested that, one way or another, Soviet and American
leaders would certainly have found a way to avoid war over the
missiles in Cuba.[36] But Robert Kennedy's revelation about the
recommendations of the Joint Chiefs of Staff, one of whom was a
vice-presidential candidate in 1968, should go a long way toward
dispelling any overoptimism. It takes no great act of imagination
to conceive of another president facing a similar situation who

---

* Sorensen, *Kennedy*, p. 726. Sorensen observed that the missile crisis significantly affected Kennedy's feelings about foreign affairs: "His perspective, too, had
changed after looking down the gun barrel. After the first Cuban crisis he had
stressed to the nation's editors that 'our restraint is not inexhaustible.' After the
second Cuban crisis, questioned by the same audience about that statement, he
replied: "I hope our restraint—or sense of responsibility—will not ever come to
an end." *Ibid.*, pp. 726–27. See also Arthur M. Schlesinger, *A Thousand Days*
(New York: Houghton-Mifflin Co., 1965), p. 893.

would be willing to rely very heavily upon the advice of his military commanders.* In such circumstances, it is difficult to believe that Russian leaders would have shown the restraint necessary to avoid a Soviet-American war. More generally, it would be a potentially tragic misreading of history to assume, on the basis of the Cuban missile crisis, that a "way out" will always be found.

The availability of the United Nations as a systemic institution for communication and negotiation may also have been a factor. Public discussions between Soviet and American representatives at the Security Council were used primarily to score debating points, but some useful private contacts between Stevenson, Zorin, and their staffs may have been facilitated. Nevertheless, the public evidence to date suggests that the most important channels of communication were those outside the United Nations. In 1914, on the other hand, the so-called Concert System was in fact a series of *ad hoc* conferences and efforts to convene it at the height of the crisis were wholly unsuccessful.

A second possible explanation for the different outcomes in 1914 and 1962 can perhaps be found in the *crisis-management experiences* of the leaders involved. By 1914, Balkan crises had come and gone for a generation without leading to general war. On the surface it appeared to many that European leaders were able to cope with such recurring disturbances, at least to the point of limiting the use of violence to local areas. There is some evidence, admittedly anecdotal, of confidence that the crisis triggered by Franz Ferdinand's assassination was also a situation which could be settled peacefully by reasonable men. Even such a political "realist"—or in more contemporary terminology, a "superhawk"—as Winston Churchill, British first lord of the admiralty, wrote that less than three days before the outbreak of war, "I went to bed with a feeling that things might blow over . . . we were still a long way, as it seemed, from any danger of war." [37]

In contrast, American leaders in 1962 had, less than two years

---

* Even Harry S Truman and Dean Acheson, architects of perhaps the most creative era in the history of American foreign policy, permitted themselves to be guided by General Douglas MacArthur's advice in Korea—with catastrophic consequences—until it became indelibly clear that the general had no intention of acceding to any foreign-policy directives from Washington.

earlier, experienced an almost classic case of how not to handle a crisis. Whatever sense of overconfidence about the management of foreign affairs the Kennedy administration may have possessed upon coming to office in early 1961 must surely have been diminished by the disastrous events surrounding the Bay of Pigs invasion. The bitter lessons of 1961 may well have contributed to the skill with which the president and his advisers managed the much more dangerous situation eighteen months later. If nothing else, the Bay of Pigs fiasco taught the president to be properly sceptical about the quality of advice he received from military sources.

A third possible explanation is that *situational factors* in 1914 and 1962 were different in one critical respect: perhaps the Cuban situation did not reach a stage that was as stressful as that in the latter days of the 1914 crisis.* The evidence at this point is at best mixed, and interpreting it is virtually impossible. Most accounts of the decision-making process in Washington indicate no evidence of the type of personal breakdown under duress that the kaiser apparently suffered in late July, 1914. Nevertheless, as Robert F. Kennedy's memoir of the crisis makes clear, tensions during some days of the crisis reached an almost unbearable intensity, and "some [American decision makers], because of the pressure of events, even appeared to lose their judgment and stability." [38]

On the Soviet side it is also clear that the pressure of events was intense. William Knox, who met with Khrushchev on 24 October, described the Soviet premier as "in a state of near-exhaustion" and "like a man who had not slept all night." [39] There is considerable controversy surrounding Premier Khrushchev's message to President Kennedy on the evening of 26 October (the only message from either Washington or Moscow that has never been made public). Of the few that have seen it, some have asserted that it reveals the incoherence of a person on the verge of

---

* Schelling, for instance, has described the events of October 1962 as a "mild crisis." *Arms and Influence* (New Haven: Yale University Press, 1966), p. 242. Whether or not this is an "objectively" valid assessment, memoirs of the missile crisis by Robert Kennedy and others lead me to believe that at least those responsible for crisis management in 1962 regarded the situation as far more severe.

a total collapse; others have interpreted it as the message of a concerned but nevertheless wholly coherent individual.

The latter point suggests at least the possibility that not only is the level of stress important in crisis decision making, but also that there may be significant individual differences in tolerance for stress. Although time pressure weighed heavily on American leaders during the Cuban crisis, reactions to short decision time were far from uniform. President Kennedy took a number of steps to reduce its potentially adverse effects on both American and Soviet decisions. In contrast, when Senators Richard Russell and William Fulbright were informed of the situation in Cuba they argued that a blockade could not be effective in the short time remaining before the launching sites in Cuba became operational. Their demand for an immediate invasion to remove the Soviet missiles, if satisfied, almost certainly would have altered the outcome of the crisis. Did their reactions stem from the fact that their roles differed from that of the president? from different information about the situation? From personality or other idiosyncratic differences? Would Kaiser Wilhelm and Tsar Nicholas (or Richard Nixon and Alexei Kosygin, or Lyndon Johnson and Leonid Brezhnev) have reacted differently to the Cuban missile crisis than did Kennedy and Khrushchev? These are, of course, unanswerable questions. The only value of asking them in this context is to raise the possibility that consequences of intense stress on human performance may vary according to personal attributes which have not been considered here.

Not the least reason why it is so vital to avoid intense international crises is precisely because there will always be an element of unpredictability in human reactions to such situations. To be sure, we are not wholly without evidence on the psychological dimensions of political leadership, including styles of coping with crises.[40] But it is also worth recalling the conclusion of a major study on the reactions of air crews to stress: "No matter how 'normal' or 'strong' an individual is, he may develop a neurosis if crucial stress impinging on him is severe enough. . . . Furthermore, it has been learned that the important psychological predispositions to 'operational fatigue' are usually latent and therefore difficult to detect until they are uncovered by catastrophic events." [41] It is not altogether reassuring to contemplate that perhaps the only sure test of a statesman's ability to cope with intense stress is to have him experience it in catastrophic proportions.

Chapter Eight

CONCLUSION

SOME THOUGHTS ON POLICY IMPLICATIONS

> T. S. Eliot once spoke of a world that
> ends "not with a bang but with a
> whimper." What we have to fear is that
> the bang will come, preceded by the
> contemporary equivalent of the whimper
> —a faint rustle of paper as some self-
> convinced chief of state, reviewing a
> secret memo full of comfortable
> rationalizations just repeated at the final
> conference, fails to muster the necessary
> intelligence and wit and miscalculates
> the power and intent of his adversaries.
>
> Harold Wilensky

THE CONCLUSION IS SOBERING: men rarely perform at their best under intense stress. The most probable casualties of high stress are the very abilities which distinguish men from other species: to establish logical links between present actions and future goals; to create novel responses to new circumstances; to communicate complex ideas; to deal with abstractions; to perceive not only blacks and whites, but also the many shades of grey which fall in between; to distinguish valid analogies from false ones, and sense from nonsense; and, perhaps most important of all, to enter into the frames of reference of others. With respect to these precious attributes, the law of supply and demand seems to operate in a perverse manner; as crisis increases the need for them, it also appears to diminish the supply.

Evidence from the 1914 crisis revealed that with increasing stress there was a vast increase in communication; information which did not conform to expectations and preferences was often disregarded or rejected; time pressure became an increasingly salient factor in policy making; attention became focused on the immediate rather than the longer-range consequences of actions; and one's alternatives and those of allies were viewed as limited and becoming more restricted with increasing stress, whereas those of the adversary were believed to be relatively free from constraints. As a consequence European statesmen felt a declining sense of responsibility for their actions and the consequences to which they might give rise. These findings clearly deviate rather sharply from some of the common precepts of calculated decision making.

Analysis of the Cuban missile confrontation confirmed that communication, time pressure, and identification of alternatives are highly salient aspects of crisis decision making. More importantly, it revealed that the 1914 pattern of escalation is not inevitable, that there are techniques of crisis management for reducing, if not eliminating, some of the most dangerous characteristics of crises.

How far can we generalize about the effects of intense stress from these two episodes? Nineteen fourteen and 1962 are clearly not "typical" international crises, and there is no intention here of presenting them as representative, in the sampling sense, of a larger universe of events. If no further evidence could be adduced, generalizations about crises drawn from these cases alone would at best be highly tentative. Unfortunately (from the viewpoint of international stability) other findings appear to provide substantial corroboration. Although statesmen operate within complex bureaucratic environments which are intended to minimize the effects of emotional and other nonrational factors, their reactions to stress are often disturbingly similar to those of subjects in experimental settings. That diverse methods should yield similar results enhances our confidence in both bodies of evidence. Studies of historical events which address themselves to like questions also provide some support,[1] as does research which shares the definition of crisis used here.[2]

A more important and far more difficult question remains: can we adduce any "practical lessons" from the study of past crises? Whether useful guidelines can be drawn from history is, to understate the point, a controversial question among historians themselves. Santayana's widely cited dictum—those who are unable to learn from history are doomed to repeat it—is more quotable than useful. It provides no more practical guidance on use of the past than Henry Ford's equally renowned observation that "history is bunk." Noted philosophers or historians can be cited for virtually any position in this controversy but appeals to authority are scarcely a substitute for evidence. Any further effort to settle the issue, if indeed it can ever be settled, is beyond the scope of this book. It is enough to say that the question has continuing relevance, disagreements among philosophers of history notwithstanding, because men act on the basis of historical analogies: "History does not repeat itself in the real world but it does repeat itself in the 'reality world' of the mind." [3] Virtually every major foreign-policy decision or pronouncement is rooted in the belief and justified on the grounds that the experiences of some prior triumph or failure are relevant to the situation at hand. Present-day favourites include the Munich, Yalta, or Versailles Conferences, World War I, the American, French, Russian, Chinese, or Cuban revolutions, and the fall of Rome or Greece. That we look to the past is scarcely surprising; what other sources of "hard" evidence about international politics do we have? But it is also well to bear in mind de Tocqueville's warning that misapplied lessons from history may be more dangerous than ignorance of the past.[4] The enterprise is a speculative one and a stance of considerable caution towards prescriptive statements—including those in this chapter—is warranted.

Before proceeding, it may be useful to make explicit some working assumptions which bear on this issue. First, it is acknowledged that serious questions may be raised about adducing lessons from a situation—1914—which has so little resemblance to the world of the 1970s. A list of significant international changes would take up a good many pages. These differences may provide useful, if tentative, clues to explain the outbreak of war in one instance and not in the other. Later we shall examine in greater detail the impact of such considerations as the relatively much more rigid peacetime contingency planning prior to 1914.

Yet despite the many obvious modifications that have marked the international system of the twentieth century, this discussion assumes that the problem of performance under stress has not lost significance. Perhaps an analogy will make the point. The kite-like airplanes of 1914 and today's jet aircraft share only a few attributes. Acting on the assumption that the operating instructions, safety rules, fuel, or maintenance procedures of the Sopwith Camel can be mechanically applied to the Boeing 747—or vice versa—would lead to disaster. But evidence about the effects of stress on pilot performance is likely to be of interest in both cases. The modern pilot may have better mechanical or electronic instruments to assist him, but the demands on his skill may also be greater owing to increased flying speeds. In any case, as with the technological innovations available to contemporary statesmen (for example, the "hot line"), their effectiveness will be limited by the ability of pilots or statesmen to use them effectively in high-stress situations.

It is further assumed that crises as defined here will continue to occur periodically. As long as men are less than omniscient (thus capable of being surprised), are in less than complete agreement on all issues (thus likely to experience threats to important values), and are less than infinitely patient (thus likely to attach time limits to the accomplishment of certain endeavours), we are likely to be faced with international crises.

The final assumption is a negative one. It rejects as not very useful the argument advanced by some historians that had the *dramatis personae* in 1914 included Bismarck, the elder Moltke, or other statesmen of an earlier period, the disastrous world war would have been avoided. Propositions derived from the "what if" school of historical reasoning, being incapable of proof or disproof, are not worth pursuing very far. But this particular argument also contains the dangerous hidden implication that "it won't happen again" because we can explain the catastrophe of 1914 by reference to a lethal but unique combination of pathological personalities or otherwise deficient statesmen. To be sure, Bethmann-Hollweg possessed but a small fraction of Bismarck's political acumen; Kaiser Wilhelm was given to erratic and petulant behaviour; Tsar Nicholas was a living argument against hereditary rulers, as was Emperor Franz Joseph in favour of mandatory retirement at age 65; and the frankness with which Berchtold and Grey dealt with their allies and adversaries was not always consistent with the Golden Rule. But most of these men were also intelligent, eager to avoid a general war, and they had shown in the past that they could do so in spite of recurring disturbances in the Balkans and elsewhere. They were, in short, a reasonably representative sample of human strengths and frailties. Certainly it's doubtful that we would consider them a more dangerous collection of leaders than their counterparts a quarter of a century later: Chamberlain, Daladier, Hitler, Mussolini, and Stalin. Indeed, can anyone seriously suggest that they were intellectually, emotionally, physically, or morally less capable of coping with problems of war and peace than those holding high office at the time of this writing (autumn 1971) in Washington, Moscow, Peking, Paris, or London? There is scant evidence that along with more lethal weapons we have evolved leaders more capable of coping with stress. In this connection it is also worth recalling Robert Kennedy's assessment of how unpredictably men in Washington reacted during the missile crisis: "That kind of [crisis-induced] pressure does strange things to a human being, even to brilliant, self confident, experienced men. For some it brings out characteristics and strengths that perhaps they never knew they had, and for others the pressure is too overwhelming." [5] Our best hope is that from past experience we may learn how to cope with crises, but the opportunity to do so will surely be lost if we succumb to the temptations of seeking the causes of war solely in the personal failings of those in high office.

To summarize, a persuasive case can be made that crisis-induced stress often affects behaviour in ways that are inconsistent with calculated policy making. In the absence of evidence to the contrary, there is no reason to believe that the ability to cope with intense stress has materially increased since 1914. Thus, even if our findings represent tendencies rather than laws of crisis behaviour, they may provide the basis for speculation about policy making under crisis conditions. It does not necessarily follow, however, that these findings will point as clearly to a set of policy prescriptions. The paragraphs that follow address themselves to problems of crisis management identified in the previous chapters, with special emphasis on the interpretation of information, development and maintenance of policy options, and time pressure. But this discussion must frankly be labelled as highly speculative and unquestionably incomplete.

Policy options

We have seen that creativity, flexibility, tolerance for ambiguity, and the size of decision-making groups tend to decline with rising stress, whereas the sense of time pressure and urgency to act increase. These are among the many factors which may contribute to a reduction in perceived policy alternatives. But statesmen need not be helpless prisoners of the situation. Certainly the contrast between the 1914 and 1962 crises suggests steps in a number of areas which may either assist in the fruitful search for suitable policies or at least reduce the constraints imposed by the situation. These include the environment in which crisis decisions are made, the nature of military planning, alliance commitments, and the adversary's options.

THE DECISION-MAKING ENVIRONMENT

The analysis of the missile crisis in the previous chapter suggested that the unusually open discussions within the "Ex Com" contributed significantly to the substantive decisions made by President Kennedy and, ultimately, to the peaceful resolution of the crisis: "The process was the author of the policy." [6] This view is shared even by those who were in fundamental disagreement with the ultimate decisions. Dean Acheson, perhaps the most notable and cogent of the critics, has written that not only was American strategy during the Cuban crisis wrong—that it succeeded in gaining withdrawal of the missiles is attributed to "dumb luck"—but also that ascribed errors can be traced back to the "leaderless" meetings and almost endless, free-wheeling discussions and debates of that thirteen-day period. Elsewhere Acheson has written that the doctrine of keeping options open is synonymous with "avoiding decisions." [7]

The purpose of resurrecting this debate is not to speculate on "what might have been" in October 1962. Rather it is to consider the more general issue of decision-making "styles," with special emphasis on identifying and creating policy alternatives in crises.

One critical aspect of policy making in a crisis is inferring the motives and intentions of others. The range and nature of alternatives that will be given a serious hearing will depend significantly on images of other nations. Individuals and bureaucracies that are wedded to "inherent good faith," "inherent bad faith," or similar one-dimensional models of others are likely to consider a very limited repertoire of options. Compounding the problem is the very real difficulty of gaining hard and verifiable evidence about such elusive and sometimes mercurial attributes as motivations. History is not barren of instances in which disaster arose from faulty assessments of others' capabilities—witness the American estimates of Japanese and Chinese military strength in 1941 and 1950, respectively [8]—but the decidedly more difficult task of adducing intentions has no doubt created far more problems. George Kennan has observed that "in everything that can be statistically expressed—expressed, that is, in such a way as not to imply any judgment on our motivation—I believe the Soviet Government to be excellently informed about us. I am sure that their information on the development of our economies, on the state of our military preparations, on our scientific progress, etc., is absolutely first-rate. But when it comes to the analysis of our motives, to the things that make our life tick as it does, I think this whole great system of intelligence-gathering breaks down seriously." [9]

This disability is not, of course, limited to the Soviet Union, or even to totalitarian nations. Munich, Pearl Harbor, Korea, and Suez are a few of the more dramatic cases in which leaders of democratic nations seriously misread the situation. During the months prior to the Cuban missile crisis American and Soviet leaders also provided vivid evidence of their limited abilities to estimate each other's willingness to take risks. Other instances in which impending hostile actions were unforeseen because signals were overlooked, misinterpreted, or dismissed are not uncommon. In 1940, Colonel Oster of the German Abwehr [intelligence service] told J. G. Sas, the Dutch military attaché, that Denmark and Norway would be invaded on 9 March. The information was dismissed in Copenhagen as quite implausible and Sas himself did not think it worth even passing on to Oslo. A few weeks later

Oster informed Sas that the invasion of Holland was set for 10 May. Even though events had proved the earlier information about Denmark and Norway to be correct, Oster's warning was not believed in The Hague. Nor did Brussels believe it when Joseph Müller of the Abwehr told a Belgian diplomat that his country would be invaded by German armies on 10 May.[10]

Other examples may also be cited. Soviet leaders ignored all evidence and warnings that the Nazis would invade in 1941, as did the Americans with respect to the "Tet offensive" in 1968. A systematic study of thirty-two crises revealed that "warning signs are seldom decoded properly before threats of violence."[11] The reverse situation in which conciliatory actions are dismissed as tricks may occur equally often, especially under crisis conditions. Even between allies of long standing there may be difficulties in adducing motives properly, as Neustadt has noted with respect to Anglo-American diplomacy during the Suez crisis of 1956 and the Skybolt incident six years later.[12]

At minimum, sound judgments about intentions and motives require adequate information. In 1914, the volume of diplomatic communication increased steadily as war approached; the same appears to be true of most crises.[13] Moreover, in such situations policy makers often spend most of their energies in seeking out further facts. This seems to have been true of American deliberations on Vietnam policy. Often at critical junctures someone suggested that a fact-finding mission should be sent to Saigon, presumably on the assumption that repeated disappointments in the course of the conflict could be traced to a lack of "facts."[14] It is perhaps of some significance that in March 1968 the impending retirement of Defense Secretary McNamara precluded his going once again to Vietnam for a first-hand briefing by local commanders. Instead, Clark Clifford, McNamara's successor, and others turned the discussion to more fundamental issues about American policy. The problem of information, then, is more likely to be qualitative than quantitative; there may be an immense flow of diplomatic correspondence, but the information contained therein may lend itself to multiple inferences.

Thus, perhaps even more important than raw information is a valid theory to give it meaning and relevance; rarely do "the facts speak for themselves." A single fact or even a set of data is usually consistent with several theories. It is quite probable that most international disasters can be traced not to the inadequate information, but rather to the absence of adequate models into which to place the facts. Throughout the summer of 1939, for example, London and Paris received warnings from diverse sources that a Nazi agreement with the USSR was in the offing. These were dismissed with such comments as "highly improbable." [15] The facts were not at issue—for example, Hitler's recent speeches had been devoid of their usual anti-Bolshevik diatribes and Vyacheslav Molotov had replaced Maxim Litvinov as Soviet foreign minister. The missing ingredient was a frame of reference which could assimilate and properly evaluate clues that the apparently implacable ideological enemies might find it expedient to join forces. A similar conclusion emerges from Roberta Wohlstetter's detailed analysis of the attack on Pearl Harbor: "If our intelligence system and all our other channels of information failed to produce an accurate image of Japanese intentions and capabilities, it was not for want of the relevant materials. Never before have we had so complete an intelligence picture of the enemy." She goes on to point out that too much information, bureaucratic rivalries, and normal limitations on human perceptions were at the root of the failure. If there is any antidote to these problems it is to be found in a "willingness to play with materials from different angles and in the context of unpopular as well as popular hypotheses." [16]

These examples illustrate the need for a set of alternative premises and theories against which the evidence can be tested. Well-established psychological principles suggest that few persons can effectively examine evidence from more than one or two views of reality. And although the complex bureaucracies that characterize all modern governments are intended to reduce the effects of idiosyncratic elements, even organizations can become single-minded advocates of a preferred viewpoint. Thus, decision-making groups should be sufficiently large and diverse in outlook to ensure that the available information is subjected to vigorous probing from multiple perspectives, not merely from the view of the prevailing conventional wisdom. Encouragement of multiple advocacy also provides some degree of protection against the fallibility of all advisers. Senator William Fulbright, for instance, was one of the very few who warned the president against supporting the disastrous plan to invade Cuba in 1961. Eighteen months later, Fulbright demanded bombing and an invasion of that island to remove Soviet missiles, an enterprise that would almost certainly have given rise to a far different outcome of the missile crisis.

The advice that every foreign office needs "devil's advocates" is often given [17] but apparently hard to implement. It appears that the ability to create a decision-making environment receptive to both "popular and unpopular" hypotheses is a rare talent.° That dissenters in totalitarian systems rarely enjoy long public careers is a point that requires little elaboration. One example is sufficient to make the point. Joachim von Ribbentrop, Hitler's foreign minister, had an unshakeable conviction that Great Britain would never go to war against Germany. All members of his staff received a directive warning that: "If it came to my notice that anyone had expressed a contrary opinion [on the question of British policy] I would kill him myself in his office, and take responsibility before the Führer for it." [18] Even a less extreme warning would no doubt have sufficed to protect von Ribbentrop from the discomforts of dissent.

It is, however, far more instructive to illustrate how easy it is even in a non-totalitarian political system to exclude unpopular ideas from policy-making councils, especially in crises. Earlier we cited the cases of two ambassadors—Prince Lichnowsky in 1914 and Henry Byroade in 1956—whose accurate warnings of impending trouble were dismissed as nonsense. In 1938 Anthony Eden, the British foreign secretary, and Robert Vansittart, the top-ranking civil servant in the foreign office, were in effect serving as devil's advocates in the appeasement-minded Chamberlain government. The prime minister conspired to force Eden's resignation and he "promoted" Vansittart into a less sensitive position. The latter continued to prepare memoranda warning of Hitler's ambitions and of the probably disastrous consequences of British policy. Suspecting that they were not being read, Vansittart

---

° Richard E. Neustadt points out that Franklin D. Roosevelt's ability to surround himself with multiple sources of information—both formal and informal—was a major element in his success. *Presidential Power* (New York: Signet Books, 1964), pp. 146–151.

began submitting his papers shuffled out of order; they were returned in the same order, confirming his suspicions. Later he used the same trick to discover that even dispatches from British envoys abroad went unread. During the same period the French air attaché in Germany was reprimanded for repeatedly warning Paris of German intentions. He was ordered to confine his future reports to aviation matters.[19]

Recent American administrations provide further examples of how easily open debate may be discouraged. In some respects the problem can be traced to isolation of national leaders and size and complexity of contemporary governments. Most American presidents have come to office vowing that they will avoid the isolation of their predecessors, that theirs will be an "open administration." None has been very successful in this respect; the gap between aspiration and performance has been especially notable during some recent foreign-policy crises.°

George Reedy, an assistant to President Johnson, recalled that rarely if ever were top-level meetings about Vietnam with the president "fist-banging sessions" in which alternative premises and conclusions were vigorously debated. The usual pattern, according to Reedy, was for advisers to fall all over each other telling the president what they believed he wanted to hear. Conversely, no one ever responded with a blunt "That's stupid" to a presidential suggestion, even to one which richly merited it.[20] This may reflect something about the quality of the advisers or the sense of awe and respect with which they held the presidential office. But Johnson himself also contributed to the problem by being less than vigorous in seeking advice on Vietnam which may have challenged his own premises about the war. For example, he appointed his close friend Clark Clifford as secretary of defense in part because Clifford was seen as a staunch supporter of administration policies in Vietnam. Clifford began doubting the wisdom of those policies when the Joint Chiefs of Staff were

---

° There is substantial evidence that anxiety-producing situations, of which crisis is one example, result in reduced tolerance by members of a group for those who deviate from its norms. See, for example, Leonard Weller, "The Effects of Anxiety on Cohesiveness and Rejection," *Human Relations*, XVI (1963), 189–197; and Lewis Coser, *The Functions of Social Conflict* (New York: The Free Press, 1956), pp. 103–104.

unable to provide satisfactory answers to the most basic questions about the conduct of military operations and their consequences. After that the president refused ever again to meet privately with his secretary of defense. In the salty language of one participant, "The President was colder than a whore's heart." ° Earlier Vice-President Humphrey had suffered virtual banishment from top-level policy discussions for questioning administration policy on the war. Whether or not the doubts entertained by Clifford and Humphrey were valid, incidents such as this are bound to affect other advisers. Only the most courageous—or foolhardy—would have failed to draw the conclusion that unpopular opinions are neither welcomed nor rewarded.

Compounding the problem was the president's reliance upon Walt W. Rostow, described by one colleague as "a dedicated partisan whose mind automatically filtered out evidence that did not support his own established beliefs," who shielded Johnson from contrary opinions by means of "selective briefings." It also appears that Secretary of State Rusk discouraged dissent on the issue of Vietnam. As a result, discussions of Vietnam took place in a "climate of cozy, implicit agreement on fundamentals," within inner councils "where never was heard a disparaging word." [21]

Clifford's role in the discussions of March 1968 that led to the reversal of American policy on Vietnam is also instructive for another reason. At the time of his appointment to the Pentagon he was engaged in his private law practice. Coming from outside the government he had not developed a personal stake in any given policy on Vietnam, and thus he was better able to view claims and counterclaims with a fresh and sceptical eye. Clifford's "defection" was clearly not welcomed by the president, but it did ultimately impel Johnson to seek further outside advice, including that of Dean Acheson. The former secretary of state bluntly told the president that he was "being led down a garden

---

° Charles Roberts, "Inside Story: LBJ's Switch on Vietnam," *Newsweek*, 10 March 1969, p. 32. According to a perceptive analyst, the first article of "Lyndon Johnson's common law" was that he must not be criticized, especially in public. Philip Geyelin, *Lyndon B. Johnson and the World* (New York: Frederick A. Praeger, 1966), p. 154.

path" by the Joint Chiefs of Staff "who don't know what they're talking about." [22]

Richard Nixon has established a style of decision making which further accents the isolation of the chief executive and protects him against probing questions about his basic premises. Nixon himself has commented about his "passion for privacy" and his distaste for having "a lot of people around." [23] These personal preferences have been reflected in the conduct of public affairs. Even in the normal day-to-day conduct of his office he has established procedures which insulate him from all but a small handful of like-minded advisers. Charges made in the "Hickel letter" that members of the cabinet were rarely consulted by the president have been confirmed and defended by an administration spokesman: "We can't have a lot of Cabinet guys [sic] running in to the President or he'd never have a question refined to where it's worth making a decision." * In crisis situations this pattern has been accentuated, as Nixon appears to withdraw into almost total isolation and to rely on communion with his yellow lined pad rather than in free-wheeling exchanges with his colleagues. Characteristically, his decision to send American troops into Cambodia in 1970 was made in the solitude of the presidential retreat at Camp David rather than, as in the case of Kennedy's decisions during the missile crisis, in an environment of vigorous advocacy for many different strategies. The only senator with whom the president discussed his plans was John Stennis of Mississippi, an acknowledged supporter of the war in Southeast Asia. Nor was any vigorous dissent to the planned invasion likely to emerge from Nixon's briefings of George Meany, Norman Vincent Peale, Billy Graham, Harry Dent, Robert Haldeman, or John Ehrlichman.[24] Secretaries Melvin Laird and William Rogers reportedly argued against the president's decision, but the overall picture which emerges is one of Nixon acting as "his own gray

---

* Richard F. Janssen, "An Inaccessible Nixon Stirs Anger and Despair within Administration," *Wall Street Journal*, 8 May 1970, p. 1. Compare this to President-elect Nixon's pledge at the introduction of his cabinet in December 1968: "Every man in this Cabinet will be urged to speak out in the Cabinet and within the Administration on all the great issues so that the decisions we make will be the best decision we can possibly reach."

eminence."[25] This pattern of distrusting advisers, of failing to consult with those who question preferred options, and of relying upon his own instincts and judgment in crises is apparently a recurring one in Nixon's career.[26]

These examples could be multiplied many times over. They point up the fact that it is not sufficient merely to appoint and then tolerate with ill-disguised impatience those who question the conventional wisdom, who report unpopular information, or who propose alternatives which fly in the face of established policies. In the absence of strong support for such persons the lessons will quickly become clear to other advisers and bureaucrats: the only safe position is that which confirms what top leaders are presumed to prefer; those who "rock the boat" will be left to sink, or will be thrown overboard.

One episode just preceding the missile crisis illustrates how the knowledge that certain information and interpretations are not welcome may affect the flow of information within and between bureaucracies. In August 1962, John McCone, director of the Central Intelligence Agency, privately told the president of his suspicions that Soviet offensive missiles were being introduced into Cuba. Kennedy's cool reception to this intelligence became known.* For this reason later warnings by McCone about Cuba —accurate ones as it turned out—were not distributed outside the CIA.[27]

There is the practical aspect of the issue, however. As a sympathetic observer of the Nixon administration put it: "How realistic is it to expect a President to surround himself with dissenters, particularly in embattled times like the present? Mr. Haldeman, John Ehrlichman and Henry Kissinger are sitting at the right hand of power today because Mr. Nixon feels comfortable with them because they see the world much as he does."[28] But at what times other than embattled ones is the question even relevant? Does a prime minister or president really need to be confronted with alternative perspectives when his working day is highlighted by a round of golf, greetings to a convention of the Amalgamated Widget Workers, a statement proclaiming Na-

---

* Kennedy's doubts about CIA information on Cuba stemmed largely from the Bay of Pigs episode.

tional Sauerkraut Week, or a public appearance with the "Heroine Mother of the Year" and her brood of fifteen children? It is precisely during periods of intense conflict, and especially during crises, that those who ask penetrating questions and suggest alternative—and perhaps even unpopular—ways of defining the situation are most urgently needed. And surely the least important measure of an adviser's worth is whether he makes his colleagues "comfortable." Anyone who consistently does so, whether because of fatigue, group pressures for conformity, personal ambition, sycophancy, or vested interest in a given policy, has outlived his usefulness.

MILITARY ADVISERS

A closely related issue concerns the role of military advisers. Their views almost always take on special importance during international crises—and legitimately so. But in the absence of broad consultation with persons who represent a variety of personal and bureaucratic viewpoints, all too often technical military considerations will prevail over diplomatic and political ones. Brodie's assessment of World War I generals— "It was their horizons rather than their skills which proved so disastrously limited" [29] —may have relevance for other times and places. The missile confrontation illustrated the tendency of military advisers to view crises from a purely military perspective. The Joint Chiefs of Staff stood solidly in favour of bombing the missile sites rather than using a minimal level of force—the blockade—as a lever with which to seek a political solution of the situation. Indeed, use of atomic weapons was urged by at least one of the service chiefs.

A cogent analysis of this problem has been written by Stewart Alsop, hardly a wild-eyed critic of the military. He suggests that there are role, bureaucratic, and historical reasons why professional diplomats are likely to be cautious in proferring advice, why they are likely to raise such invaluable—but not always appreciated—questions as: "Have you considered all the possible consequences, sir?" In contrast, the typical military adviser's response is, "Can do." On occasion this answer falls short of being the complete truth. During the Cuban missile crisis, for instance, the Joint Chiefs of Staff misled the president about their ability to carry out a "surgical strike" which would eliminate the missile sites at the least possible cost of life.[30] Alsop goes on to point out that in recent years American foreign-service officers have rarely been consulted in crises; the notable exception was the Cuban missile crisis during which Llewellyn Thompson played a central role in dissuading the president from following the military advice to bomb the missile sites in Cuba. In Alsop's words: "In the decade now ending (the 1960's), the military professionals have largely usurped the role of the foreign-policy professionals." [31] There is certainly no indication that this trend is being reversed; if there has been any change, it has been in the direction of further downgrading of the diplomats.

The reasons for suggesting that the counsel of military advisers should not be accepted uncritically are not the frequently made charges (which may or may not be true in any given instance) that military personnel tend to be authoritarian, biased toward political conservatism, or innately aggressive. Rather, it is because the perspectives of military advisers, derived in part from role considerations, may not be sufficiently broad for an acute crisis in which the critical questions of war and peace remain to be resolved.

Quite understandably, the most salient aspect of the situation to the professional soldier is the possibility that the crisis may lead to the outbreak of war. Among the questions which will be uppermost in his mind are the following. What preparatory steps must be taken in order not to be caught at a disadvantage should war break out? How can we ensure success in these circumstances? What if the adversary is planning a surprise attack? These and related technical questions are not only legitimate ones for the soldier to consider; satisfactory performance of his job requires him to do so. But in taking steps to counter the most aggressive action the enemy is able to undertake, he may be counselling policies which materially reduce the scope of diplomatic options, if not actually increase the probability of war. For example, in the face of a suspected mobilization by the adversary in the near future, the "safe" course from the perspective of one who may be called upon to fight a war is to alert or mobilize his forces. This may, in turn, be precisely the action which tips the balance in favour of mobilization by the other side, thereby setting the stage for another round of escalation.

There are, of course, instances in which the threat or even the use of force at an appropriate level and in controlled increments may be stabilizing and contribute to eventual de-escalation of a crisis by persuading the adversary to revise his calculations.[32] What constitutes an "appropriate level" will vary from instance to instance, but it certainly means avoiding the sort of reasoning which goes something like this: if force is to be used, the "safest" strategy is to employ all available capabilities in the first instance to ensure victory; otherwise, it is better not to use force at all. As shall be pointed out later, 1914 and 1962 are not the only crises in which military advisers have attempted to dichotomize the options in this manner.

This is not to say that military advisers are unique in defining the situation on the basis of role considerations. Presumably legal advisers, professional diplomats, or any other persons will also do so. Military advisers have been singled out here for special attention because they are almost invariably consulted during international crises, they usually have a significant if not deciding influence on policy choices, and there is some evidence that this has increased in recent years. The point, then, is not to eliminate military personnel from policy-making groups during an international crisis. Rather, it is important to bear in mind that the soldier may tend to view crisis developments from the perspective of gaining an advantageous military position should diplomacy fail to resolve the situation. But the very actions which may advance that end may also impede crisis-management efforts by *increasing time pressure* even further and by *restricting policy options*.

There is a further reason for evaluating military advice with a critical eye during a crisis. Military planners can, of necessity, only develop a limited number of contingency plans to meet the most probable types of situations. These are then practiced repeatedly to gain precision and coordination. In any given crisis military advice is almost bound to be coloured by the kinds of plans which have been developed—even if the situation is one for which no plans exist.

We have already seen that in 1914 the Russian generals, unprepared for a partial mobilization against Austria-Hungary, pressured Tsar Nicholas into accepting the only option (other than doing nothing) for which they had planned—a full mobilization to include the German sector of Russia's eastern frontier. Whether or not the many historians who cite this action as the "point of no return" are correct, it was undoubtedly a critical decision which gave rise to such immediate consequences as the German and French mobilizations two days later.

Nor were German plans, especially as interpreted by Schlieffen's successors, any more flexible.* German generals were so thoroughly wedded to the strategy that they had been preparing for years that they could not countenance the possibility of reversing it at the last moment. The kaiser's sudden and short-lived impulse to avoid a two-front war by reversing the Schlieffen plan —to attack toward the east instead of the west—literally caused Moltke to collapse. It was simply impossible to overlook the years devoted to fine-tuning one basic strategy because of unforeseen political developments which arose during the course of the crisis. Similarly, the inability of the Austro-Hungarian army to undertake a limited action against Serbia in accordance with the "Halt in Belgrade" plan, proposed in various capitals as a last-ditch alternative to full-scale war, effectively ruled out adopting this fairly promising effort to localize the crisis.[33]

The absence of flexibility in military plans thus contributed to the speed with which the Austro-Serbian conflict escalated. But the "all-or-nothing" character of military planning and advice have not been confined to 1914. Advice from the Pentagon apparently led President Nixon to conclude that the United States had only two options in Cambodia: to commit American troops to a full invasion of the Fishhook and Parrot's Beak areas, or to do nothing about the North Vietnamese threat to the Lon Nol government.[34] In 1936, although there had been substantial prior evidence that Hitler would soon make a move into the Rhineland, the French General Staff had no prepared plans for such an

---

* Rigidity also marked execution of the Schlieffen plan. In the event of a failure to defeat France within weeks, Schlieffen had called for efforts to negotiate a peace. Instead, after German forces had been stopped at the Marne, four years of bloody stalemate followed on the Western front. Brodie, *Strategy in the Missile Age* (Princeton: Princeton University Press, 1959), p. 35.

event. When a small, ill-equipped contingent of Germans occupied that demilitarized area, General Gamelin and his colleagues could offer but two alternatives: to order a full mobilization of 1.2 million Frenchmen, or to do nothing. Given only these two options, it is perhaps understandable that the latter course was selected, even though Hitler's forces were pathetically weak and a demilitarized Rhineland was crucial for French security.° Whether the availability of a plan to expel the German invaders with the limited French forces required to carry out the task would have led to its adoption is, of course, open to speculation. It is clear, however, that the costs and risks of the full mobilization option impelled French leaders to choose the only other alternative of making feeble and totally ineffective protests against the German action.

ALLIANCE COMMITMENTS

Policy options may also be reduced materially by initiating or increasing alliance commitments during a crisis, especially with partners who cannot be depended upon to view the resulting obligations as reciprocal. Such pledges may ultimately force a choice between two unpalatable alternatives: reducing the commitment under threat, thereby seriously eroding one's credibility in the future; or backing the promise to the hilt, with the possibility of becoming a prisoner of the ally's policies. New or expanded pledges of support to small allies may also complicate rather than facilitate the resolution of crisis situations by introducing further—and often irrelevant—issues into crisis negotiations. Fidel Castro attempted to inject such issues into Soviet-American bargaining during and immediately after the resolution of the missile crisis. It is probably fortunate that Soviet leaders, who had serious and probably justified doubts about the quality

---

° Hitler's own assessment of the German forces is revealing: "We had no army worth mentioning; at that time it would not even have had the fighting strength to maintain itself against the Poles. If the French had taken any action, we would have been easily defeated; our resistance would have been over in a few days. And what air force we had then was ridiculous. A few Junker 52's from Lufthansa, and not even enough bombs for them." Albert Speer, *Inside the Third Reich*, trans. by Richard and Clara Winston (New York: Macmillan Co., 1970), p. 72.

and volatility of Cuban leadership,[35] did not irrevocably commit Soviet policy and prestige to whatever demands may have emerged from Havana.

Quite apart from the very real constraints that may be imposed by inflexible contingency planning, there is evidence that persons under high stress tend to define the situation in "either-or" terms. Other nations, for instance, may be viewed as either friends or enemies, but rarely as genuine neutrals.* Related to this dichotomization is the belief that one has no common interests with adversaries. The dangers in such a situation have been explored at length and require no elaboration here. Less attention, however, has been devoted to another kind of dangerous stereotype —the belief that *all* one's interests are shared by allies.[36] The tendency to rely on such "inherent good faith" models may be accentuated during crisis situations. History reveals a number of instances in which major powers undertook strong commitments of support to allies in a crisis, only to discover later that their policy options had been restricted to a far greater degree than they had foreseen.

The German pledge of support to Austria-Hungary, given only a week after the assassination of Franz Ferdinand, is a case in point. Germany was faced with a cruel dilemma. Having accurately judged that Italy was a weak and perfidious member of the Triple Alliance and that Rumania could not be counted on either, Berlin knew that Austria-Hungary was Germany's only real ally. This fact was also appreciated in Vienna and it was used to generate considerable diplomatic leverage within the alliance. German intent in its "blank cheque" commitment to Vienna is still debated among historians. Less open to question is the fact that Austro-Hungarian leaders interpreted German support as unconditional. As a consequence they kept Berlin poorly informed on many policy developments during subsequent weeks, including the details of the ultimatum to Serbia. Most importantly, all German efforts to restrain their ally after the Serbian reply to the ultimatum fell on deaf ears. Indeed, some of the most urgent messages from Berlin recommending moderation in

---

* A clear example is the kaiser's image of the political map of Europe during the first few days of August, 1914.

Vienna were not even answered. The kaiser fully shared and encouraged Austro-Hungarian ambitions for a major diplomatic triumph, but he believed that goal had been achieved with the Serbian response of 25 July. Wilhelm's complaint that "the stupidity and clumsiness of our ally has made a hangman's noose for us," [37] although a self-serving rationalization, was not a wholly unfair assessment of Viennese diplomacy.

Other examples may also be cited. During the crisis arising out of the German invasion of Czechoslovakia in March 1939, the Chamberlain government in London finally realized that promises of peaceful intent by Hitler at Munich and elsewhere were absolutely worthless. In an almost reflex reaction, the British government committed itself to guarantee the security of Poland, a pledge extended to Rumania and Greece two weeks later.° However worthy the motives for this action may have been, it was based in part on the erroneous belief that Polish armed forces were capable of determined and effective resistance against any German attack; indeed, virtually all British and French military advisers believed that the Polish army was stronger than that of the Soviet Union! [38] Moreover, the British accepted at face value Warsaw's assurances that Polish-German relations were cordial when, in reality, these two nations were on the verge of war over the Polish Corridor and Danzig. In subsequent months the British were to discover, further, that there was little inclination among the colonels who ruled Poland to accept British advice or to coordinate alliance strategy. On the issue of an Anglo-French alliance with Russia and during the last minute Anglo-German discussions on the Polish crisis, Warsaw did everything in its power to prevent agreement. Instead, the Poles stuck firmly to the belief that they were in control of the situation; if war broke out, the Polish army, led by its cavalry—mounted on horses, not in tanks—would march triumphantly into Berlin. There is a substantial element of truth in Duff Cooper's bitter observation made at the time of the British commitment to Poland that for the first time in history "we left it in the hands of one of the

---

° A secret protocol specified that this commitment applied only to a German attack against Poland. Hence Britain was not forced into war against both Germany and Russia when Hitler and Stalin carved up Poland in the autumn of 1939.

smaller powers the decision whether or not Great Britain goes to war." The Rumanian foreign minister was even harsher: "The British must be mad. Poland is the least moral country in Europe." [39] If the Nazis also viewed Britain's action as unprecedented and irrational, it would scarcely have caused them to revise their belief that Britain would not fight to the bitter end for Poland.

The American experience in Vietnam further underscores the danger of increasing commitments made under crisis conditions to weak and not wholly responsible allies. Repeated statements of American support have given the South Vietnamese government a greater ability to act independently of, or even contrary to, American interests. The operating premise that the commitment to Saigon was an *"ipso facto* blank check" [40] reduced rather than increased Washington's leverage vis à vis its ally.

Lest this discussion has left the impression that alliances invariably create difficulties in crisis, it is worth making two further distinctions: pre-existing commitments should be distinguished from those that are suddenly undertaken during the course of a crisis, sometimes in a desperate effort to bolster the credibility of one's policy. Similarly, pledges of support to nations able and willing to make a serious effort to defend their own security should be distinguished from those offered to nations whose romantic illusions are surpassed only by the absence of will, capabilities, and popular support to sustain concerted action on their own behalf.* The tragedy of British and French policies during the late 1930s is that they failed to honour their commitments to Czechoslovakia, a nation possessed of a large and well-trained army, a powerful armaments industry, superb geographical location and strong popular support, except among Sudeten Germans.† Having assisted in the destruction of this ideal ally, Brit-

---

* Binding one's policy to that of an irresponsible partner may also be viewed as a special form of the "rationality of the irrational" strategy, a topic to be considered in more detail below. But note that *the less rational such a pledge seems, the more difficult it will be to convince adversaries that the commitment even exists.*

† "The Czech border fortifications caused general astonishment. To the surprise of experts a test bombardment showed that our weapons would not have prevailed against them. Hitler himself went to the former frontier to inspect the arrangements and returned impressed. The fortifications were amazingly massive,

ain then undertook a frantic and poorly conceived pledge of support to Poland, called by some the most romantic and corrupt nation in Europe. Similarly, we would distinguish Greece in 1947, South Korea in 1950, and Israel or West Germany today— all nations with a fierce determination to defend their own security—and such dubious allies as the succession of regimes in Saigon.

The problem of establishing credibility is a legitimate one for any nation. It is also vital to international stability because it lends a degree of predictability to foreign relations. There is thus a very real element of truth in the dictum that unwillingness or inability to honour one commitment will jeopardize all of them. But credibility may also be eroded by staking immense resources on an ill-conceived undertaking which must ultimately be dropped short of success. Although the final scenes in the Indochina drama have yet to be acted out, it is not inconceivable that US support of Saigon—a policy initiated to bolster American credibility not only in Southeast Asia but in other areas of the world as well—will have precisely the opposite long-term effect and hence provide a "domino effect" by having originally selected a weak domino. Thus, a relevant aspect of the issue is also "where to do it." Is any spot on the globe equally good, or is it important to select one's allies with some care? Moreover, timing would seem to be an important factor. Wise parents, labour and management negotiators, and skilled diplomats know that in a conflict situation one should not abandon a previously established position under the threat of force. Perhaps an equally valuable corollary is: exercise caution in making new commitments or increasing existing ones in the heat of a crisis.

THE ADVERSARY'S OPTIONS

The discussion to this point has focused on the internal and intra-alliance aspects of identifying and creating policy alternatives and choosing between them. Even more difficult problems arise

he said, laid out with extraordinary skill and echeloned, making prime use of the terrain." Speer, *Inside Third Reich*, p. 111. For a different assessment of Czech capabilities, see Laurence Thompson, *The Greatest Treason* (New York: William Morrow & Co., 1968).

in trying to manipulate and influence the adversary's options. The danger of war is never greater than when a nation's leaders define the situation as one in which the options are reduced to a war or humiliation with a crippling loss of "face." By the end of July 1914, most leaders in Berlin, Vienna, St. Petersburg, Paris, and London had come to the conclusion that this was precisely the situation in which they found themselves. It is on the one hand necessary to avoid appeasing the adversary's illegitimate demands and to impress on him the dangers of pressing them; on the other, it is equally important to avoid placing the opponent in a position where large-scale violence is perceived as the least distasteful, or perhaps the sole, alternative. The task, in short, is to demonstrate to the adversary by actions and words that his self-interest can best be served in choosing the path of de-escalation. The trick, of course, is to map this path in clear terms and to make it appear as the most attractive alternative. Among the crisis management techniques which may enhance the likelihood of success are the following.

Perhaps the first prerequisite is a sensitivity to the adversary's frame of reference. To assume, as many statesmen came to believe in 1914, that only leaders of the opposing nations were free to end the crisis by taking appropriate steps is a convenient and self-serving rationalization, but it also amounts to abdicating responsibility for future developments. This is *not* to say, however, that one must agree with the opponent or appease his demands; empathy is not synonymous with sympathy. Rather, the point is that one can scarcely hope to influence others without a realistic image of the situation they find themselves in, of the hopes and fears which may motivate them, of the intra- and inter-bureaucratic pressures which may impinge on them, and of the "operational codes" which may dictate their strategies and tactics. It also pays never to forget that the opponents, too, are making choices under highly stressful conditions. First-hand accounts of the missile crisis reveal that President Kennedy and his advisers exhibited an unusual ability to place themselves in the shoes of the men in the Kremlin.° The counsel of Llewellyn Thompson,

° Note, however, that only months earlier the president and his advisers had been almost uniformly wrong in assuming that, from the perspective of the Kremlin, it would make no sense to deploy offensive missiles in Cuba. Similarly, al-

former American ambassador in Moscow, was especially useful because it was based in part on his informed assessment of Premier Khrushchev's likely behaviour under high stress. It goes without saying that the ability to project oneself into an accurate reconstruction of another's frame of reference is a skill in short supply; it may also be viewed by harried policy makers as an "unnatural diversion of a busy man's attention." [41] Nevertheless it appears to be a necessary if not sufficient condition for successful crisis management.

Avoid taking steps which seal off "escape routes." This is a real test of diplomatic skill, especially as there is reason to believe that the ability to improvise creatively under stress is not a widely shared attribute. It is rarely easy to convince an adversary that efforts to de-escalate a crisis are not tricks. Even under normal circumstances gestures of good will by enemies may not be accepted at face value; they are even less likely to have an impact in the midst of a severe crisis. Most difficult of all is the problem of devising strategies of "coercive diplomacy" which are credible and yet do not provoke the adversary to escalate. The Russian decision in 1914 for a partial mobilization which would not involve troops on the German frontier and President Kennedy's choice of a blockade rather than an air strike are examples of forceful actions which nevertheless left the adversary with options other than recourse to full-scale violence. Conversely, Russia's later full mobilization, coming on the heels of an admission that secret military preparations had begun almost a week earlier, placed the Germans in a terrible dilemma, much as a massive air strike against Cuba would have confronted Soviet leaders with a choice between acquiescing to large-scale Soviet casualties or retaliating in some manner. It has been suggested by several students of Soviet conduct that Leninist doctrine extols rather than condemns even humiliating retreats (e.g. Brest-Litovsk) in the face of massive opposition. But evidence of substantial disagreement among Soviet leaders on correct handling of the missile confrontation [42] suggests that at best this is only a partial expla-

---

though Khrushchev and his colleagues apparently drew the proper conclusions about the dangerous dilemma which the missiles had created for the Kennedy administration, earlier, when deciding to send the weapons to Cuba, they appear to have completely miscalculated the likely American response.

nation of Soviet conduct. In any case, if it were a generally accepted rule of crisis management that any nation need only be confronted with sufficient force to make a humiliating retreat "rational"—and therefore palatable—it would no doubt increase the incidence and magnitude of international violence.

Reducing the adversary's incentives to escalate will probably require a combination of incentives and threats. The limited utility of either threats or promises alone for influencing the conduct of others is amply documented. There is also rather impressive evidence that severe threat is not a particularly effective method for altering behaviour.[43] Parents armed with a repertoire of child-management tactics which includes carrots without sticks, or vice versa, soon learn that taken alone neither is sufficient. Somehow the point seems less widely believed about international politics. A. J. P. Taylor, for instance, has suggested that consistent use of either deterrence (the stick) or appeasement (the carrot) during the 1920s and 1930s would have prevented World War II.[44] Evan Luard's conclusion, based on a survey of the interwar and postwar eras, that effective diplomacy requires a skilful blending of deterrence and conciliation appears sounder and more relevant for crisis management.[45] To oversimplify the point, if the function of deterrence is to convince the opponent that certain options are unacceptable and that he cannot improve his bargaining position by escalation, the role of diplomacy is to create a situation in which there are acceptable alternatives, and to persuade him that these are more compatible with his self-interest.

In crisis diplomacy, as in other forms of communication, actions tend to speak louder than words. When Premier Khrushchev seemed to question the credibility of certain American policy pronouncements, President Kennedy is reported to have complained, "That son of a bitch won't pay any attention to words. He has to see you move." [46] The complaint was not quite fair because the Soviet leader was merely exhibiting a fairly widespread human trait. Certainly when there is a discrepancy between words and deeds, the latter are likely to be the more highly valued evidence, especially in high-stress crisis situations. Thus, if one's words convey a message of peaceful intent but one's actions indicate further escalation and war, only the naive

Neville Chamberlains or Georges Bonnets of this world will believe the former. For maximum impact it is useful to orchestrate declarations of intent and actions so as to employ multiple channels of communication to convey the same message, whether it is one of deterrence, conciliation,or a combination of the two.

Make every effort to slow the pace of crisis events. As shown repeatedly in previous chapters, intense time pressure is rarely consistent with calculated decision making. Discussion of steps which may lengthen decision time will be deferred until the next section.

During a crisis responsible policy makers should be in control not only of broad strategic decisions, but also of the details of implementation. It is especially important that efforts to de-escalate or slow the pace of events are not sabotaged, inadvertently or otherwise, by subordinates. In 1914, Russian and German officers effectively undermined last-minute—and at best not overly promising—efforts by the two monarchs to avoid a European war. Moltke's wire urging Austria-Hungary to mobilize immediately against Russia ensured that efforts by the kaiser and chancellor to restrain Vienna would be ineffective. Bethmann-Hollweg had personally failed to carry out precisely Wilhelm's instructions to notify Vienna that "no more cause for war exists," for fear of antagonizing Austria-Hungary; his telegram had been less forceful in requesting adherence to the "Halt in Belgrade" plan.[47] At the same time the tsar's military staff was waging a successful campaign to supersede the order for partial mobilization with a full-scale call to arms. These are by no means isolated incidents. Until his dismissal in 1951, General Douglas MacArthur repeatedly made public policy statements which were in direct conflict with Washington's diplomatic stance on the Korean war and general Far Eastern policy. In contrast to the almost unbelievable tolerance exhibited by President Truman, Secretary Acheson, and the Joint Chiefs of Staff toward MacArthur, President Kennedy and Defense Secretary McNamara maintained fairly effective control over the minutest details of strategy and tactics during the missile crisis, even in the face of the intense displeasure of Naval Chief George W. Anderson. Nevertheless, at least two failures of presidential control introduced potentially dangerous elements into the crisis. In one case an order issued in

August 1962 to withdraw short-range missiles from Turkey had never been carried out, and the continued presence of these weapons near the Soviet Union gave Premier Khrushchev a pawn with which he attempted—unsuccessfully—to bargain during the crisis. The other incident involved an unarmed U-2 aircraft that took its bearings on the wrong star and headed for Moscow rather than Alaska, despite orders that such flights be cancelled. Although the U-2 was merely on an air sampling flight, there was no way for the Soviets to know that it was on an innocent mission.[48]

These are a few of the crisis-management techniques which may reduce some of the less desirable effects of stress on consideration of policy alternatives. In many ways they overlap and supplement those suggested by other analyses of crisis diplomacy.° They are, however, almost diametrically opposed to strategic theories which stress the value of forcing the opponent's capitulation by a policy of calculated recklessness. Illustrative of this viewpoint is the "protracted conflict" approach to crisis management, which is based on two fundamental principles.[49] One must have military capabilities which are superior in all respects to those of the adversary. Anything less is unacceptable because rapid technological changes may render them insufficient in short order. Better to acquire "genocidal" capabilities in order to provide an ample margin for error. No less important is the psychological and political value of displaying sufficient intestinal fortitude to use—or at least threaten to use—all necessary force to compel total defeat of the adversary in any crisis situation.

Canons of crisis management are deduced from these basic principles. Command and control precautions against accidental war are condemned because they are likely to hinder the use of weapons systems as well as to raise doubts about one's determination to use them. Automatic use of force is favoured in a num-

° Compare them, for example, with Alexander George's "requirements for controlled, measured use of force and effective crisis management": presidential control of military options; pauses in military operations; clear and appropriate demonstrations; military actions coordinated with political-diplomatic action; confidence in the effectiveness and discriminating character of military options; military options that avoid motivating the opponent to escalate; and avoidance of impression of resort to large-scale warfare. Alexander L. George, David K. Hall, and William R. Simons, *The Limits of Coercive Diplomacy: Laos, Cuba, Vietnam* (Boston: Little, Brown and Co., 1971), pp. 9–11.

ber of circumstances as a means of maintaining credibility. One must not, moreover, make a distinction between threats to central and peripheral values; doing so reduces credibility. Concern that a minor crisis may thus quickly escalate into a general war is dismissed from consideration. Nor should employment of military force be delayed. Indeed, Ward questions the value of invulnerable weapons such as the Polaris precisely because they permit delay in the use of force, thereby inviting the adversary to use blackmailing tactics.[50] Thus, military power should be employed as soon as possible and with sufficient freedom from constraints to ensure the rapid and complete defeat of the enemy.

Finally, although deterrence is defined by the protracted conflict strategists as a policy addressed to the psychology and rationality of the opponent, one's own actions should be unpredictable, avoiding even the appearance of caution: "In strategy, the most reckless course of action—'calculated madness'—often pays off the best."[51] The adversary, it is assumed, will respond to recklessness by greater rationality. Should he fail to back down in the face of this strategy, it will confirm his willingness to go to war. While the costs of the ensuing war may be high, consolation is to be found in the fact that "the defense of civilization is tantamount to destruction of the communist movement throughout the world."[52]

It is, of course, possible to achieve foreign-policy objectives by bluff, by appearing to be irrational or insane, or by deliberately losing control of the situation. The point of these ploys is to impress the adversary that *he* must give in to avoid a mutual disaster. Thomas Schelling and others have demonstrated that the game of "chicken" played by teenaged hot-rodders has its counterparts in many other areas of life, including international politics.[53] But "chicken" is a dangerous game under the best of circumstances; for reasons that have been emphasized throughout this book, it is doubly perilous when played in high-stress situations. There are no guarantees that one can repeatedly be successful by creating an image of recklessness; surely the same methods can be employed by both sides. Strategies of calculated irresponsibility, moreover, even if successful, also incur longer-range costs which must be paid in the premium currencies of reputation, credibility, desirability as an ally, and the like.

Time Pressure

Probably the most pernicious attribute of crisis is time pressure; the aphorism that "haste makes waste" can take on a terrible new meaning in nuclear confrontations. Not only is short decision time likely to constrain full exploration of policy options, it may also materially increase the probabilities of unintended escalation and war. Let's assume that military technology has made nuclear war as an instrument of policy "unthinkable" because it has become too costly even for the "winner." A similar argument was, incidentally, also quite popular during the decade before 1914. But we cannot totally overlook the unintended ways in which war might occur: escalation of limited war into a thermonuclear holocaust; catalytic war, in which major powers are drawn into a conflict initiated by other nations; war arising from an accident, a breakdown in discipline among subordinate military personnel; and, a war resulting from erroneous intelligence, faulty interpretation of radar images, or from other types of communication difficulties.[54]

Most of these occurrences are extremely unlikely owing to complex devices and procedures designed to circumvent accidents. For example, a number of aircraft armed with nuclear weapons have crashed without a nuclear detonation owing to safety devices built into the triggering mechanism. The presence of such safeguards does not, however, provide absolute insurance against errors of human perception, judgment, and performance. But in the absence of time pressure, these scenarios can perhaps be dismissed as too improbable for serious concern. This section will consider several aspects of military capabilities and strategic doctrines which may assist in reducing the time pressures under which statesmen must act in crises.

ATTRIBUTES OF WEAPONS

Although the distinction between "offensive" and "defensive" weapons lives on in debates about strategy and disarmament, it is not very useful for our purposes because most defensive weapons can also be used to attack. Nevertheless, it is a mistake to assume that "a weapon is a weapon." Some armaments convey such clear implications of "first strike" that they draw everyone's finger a little closer to the trigger, especially in crisis situations. The German army in 1914 did precisely this. It was widely recognized that Germany hoped to offset the disadvantages of a possible two-front war by rapid mobilizations, a quick victory over France while the ponderous Russian army was being mobilized, and, after France was defeated, a decisive deployment of German forces to the Russian front.

The speed, range, and destructive capacity of modern weapons may under some circumstances provide a potential attacker with the opportunity and temptation to destroy the adversary's military forces with a surprise attack. If one nation's leaders believe that a surprise attack will permit quick victory without much likelihood of retaliation, because the enemy nation's weapons can be destroyed before they are used, the two countries have an inherently unstable relationship. Virtually all European leaders in 1914 defined the situation as one in which great—and possibly decisive—advantages would accrue to the nation or alliance which struck the first military blow. The same belief was held by several persons during the missile crisis; fortunately the president was not among them. Vulnerable military capabilities not only invite a possible enemy attack but, even worse, that knowledge creates immense pressures to use them before they are destroyed.[55] And, of course, the adversary will realize the implications of this dilemma for his own planning: in order to forestall the possibility of a pre-emptive blow the only "safe" option may be to unleash a desperate last minute effort to blunt the other side's attack. Under these circumstances, the conservative strategy is to assume the worst and to act as if an attack were imminent.

Vulnerable forces greatly magnify time pressures on policy makers because they provide no incentive to delay response. Knowledge that the opponent can launch a crippling surprise attack reduces decision time, and increases pressure to launch a pre-emptive strike at the first signal (which may turn out to be false) that such an attack is imminent. When both nations' deterrent forces are vulnerable the situation is even less stable, as neither side can afford to delay. Each may prefer to back off, but neither can be certain of not having his rationality exploited. A delay of hours, or even minutes, might make the difference between being able to retaliate and having one's military capabilities destroyed. Compressed decision time and the need for a hair-trigger on retaliatory forces thus significantly increase the probabilities of accidental war. Consider, for example, the situation of a single nuclear explosion over an American or Soviet city. Without adequate time for investigation of its causes, it might be impossible to determine whether it was the result of an accident, forerunner of an all-out attack, or some other cause. In these circumstances the pressures for immediate retaliation against the presumed attacker might become irresistible.°

Conversely, invulnerable strategic forces—those which cannot be eliminated, even by the most severe attack that the enemy can mount—*may* mitigate some of the more severe time pressures attending a crisis. Knowledge that one's forces are secure reduces the motive to "shoot first and ask questions later." The temptation to launch a first strike should diminish as the certainty and probable costs of devastating retaliation increase. Equally important, when retaliatory systems are invulnerable the incentive to undertake a pre-emptive attack in the absence of complete information (as in the example of the explosion of unknown origin) declines as the ability to delay response increases decision time.

Survival capability of deterrent forces can be enhanced by a number of methods. *An increase in quantities of weapons* can, at least temporarily, make it more difficult for the attacker to succeed in a first strike. This method is relatively crude and will be effective only if the adversary does not increase his forces proportionately. The search for numerical superiority may decrease vulnerability in the short run, but its long-term consequence is likely to be an arms race which leaves neither side more secure.

° As the number of nations possessing nuclear weapons and delivery systems increases, and the size of weapons decreases, the problem of identifying the attacker will become more serious. The miniature bomb capable of delivery by a single agent is no longer in the realm of science fiction. J. T. Coffey, "The Chinese and Ballistic Missile Defense," *Bulletin of the Atomic Scientist*, XXI (December 1965), 17–19.

Although this discussion is illustrated by problems of deterrence between nuclear powers, the same considerations hold for deterrence situations among smaller nations, or for prenuclear situations.

Dispersal of forces at home and in overseas bases may also provide some protection, but this alternative is becoming less attractive as missile guidance systems become more accurate and the political costs of foreign bases increase. *"Hardening" retaliatory weapons* by placing them in underground shelters, although relatively expensive, can provide adequate protection against all but a direct strike. Hardening requires the attacker to expend more weapons on each target, thereby reducing the probability of a crippling first strike. But as missiles become more accurate, the effectiveness of this measure is eroded. Placing retaliatory sources at the *maximum possible distance* from a potential enemy ensures their survival only as long as the gap in distance is not closed by longer-range delivery systems. A further measure of protection can be provided by *concealment*, but this method is already vulnerable to advances in the technology of detection. American U-2 flights over the Soviet Union proved that high-altitude photography can yield considerable intelligence information. Orbiting "spy" satellites have been even more effective than the U-2, without incurring any of the political costs of manned overflights.

Presently, the most reliable method of decreasing vulnerability appears to be *mobility*. Polaris missile-launching submarines have become a major component of American defence forces and the Soviet Union has subsequently acquired similar capabilities. These weapons combine high mobility with capabilities for dispersal, distance, and concealment; unlike missile sites or air bases located near cities, they provide the adversary with no incentive to attack major population centres; and they do not require foreign bases.°

Submarine-based missiles, hardened launching sites, and dispersal of retaliatory weapons by both superpowers have reduced but not eliminated the incentives to strike first. Certainly there is little reason for complacency about the future. There is, in the

---

° The Polaris may also remain beyond striking distance of its target (communicating reassurance) but can rapidly be brought into firing position (communicating threat) without losing its invulnerability. The implications of this attribute for arms control are discussed in John R. Raser, "Weapons Design and Arms Control: The Polaris Example," *Journal of Conflict Resolution*, IX (1965), 450–462. See also Raser, "The Failure of Fail-Safe," *Transaction*, VI (January 1969), pp. 11–19.

first place, a not insignificant group of civilian and military strategists who continue to press for adoption of first-strike doctrines
and deployment of the appropriate weaponry. Among the most
prominent of these is the "protracted conflict" school, whose
views were examined earlier. Their counterparts certainly exist
in the Kremlin.[56]

Secondly, the anti-ballistic missiles systems (ABMs) and multiple warhead missiles (MIRVs) deployed by the Soviet Union and
the United States have some disturbing first-strike implications.
Even if the intention is merely to augment retaliatory second-
strike capabilities, it is by no means certain that the other side
will not draw the opposite conclusion. Weapons such as Polaris
submarines may, to be sure, be used for pre-emptive attacks as
well as for retaliation. But their capabilities are such that they
appear to "make more sense" for the latter purpose; hence they
give credence to and reinforce denials of first-strike intentions.
ABMs and MIRVs, on the other hand, are at least equally consistent with strategies of first strike. If one takes seriously the claims
of effectiveness made on behalf of ABMs by their supporters,*
then one must also question whether these weapons may not result in the dangerous belief that there are advantages in striking
first. A continued arms race in such weapons may lead to a
1914-like situation in which the fears and temptations associated
with first-strike capabilities—whether real or perceived—heighten
the pressures of time under which crisis decisions are made. This
would scarcely contribute to reducing the stress accompanying
crisis.

Thirdly, although strategic weapons of any kind are costly, invulnerable ones are by far the most expensive; they are almost
certainly beyond the resources of all but the major powers. In

---

* If one does not—and many knowledgeable scientists have disputed both Soviet
and American claims—then one can question deployment of ABMs on other
grounds; for example, that they buy no additional security at a fantastic cost. See,
for example, Jerome B. Weisner and Herbert York, "National Security and the
Nuclear-Test Ban," Scientific American, CCXI (October 1964), 27–35; Herbert
York, "ABM Technology and National Security," Scientific American, CCXXI
(August 1969), 17–29; Abram Chayes and Jerome B. Weisner (eds.), ABM: An
Evaluation of the Decision to Deploy an Antiballistic Missile System (New York:
Harper and Row, 1969). For a different evaluation, see D. G. Brennan and Johan
J. Holst, Ballistic Missile Defence: Two Views (London: Institute of Strategic
Studies, Adelphi Paper No. 43, November 1967).

these circumstances it is predictable that the spread of nuclear weapons to small nations will take the form of vulnerable systems, with deleterious consequences for both regional and international stability.

Finally, although the case for replacing vulnerable weapons with invulnerable ones is strong, it should not be overstated. Weapons which can withstand a first strike may be a necessary condition for successful (i.e. peaceful) deterrence, but they are probably not sufficient. We cannot, for instance, explain the haste with which armed forces were alerted, mobilized, and sent across frontiers in 1914 solely by reference to military technology. None of the European nations in 1914 had the ability to unleash a sudden destructive attack, crippling the opponent's ability to retaliate militarily. But in the tense days preceding the outbreak of general war, policy makers in the capitals of Europe increasingly attributed to their potential enemies both the *ability* and the *intent* to do so. They chose the "safe" strategy of taking precautionary steps—sending ultimata, secretly alerting armed forces, mobilizing, and the like—to offset any advantage in time which might accrue to their adversaries. And, just as logically, the latter interpreted these moves as confirmation of their own suspicions that the time remaining for them for similar steps was becoming very short indeed. Military technology in 1914 appears to have permitted efforts to delay the process of escalation without potentially catastrophic risk to any country, but the situation as defined by many European leaders was quite different, and it was this definition of reality that ultimately dictated policy decisions. The ability to delay response is therefore not likely to contribute to crisis management unless policy makers perceive that the risks of acting in haste are greater than those of using a strategy of delay and, equally important, unless they are willing to attribute the same preferences to the adversary's leadership.

STRATEGIC DOCTRINES

The problem thus concerns not only military technology, but also the prevailing doctrines and norms of military strategy. In 1914 the putative "lesson" of the Franco-Prussian war was that rapid mobilization was the key to military victory. Not untypically, the experiences of the previous war were uncritically applied by general staffs to a different situation with disastrous consequences for everyone, although the Schlieffen plan may have come close to succeeding.° By 1914 the machine-gun had been developed into a potent weapon that rendered offensive action against entrenched positions prohibitively costly: in December 1915 Lloyd George informed the House of Commons that about eighty per cent of British casualties had been inflicted by the machine-gun. Moreover, since at least the Franco-Russian military convention of 1892 it had been explicitly recognized that the act of mobilization was tantamount to a declaration of war. The records of the negotiations leading to that treaty stated: "General Obrucheve emphasized finally the necessity of the immediate and simultaneous mobilization of the Russian and French armies at the first news received by either of the two countries of a mobilization of the forces of the Triple Alliance. He understands further that this mobilization of France and Russia would be followed immediately by positive results, by acts of war." [57] A government may have wished to mobilize as a purely defensive measure, but it could not do so without signalling the intent to declare war. Stated somewhat differently, the norm of equating mobilization with war erased the distinction between what might otherwise have been two quite different steps taken for vastly diverse reasons. It did not, moreover, permit a nation to use mobilization as a signal of resolve and determination without also conveying the message that war was imminent.

A related aspect of military doctrine was the widely accepted dictum that anything other than a rapid offensive movement represented a dereliction of duty to the nation. Typical was the advice of Colonel F. M. Maude, presented at the turn of the century in his introduction to a new edition of Clausewitz' On War: "Vic-

---

° The conventional view is that the Schlieffen plan failed only because of Moltke's incompetence and the French "miracle" at the battle of the Marne. A very convincing counterargument is that there were predictable reasons for the French success at the Marne. More importantly, even military success of the Schlieffen plan would not have resulted in a quick German victory because France would have continued fighting as long as she had the support of Britain and Russia. L. L. Farrar, Jr., "The Short-War Illusion: The Syndrome of German Strategy, August–December, 1914" (University of Washington: mimeographed, 1971).

tory can only be insured by the creation in peace of an organization which will bring every available man, horse, and gun (or ship and gun if the war be on the sea) in the shortest possible time, and with the utmost possible momentum, upon the decisive field of action. . . . The statesman who, knowing his instrument to be ready, and seeing war inevitable, hesitates to strike first, is guilty of crime against his country." [58] These ideas were by no means confined to Schlieffen and his successors. French military journals had raised the dictum that "the offensive alone can obtain decisive results" into a virtually unquestioned article of faith.[59]

The widespread acceptance of this viewpoint no doubt contributed to the pressures of time felt in European capitals during the 1914 crisis and the unwillingness of European policy makers to delay taking military actions; instead, they actually sanctioned a good deal of military preparation prior to the issue of formal orders for mobilizations.

FLEXIBILITY

Availability of a wide range of military options may also reduce time pressures. As noted earlier, general staffs in 1914 had devoted years or even decades to developing and refining a small number of very elaborate plans. In no country could these be substantially modified to meet political requirements. Aside from the constraints which military staffs had thus imposed on their political counterparts, their plans virtually precluded the use of military power for any purpose other than attack. Actions that might be used merely in prudent self-defence, for diplomatic bargaining, or to demonstrate determination were identical with those that would be taken as a prelude to an all-out attack. And, once set in motion, it was virtually impossible to stop mobilization without creating such vast confusion as to leave oneself militarily vulnerable. Even the tactic of employing a naval show of force had lost its value as a signal of determination; it has been used so often in the past that it had lost its meaning as a sign of extraordinary concern.[60] In one respect at least the contemporary situation is equally dangerous: once fired, nuclear-armed missiles cannot be recalled; moreover they are not equipped with mechanisms which permit them to be destroyed en route by the attacker. Hence it is all the more important that the decision to use such weapons never be taken in the belief that it is safer to attack than to wait.

In contrast to 1914, both Kennedy and Khrushchev could convey their resolve by various means without invoking a direct threat of a nuclear first strike on the other. For example, 150,000 American reserves were mobilized and a good deal of military movement took place within the United States. The Soviet Union alerted Warsaw Pact forces following the president's speech on 22 October. But the important point is that none of these forces threatened destruction of the adversary's homeland. Their value was as much diplomatic and symbolic as military. They might, to be sure, have been used to threaten Cuba or West Berlin, but the geographic facts of life rendered both these outposts vulnerable even before the Soviet and American deployments. The more important point is that both sides possessed the ability to undertake essentially symbolic military actions to demonstrate their determination, and to do so without conveying the message that general war was imminent.°

One caveat is worth mentioning. A broad range of available capabilities is not an end in itself. Nor does it ensure that from the wide spectrum of options which it makes possible, choices will be made wisely. In 1954, some six months after Secretary of State Dulles' "massive retaliation" speech, the Eisenhower administration decided against intervention in Indo-China, partly on the grounds that American conventional forces were insufficient for the task. In response to the logical and political shortcomings of massive retaliation—these had been recognized by Dulles less than four years after the 1954 speech—the Kennedy and Johnson administrations undertook a large build-up of conventional forces to redress existing imbalances. But the availability of multiple military options also made it possible to become committed, step by almost imperceptible step, to a tremendously costly war in Vietnam.[61] The value of flexible capabilities is thus no greater than the wisdom with which they are deployed.

° This did not ensure that signals of determination would not be misinterpreted as the prelude to an all-out attack, thereby triggering a general war. Indeed, the evidence presented in the first seven chapters suggests that under stress misinterpretations of this type are more likely than in non-stress situations.

In summary, the pressures of time in crisis, and consequently the probabilities of uncontrolled escalation, may be reduced if both sides possess weapons capable of withstanding *any* first strike, if military doctrines stress the importance of delay rather than haste in employment of force, and if both sides possess sufficiently varied capabilities that each military deployment need not be interpreted as a prelude to attack.

Some will no doubt find this argument repugnant because it fails to suggest disarmament as the answer to crisis management. Yet even if we assume the achievement of total nuclear disarmament and massive reductions of conventional arms, the logic of this discussion would still be valid. If it were widely believed that launching a surprise first strike (with rifles, cross-bows, or whatever weapons were available) would be decisive, the pressures to do so in an international crisis might become insurmountable, as they did in 1914. "He who hesitates is lost" may be a sound rule for card players; we can scarcely afford to have statesmen act on that principle. The ideal deterrence system is one which clearly and continually impresses everyone with the fact that striking first is the reckless, not the "safe" choice. This is *not* to say, however, that nuclear deterrence based on the threat of mutual annihilation is the ideal means of preserving peace and international order. At best it is only a short-run expedient which is susceptible to failure for reasons that have been spelled out repeatedly in the previous chapters.

Conclusion

Not all crises result in war, nor do all wars arise from crises which get out of control. It would be stretching the present findings beyond all recognition to suggest that important international events such as the invasions of Poland and Finland in 1939, South Korea in 1950, or Czechoslovakia in 1968 resulted from the adverse effects of stress on policy making. Our concern has not been to explain all outbreaks of international violence, much less the entire domain of international politics. Most events can be understood adequately without reference to the effects of stress on decision making.

Our attention has thus been directed at a very small segment of the rich and varied scenarios that constitute international politics, but one of continuing practical relevance. Only a twentieth-century Pangloss would maintain that we have developed adequate protection against human failure in crises. The attempt in this chapter to speculate about some steps in this direction is no doubt inadequate when measured against the importance of the problem, one which remains high on an already overcrowded agenda of potentially catastrophic dangers against which we must devise better safeguards. There would be little consolation in learning that a nuclear holocaust was not the result of malice but of another human trait—our limited ability to perform at peak effectiveness under intense and sustained stress.

Appendix

TABLES AND METHODOLOGY

IN ORDER TO keep the text relatively free of detailed tables and discussions of methodology, these have been deferred to this appendix. The following tables present the 1914 data on a daily basis for each nation. Each table is accompanied by definitions and other methodological information, unless it is readily available elsewhere. In that case the present discussion will be brief and citations to other sources are provided. For example, the methods of content analysis used for some of the 1914 data have been described in a research handbook.[1] Similarly, the statistical methods used in Chapters 2–6 are described in virtually any textbook.

ACTION DATA (CHAPTER 2)

The action data were gathered from various sources the most useful of which were the multivolume diplomatic histories by Fay and Albertini.[2] Each action was typed on a card in a uniform format consisting of the *acting nation*, the *action*, and the *target*. In some cases more than a single target might have been identified. A German statement of support for Vienna in its policy toward Belgrade, for instance, could have had either of two targets: Austria-Hungary or Serbia. In every such instance the target was coded as the nation in the opposing alliance. The example above was thus coded as a German action toward Serbia, and in the subsequent scaling judges were asked to assess the level of threat in the action accordingly. This arbitrary rule reflected the primary interest in relations between nations in opposing alliances, rather than in intra-alliance politics.

The set of 448 actions was given to two judges for Q-sort scaling, a technique in which judges are instructed to place themes into a nine-point scale. This is a rank-order method with a fixed number of permissible tied scores at any point in the scale. The distribution of scores approximates a normal (bell-shaped) curve:

					INTENSITY				
	Low								High
Category	1	2	3	4	5	6	7	8	9
Percentage of Items in Category	5%	8%	12%	16%	18%	16%	12%	8%	5%

Thus for any set of Q-sorted data the mean is 5.00 and the standard deviation is 2.08.

The final score assigned to any item was the mean of the two judgments. Thus, if the first judge placed an item in category 7 and the second scored it as 8, it was assigned a final score of 7.50. All the action data were coded by the author and thus no inter-coder coefficient of agreement can be provided. Inter-judge reliability on the scaling operation was .853, as measured by the formula:

$$r = 1 - \frac{\Sigma d^2}{\frac{864 \, (N)}{100}}$$

N is the number of items scaled, and d is the difference in the category assigned for each item. Another way of describing the level of agreement is to summarize the distribution and extent of disagreement for the entire set of 448 items:

	Number
Judges placed item in same category	161
Disagreement on item by 1 category	193
Disagreement on item by 2 categories	94
Disagreement on item by 3 or more categories	0
Total	448

Table A presents the action data for each nation on a daily basis.

PERCEPTIONS OF INTERNATIONAL HOSTILITY (CHAPTERS 2–6)

Of the 5078 themes extracted from the diplomatic documents by content analysis, 1096 were coded as perceptions of international hostility. The unitizing, coding, and masking procedures have been described in a research handbook, to which the reader should turn for a more detailed description.[3] Inter-coder agreement for the hostility data was .80. The set of 1096 themes was then Q-sorted by three judges using the same procedures described above for the action data. Composite inter-judge agreement was .74, or an average disagreement of less than 1.5 points per items on the Q-sort scale.

Table B summarizes the number and mean (average) intensity of perceived hostility for each nation on a daily basis.

In two instances Table B includes perceptions of international hostility even though subsequent tables on communications indicate that there were no documents written by top-ranking officials on that data. This is true, for example, of the German data for 2 July. The explanation is that the perceptions of hostility were coded from annotations, such as the kaiser's marginal notes, added to documents written by other persons.

COMMUNICATIONS (CHAPTER 4)

Tables C-G include all messages published in the five major collections of documents, except for a very few which did not fit into any of the categories because they were neither sent nor received by the foreign office. If, for instance, the French military attaché in Belgrade prepared a report for the French ambassador there, it was not included unless the latter forwarded it to Paris. The number of excluded messages was extremely small.

PERCEPTIONS OF TIME (CHAPTER 5)

All references to time as a factor in policy making are presented in Table H. These statements were further classified as being concerned with either the "immediate" or "distant" future. The former category includes those which considered time only within the context of the situation immediately at hand. The following examples are illustrative.

TABLE A
Crisis Actions: Frequency and Mean Intensity of Threat

Date	Austria-Hungary N	Int.	Germany N	Int.	France N	Int.	Great Britain N	Int.	Russia N	Int.	All Other Nations N	Int.
27 June												
28					1	4.00					1	8.50
29	1	4.00										
30			1	5.00					1	4.00		
1 July	1	5.00										
2					1	3.50						
3			1	4.50								
4			1	5.50							1	1.50
5	1	6.00	1	6.50								
6			2	3.00								
7	4	5.75	1	4.50	1	4.50			1	1.00	1	5.00
8			1	4.50								
9			1	3.00								
10			1	5.00	2	3.50						
11			1	4.50	1	5.00						
12					1	3.00						
13							1	2.00	1	4.50		
14			1	5.00	1	3.00						
15			1	3.00	1	3.00	2	2.00			2	7.00
16					1	4.00					1	7.00
17					3	3.67	1	3.00			2	3.25
18							1	3.50			1	2.50
19							1	3.00			1	6.00
20			3	4.00	1	2.00					1	5.00
21												
22			1	2.00	1	2.50	1	3.00				
23	3	6.50			2	5.25						
24	2	5.25	2	4.75	3	3.50	3	1.83	4	6.13		
25	7	5.71	3	4.17	4	4.88			5	5.60	4	6.00
26	7	5.64	6	4.67	3	5.33	5	2.60	9	5.78	5	3.40
27	3	6.50	6	3.25	4	4.63	2	5.00	4	5.75	1	1.50
28	9	6.67	4	5.75	3	4.67	3	3.67	3	4.33	7	4.79
29	5	6.20	15	4.23	4	4.38	4	5.50	4	6.88	8	3.63
30	6	7.17	18	3.75	5	5.10	11	4.55	5	5.60	17	3.74
31	4	7.63	12	6.04	1	4.50	5	4.90	4	6.75	9	3.56
1 August	1	4.00	9	6.11	10	5.60	2	4.25	5	6.40	11	3.18
2			9	6.17	3	6.67	4	6.88	2	7.75	12	4.42
3	1	7.00	8	7.81	1	6.00	5	4.20	2	5.75	11	4.68
4	3	8.00	8	6.19	2	6.75	7	7.29	1	5.00	8	4.31

Perceptions of Hostility: Frequency and Mean Intensity

Date	Austria-Hungary		Germany		France		Great Britain		Russia	
	N	Int.	N	Int.	N	Int.	N	Int.	N	Int.
27 June	57	2.94								
28										
29										
30			1	3.67			1	4.67	4	5.04
1 July									1	3.00
2	28	4.29	2	2.33						
3										
4									8	4.00
5									3	3.67
6			13	3.31					3	3.50
7	6	4.89							1	3.33
8	13	3.79					2	4.66		
9									3	3.67
10									11	4.55
11	2	3.33	2	3.33						
12	2	3.50	6	4.39						
13										
14	1	3.00	15	3.75					1	2.00
15			10	2.83						
16	1	3.67	1	1.67					2	5.75
17			2	3.33						
18	1	4.00	17	3.57					1	3.67
19										
20	42	3.99	3	2.44			1	4.33		
21	6	4.05	8	3.42			1	2.33		
22	15	4.31			1	3.33	1	2.33	16	4.47
23	14	4.31	7	3.90					1	6.50
24	2	4.50	3	4.78	11	3.67	6	5.33	11	6.50
25	15	4.09	1	4.67			6	4.67	8	4.83
26	32	4.79	12	4.97	22	5.01	3	5.44		
27	16	3.89	9	4.44	12	5.33	7	4.19	2	5.17
28	21	4.84	15	4.82	9	4.26	3	5.78	7	7.29
29	20	4.72	28	5.18	14	5.95	28	5.19	2	5.00
30	8	4.37	43	5.71	9	5.00	13	5.77	22	6.05
31	20	6.13	41	5.63	27	6.02	17	4.86	3	3.67
1 August			22	6.12	22	5.71	11	4.30	3	6.00
2			50	7.19	12	7.11	5	6.27	3	5.67
3			53	6.63	7	6.67				
4			12	5.67	8	7.71	21	5.48	2	2.67

TABLE C
Messages from Officials Abroad to Foreign Office
Number of Documents

Date	Austria-Hungary	Germany	France	Great Britain	Russia
27 June	3		3		
28	1		5	4	6
29	6		5	4	8
30	11	2	8	4	15
1 July	9	1	3		11
2	7	4	1	5	4
3	18		1	4	4
4	13	1	3	2	7
5	9		2	2	5
6	17	3	2	2	5
7	10	1	2	1	4
8	15	3	3		13
9	11	2	3	2	7
10	12	2	3	1	7
11	12	1	4	3	11
12	8	2	1	1	3
13	14	3	3	2	7
14	13	5	4	1	8
15	13	2	6	1	10
16	16	6	3	5	10
17	21	4	3	4	7
18	19	2	1	7	5
19	10	2	4	2	9
20	19	5	3	3	6
21	23	9	10	2	9
22	19	8	7	6	17
23	22	10	5	10	9
24	45	17	17	13	14
25	42	26	27	22	25
26	42	30	23	17	22
27	52	25	47	26	31
28	46	27	31	32	30
29	57	28	39	30	43
30	72	37	49	40	38
31	62	29	56	39	27
1 August		42	48	45	44
2		32	40	42	25
3		40	44	45	29
4		29	44	37	36

Messages from Foreign Office to Officials Abroad
Number of Documents

Date	Austria-Hungary	Germany	France	Great Britain	Russia
27 June	3				
28			2		1
29				1	2
30				1	1
1 July	2	1			3
2	3				5
3	1				2
4	10				2
5	2				
6	1	3	5	2	3
7	9		3		2
8	3		3	2	2
9	2	2	5	1	3
10	7		2		1
11	9	2	1		1
12	3	2			2
13	9	1	1		4
14	3	4			9
15	10	3			3
16	4	1	1		2
17	6	1	6		2
18	2	3			1
19	6	1	6		2
20	30	3	6	2	1
21	8	3	13	1	2
22	17	4	12	1	3
23	57	3	14	1	1
24	30	9	37	15	9
25	66	4	28	21	8
26	31	10	16	10	16
27	55	10	30	14	11
28	40	16	59	19	11
29	52	9	48	15	12
30	32	21	45	18	11
31	49	19	58	11	24
1 August		18	60	23	10
2		24	44	13	4
3		23	42	6	2
4		15	39	35	14

Messages Within Foreign Office
Number of Documents

Date	Austria-Hungary	Germany	France	Great Britain	Russia
27 June	1	1			
28	2				
29	3				3
30	2				1
1 July	6		1		1
2	10				1
3	15				2
4	5				1
5	5				1
6	3				5
7	10				4
8	10				1
9	5	2		2	
10	4				1
11	6	2	1		1
12	5				
13	5		1		2
14	2				1
15					2
16	7	2		1	1
17	3	1			2
18	5	2			2
19	6	2			
20	9	3	1		
21	7	3		1	2
22	11	3	1	6	
23	13	4	1	2	4
24	7	4	12	5	5
25	10	4	6	6	9
26	7	3	11	4	2
27	5	5	9	12	6
28	3	12	14	10	3
29	7	4	10	13	4
30	3	10	14	3	6
31	2	14	16	14	3
1 August		7	16	12	5
2		18	6	3	1
3		16	7	12	1
4		10	6	2	

Direct Messages Sent to Central Decision Makers Abroad
Number of Documents

Date	Austria-Hungary	Germany	France	Great Britain	Russia
27 June					
28					
29	1			1	
30					
1 July				1	
2	1				
3				1	
4				1	
5	2				
6					2
7					
8				2	
9		1	1		
10					4
11				1	
12					
13					
14		1		2	1
15					1
16				1	1
17					1
18				1	
19				1	1
20			1		1
21			1	1	
22					
23			1		1
24	3	1			2
25		2		3	3
26	1	1		2	
27	1		1	1	2
28	6	3		2	6
29	1	2		4	4
30	7	3	1	2	5
31	9	5	5	4	3
1 August		4	1	5	5
2		4	4	6	1
3		4	1	2	1
4		1		8	1

Direct Messages Received from Central Decision Makers Abroad
Number of Documents

Date	Austria-Hungary	Germany	France	Great Britain	Russia
27 June					
28					
29				1	1
30					
1 July					1
2					
3					1
4					1
5		2			
6					
7					1
8			1		1
9					1
10					
11					1
12					
13					
14	1			1	2
15				1	
16				1	1
17				1	
18					1
19					1
20					1
21					2
22					1
23					1
24			2	1	1
25	2	1	1	1	3
26		1	2	1	
27		4	2	1	
28	2	3	2	4	4
29		4	3	2	2
30	2	4	2	2	3
31	2	5	7	6	6
1 August		10	5	5	4
2		8	8	6	2
3		11	4	7	
4		7	3	4	4

Perceptions of Time Pressure: Number of Themes

Date	Austria-Hungary	Germany	France	Great Britain	Russia
27 June	3				
28					
29					
30					
1 July					
2	1				
3					
4					
5					
6	1				
7	5				
8	1				
9					
10					
11		1			
12	1				
13					
14		2			
15		2			
16		2			
17					
18		2			
19	1				
20					
21					
22		2			
23					
24	2		4	5	5
25	1	6		11	2
26		1	1		
27		2	8	2	
28					1
29			4	4	1
30		5	2		1
31		11	3	4	
1 August		12	4	3	1
2		7		1	
3		4	3		
4		10		12	

In view of the colossal war preparations of Russia now discovered, this is all too late, I fear. Begin! Now!

Kaiser Wilhelm, Germany, #433.

. . . it is impossible for the powers in the short time remaining to undertake anything useful toward settlement of the complications which have arisen.

Sazonov, Russia, #23.

The "distant" category includes statements which considered the importance of time in a context beyond the immediate situation. The contradictory arguments presented by Count Alexander Hoyos and Istvan Tisza—both of which are assessments of the likely balance of power at an unspecified future data—illustrate this category.

From a military standpoint he has to emphasize that it would be much more favorable to start the war now than later since the balance of power would weigh against us in the future.

Hoyos, Austria-Hungary, #10118.

A war provoked by us would be fought under conditions unfavorable to us, while postponement of the conflict to a later date, if we exploit the time diplomatically, could lead to the improvement of our power position.

Tisza, *ibid.*, #10146.

Because the volume of communication rose during the course of the crisis, a valid test of several hypotheses examined in Chapters 5 and 6 required that this be taken into account. To obtain the *rate* of time references for each day and nation, the following formula was used:

$$\frac{\text{Number of time references on day X}}{\text{Total number of themes on day X}}$$

For example, on 4 August there were 10 time references to time as a consideration in policy making in German documents; on that date there were also a total of 83 themes coded from these messages. The rate for 4 August was thus 10/83, or .120. Any day on which there were no documents written by top-ranking official was disregarded for computing correlations in order to avoid spurious inflation of the *gamma* coefficients.

PERCEPTIONS OF ALTERNATIVES (CHAPTER 6)

The three categories used for perceptions of alternatives—"necessity," "closed," and "choice"—are defined in Chapter 6. Among statements coded in these categories are the following examples.

Necessity

The intrigues of our enemy compel us to resort to war in order to look after the interests of the Monarchy.

Franz Joseph I, Austria-Hungary, #10774.

. . . these [Serbian] actions impose the necessity on the government of Austria-Hungary to put an end to these plots which represent a constant menace to the peace of the monarchy.

Berchtold, Austria-Hungary, #10305.

Closed

Since all peaceful means are exhausted the decision will possibly be made through arms.

Berchtold, Austria-Hungary, #10714.

It is therefore impossible for me to initiate discussions with Ambassadors here.

Grey, Great Britain, #246.

Open

In regard to the Austro-Serbian conflict, the method of a direct understanding between Petersburg and Vienna as suggested by telegram 163 appears to me to be feasible.

Bethmann-Hollweg, Germany, #248.

If our direct discussions with the Vienna Cabinet should have no success, I would be prepared to accept an English suggestion, as well as any others which are able to solve the conflict peaceably.

Sazonov, Russia, #116.

The distribution of the 505 perceptions of alternatives according to nation and date appears in Tables I–Q. The rate of per-

TABLE I
Perceptions of "Necessity" for Own Nation
Number of Themes

Date	Austria-Hungary	Germany	France	Great Britain	Russia
27 June	10				
28					
29					
30					
1 July	1				
2	5				
3					
4					
5	1				
6		1		2	
7	4				
8	4				
9					1
10					
11					
12					
13					
14	1	4			
15		2			
16					
17					
18		2			
19	4				
20	7				
21					
22	5	3			
23	3	2			
24	1		1	1	2
25	4	3		1	4
26	4	6			
27	3	6		2	1
28	5	6	1		1
29	5	10	3	3	2
30	3	10		2	2
31	10	18		2	
1 August		9	4	2	5
2		9	2	2	
3		11			
4		8	2	3	2

TABLE J
Perceptions of "Closed" Alternatives for Own Nation
Number of Themes

Date	Austria-Hungary	Germany	France	Great Britain	Russia
27 June	1				
28					
29					
30					
1 July					
2		4			
3					
4					
5					
6					
7	1				
8					
9					
10					
11		1			
12					
13					
14					
15					
16					
17					
18		2			
19					
20					
21					
22					2
23					
24				3	
25	1		1	1	
26					
27		2	2	2	
28	3	2		3	
29	1	2		4	2
30		6	2	2	1
31				5	1
1 August		1		2	
2				1	1
3					
4					

TABLE K

Perceptions of "Choice" for Own Nation
Number of Themes

Date	Austria-Hungary	Germany	France	Great Britain	Russia
27 June					
28					
29					
30					
1 July					
2					
3					
4					
5					
6					
7	5				
8					
9					
10					
11					
12					
13					
14	1				
15					
16					
17					
18					
19	1				
20					
21					
22	1				
23					
24					
25					
26					
27	2				4
28		2			1
29		2		1	
30		1		1	1
31	3			2	
1 August		3	1	3	1
2		2			
3					
4					

TABLE L
Perceptions of "Necessity" for Allies
Number of Themes

Date	Austria-Hungary	Germany	France	Great Britain	Russia
27 June	1				
28					
29					
30					
1 July					
2	1	1			
3					
4					
5					
6		1			
7					
8					
9				1	
10		2			
11					
12					
13					
14		1			
15					
16					
17					
18					
19					
20					
21		2			
22					
23					
24			2		
25					
26		5		1	
27					2
28		6		1	1
29		1	1	3	
30		1		1	
31				1	
1 August			1		
2					
3					
4					

Perceptions of "Closed" Alternatives for Allies
Number of Themes

Date	Austria-Hungary	Germany	France	Great Britain	Russia
27 June	1				
28					
29					
30					
1 July					
2					
3					
4					
5					
6					
7					
8					
9					
10					
11					
12					
13					
14					
15					
16					
17					
18					
19					
20					
21					
22					
23					
24					
25		1			
26					1
27					
28					1
29					
30				1	1
31		1	1	1	
1 August			1		
2					
3					
4					

Perceptions of "Choice" for Allies
Number of Themes

Date	Austria-Hungary	Germany	France	Great Britain	Russia
27 June					
28					
29					
30					
1 July					
2	1				
3					
4					
5					
6					
7					
8					
9					
10					
11					
12					
13					
14					
15					
16					
17					
18					
19					
20					
21					
22				3	
23					
24		1	3	2	
25			1	3	4
26			1		
27		1		1	
28		2		2	
29				2	
30		2		2	
31		1		5	
1 August			1	1	
2					
3					
4					

Perceptions of "Necessity" for Enemies
Number of Themes

Date	Austria-Hungary	Germany	France	Great Britain	Russia
27 June					
28					
29					
30					
1 July					
2					
3					
4					
5					
6					
7					
8	1				
9					
10					
11					
12					
13					
14					
15					
16					
17					
18		1			
19					
20					
21					
22					
23					
24			1		
25					
26				2	
27					
28			1		1
29					
30					
31					
1 August		1			1
2					
3					
4					

Perceptions of "Closed" Alternatives for Enemies
Number of Themes

Date	Austria-Hungary	Germany	France	Great Britain	Russia
27 June					
28					
29					
30					
1 July					
2					
3					
4					
5					
6					
7					
8					
9					
10					
11					
12					
13					
14					
15					
16					
17					
18					
19					
20					
21					
22					
23					
24					
25					
26					
27					
28			1		
29					
30					
31			1		
1 August					
2					
3					
4					

Perceptions of "Choice" for Enemies
Number of Themes

Date	Austria-Hungary	Germany	France	Great Britain	Russia
27 June					
28					
29					
30					
1 July					
2	1				
3					
4					
5					
6		2			
7					
8					
9					
10					
11					
12					
13					
14					
15					
16					
17					
18					
19					
20					
21					
22				1	
23					
24				2	
25			1	3	1
26		2	2		1
27		2		1	
28		2	3	1	
29		5		5	1
30		4		3	
31		4	4	4	
1 August		2	2	1	
2		2			
3					3
4					

ceptions of alternatives was computed in the same way as for time references; that is, the number of perceptions of alternatives on any given data was divided by the total number of themes drawn from the nation's documents for the same day.

In a few instances the data in these tables differ very slightly from the results reported in an earlier paper. In the process of re-checking all of the 1914 data, a few errors were found. But in no case do they change any of the substantive findings. For example, Table 34 indicates that there were 95 Austro-Hungarian perceptions of "choice" and "necessity" alternatives, one less than reported previously.[4] Other discrepancies were equally minor.

DATA FROM THE CUBAN MISSILE CRISIS DOCUMENTS
(CHAPTER 7)

All content analyses of the 1914 documents were undertaken by manual methods. The Cuban crisis documents, on the other hand, were analysed using a version of the "General Inquirer" group of computer content analysis programs. These programs have been described in considerable detail elsewhere,[5] and the interested reader should turn to these sources for further information. The data upon which the graphs in Chapter 7 are based may also be found in another source.[6]

NOTES

CHAPTER ONE: CRISIS, STRESS, AND DECISION-MAKING

1. Henry A. Kissinger, "Domestic Structure and Foreign Policy," in James N. Rosenau (ed.), *International Politics and Foreign Policy*, rev. ed. (New York: The Free Press, 1969), p. 265.

2. Herman Kahn, *On Escalation: Metaphors and Scenarios* (New York: Praeger, 1965), p. 38.

3. Theodore Abel, "The Element of Decision in the Pattern of War," *American Sociological Review*, VI (1941), 855.

4. John Foster Dulles, "The Problem of Disarmament," *State Department Bulletin*, 12 March 1956, 416.

5. Unidentified diplomat, quoted in Chris Argyris, *Some Causes of Organizational Ineffectiveness within the Department of State* (Washington: Center for International Systems Research, Department of State Publication 8180, 1967), p. 42.

6. Dwight D. Eisenhower, Address to *Washington Post* Book and Author Lunch, quoted in *Palo Alto Times*, 1 October 1965.

7. Theodore C. Sorensen, *Decision-Making in the White House* (New York: Columbia University Press, 1964), p. 76.

8. Richard E. Neustadt, *Alliance Politics* (New York: Columbia University Press, 1970), p. 116.

9. Bernard Brodie, quoted in Philip Green, *Deadly Logic: The Theory of Nuclear Deterrence* (New York: Schocken Books, 1966), p. 159.

10. See, for example, Thomas C. Schelling, *Arms and Influence*, (New Haven: Yale University Press, 1966), p. 96; Kahn, *On Escalation*, pp. 37–38; and, Albert Wohlstetter and Roberta Wohlstetter, *Controlling the Risks in Cuba* (London: Institute of Strategic Studies, Adelphi Paper No. 17, April 1965). This assumption has been valid in a number of important instances, including the Cuban missile crisis, which we shall consider in Chapter 7.

11. See especially, Thomas C. Schelling, *The Strategy of Conflict* (Cambridge, Mass.: Harvard University Press, 1960).

12. Karl Deutsch, *The Nerves of Government* (New York: The Free Press, 1963), p. 70.

13. This definition of crisis is taken from Charles F. Hermann, "Some Consequences of Crisis which Limit the Viability of Organizations," *Administrative Science Quarterly*, VIII (1963), 61–82. There are many usages of the term "crisis."

For extensive critical reviews of these, see Charles F. Hermann, *Crises in Foreign Policy* (Indianapolis; Bobbs-Merrill, 1969); James A. Robinson, "Crisis: An Appraisal of Concepts and Theories," in Charles F. Hermann (ed.), *Contemporary Research in International Crisis*, (New York: The Free Press, forthcoming); and Kent Miller and Ira Iscoe, "The Concept of Crisis: Current Status and Mental Health Implications," *Human Organization*, XXII (1963), 195–201.

14. For a much more demanding list, see J. David Singer and Paul Ray, "Decision-Making in Conflict: From Inter-Personal to International Relations," *Bulletin of the Menninger Clinic*, XXX (1966), 303. The literature on the limits of rationality in decision making is extensive. See, for example, Herbert A. Simon, *Administrative Behavior* (New York: Macmillan Co., 1957); James G. March and Herbert A. Simon, *Organizations* (New York: John Wiley and Sons, 1958); and Richard C. Snyder, H. W. Bruck, and Burton M. Sapin (eds.) *Foreign Policy Decision Making* (New York: The Free Press, 1962).

15. Sheldon J. Korchin and Seymour Levine, "Anxiety and Verbal Learning," *Journal of Abnormal and Social Psychology*, LIV (1957), 238.

16. Dean Rusk, "Interview of Secretary Rusk by David Schoenbrun of CBS News," in David Larson, *The "Cuban Crisis" of 1962* (Boston: Houghton Mifflin, 1963), p. 268.

17. Quoted in *New York Times*, 27 June 1967.

18. *San Francisco Chronicle*, 9 June 1967.

19. See the studies cited in footnote 13, above as well as Michael Haas, "Communication Factors in Decision Making," *Peace Research Society (International), Papers*, XII (1969), 65–86.

20. Cited in Kurt Back, "Decisions Under Uncertainty: Rational, Irrational, and Non-rational," *American Behavioral Scientist*, IV (February 1961), 14–19. But in at least one study it was found that even mild stress interfered with problem solving. Wilbert S. Ray, "Mild Stress and Problem Solving," *American Journal of Psychology*, LXXVIII (1965), 227–234. Unless a specific study is cited, I have relied on two extensive reviews of the literature: Richard S. Lazarus, James Deese, and Sonia F. Osler, "The Effects of Psychological Stress Upon Performance," *Psychological Bulletin*, IL (1952), 293–317; and F. E. Horvath, "Psychological Stress: A Review of Definitions and Experimental Research," in L. von Bertalanffy and Anatol Rapoport (eds.), *General Systems Yearbook*, IV (Ann Arbor: Society for General Systems Research, 1959).

21. Alfred Lowe, "Individual Differences in Reaction to Failure: Modes of Coping with Anxiety and Interference Proneness," *Journal of Abnormal and Social Psychology*, LXII (1961), 303–308; Sara B. Kiesler, "Stress, Affiliation and Performance," *Journal of Experimental Research in Personality*, I (1966), 227–235.

22. S. J. Korchin *et al.*, "Visual Discrimination and the Decision Process in Anxiety," *AMA Archive of Neurology and Psychiatry*, LXXVIII (1957), 424–438; Robert E. Murphy, "Effects of Threat of Shock, Distraction, and Task Design on Performance," *Journal of Experimental Psychology*, LVIII (1959), 134–141; and Harold M. Schroder, Michael J. Driver, and Siegfried Streufert, *Human Information Processing* (New York: Holt, Rinehart and Winston, Inc., 1967), ch. 7.

23. Irving Janis, *Psychological Stress* (New York: John Wiley and Sons, 1958).

24. Herbert G. Birch, "Motivational Factors in Insightful Problem-Solving," *Journal of Comparative Psychology*, XXXVII (1945), 295–317; and R. M. Yerkes, "Modes of Behavioral Adaptation in Chimpanzee to Multiple Choice Problems," *Comparative Psychological Monographs*, X (1934), 1–108.

25. John T. Lanzetta, "Group Behavior Under Stress," *Human Relations*, VIII (1955), pp. 47–48.

26. Leo Postman and Jerome S. Bruner, "Perception under Stress," *Psychological Review*, LV (1948), 322.

27. E. Paul Torrance, "The Behavior of Small Groups under the Stress Conditions of 'Survival,'" *American Sociological Review*, XIX (1954), 751–755; Sheldon J. Korchin, "Anxiety and Cognition," in Constance Sheerer (ed.), *Cognition: Theory, Research, Promise*, (New York: Harper & Row, 1964), p. 67; H. Kohn, cited in Enoch Callaway and Donald Dembo, "Narrowed Attention," *AMA Archive of Neurology and Psychiatry*, LXXIX (1958), 85; L. T. Katchmas, S. Ross, and T. G. Andrews, "The Effects of Stress and Anxiety on Performance of a Complex Verbal-Coding Task," *Journal of Experimental Psychology*, LXXXV (1958), 562; Ernst G. Beier, "The Effects of Induced Anxiety on Flexibility of Intellectual Functioning," *Psychological Monographs*, LXV (1951), whole no. 326, 19; and Charles E. Osgood, G. J. Suci, and Percy H. Tannenbaum, *The Measurement of Meaning* (Urbana, Illinois: University of Illinois Press, 1957).

28. C. D. Smock, "The Influence of Psychological Stress on the 'Intolerance of Ambiguity,'" *Journal of Abnormal and Social Psychology*, L (1955), 177–182; and B. B. Hudson, quoted in Stephen B. Withey, "Reaction to Uncertain Threat," in George W. Baker and Dwight W. Chapman, *Man and Society in Disaster*, (New York: Basic Books, 1962), p. 118.

29. D. Krech and R. S. Crutchfield, quoted in Korchin, "Anxiety and Cognition," p. 63.

30. Roland L. Frye and Thomas M. Stritch, "Effects of Timed vs. Non-timed Discussion Upon Measures of Influence and Change in Small Groups," *Journal of Social Psychology*, LXIII (1964), 139–143. For an intriguing discussion of "subjective time," see John Cohen, "Psychological Time," *Scientific American*, November 1964, 116–124.

31. Samuel I. Cohen and A. G. Mezey, "The Effects of Anxiety on Time Judgment and Time Experience in Normal Persons," *Journal of Neurology, Neurosurgery and Psychiatry*, XXIV (1961), 266–268.

32. Harry B. Williams and Jeannette F. Rayner, "Emergency Medical Services in Disaster," *Medical Annals of the District of Columbia*, XXV (1956), 661; and Jonas Langer, Seymour Wapner, and Heinz Werner, "The Effects of Danger Upon the Experience of Time," *American Journal of Psychology*, LXXIV (1961), 94–97.

33. Jerome Bruner, Jacqueline J. Goodnow, and George A. Austin, *A Study of Thinking* (New York: John Wiley and Sons, 1956), p. 147.

34. Abraham S. Luchins, "Mechanization in Problem-Solving," *Psychological Monographs*, LIV (1942), whole no. 248; and John Steinbruner, "The M.L.F.: A Case Study in Decision-Making," (Ph.D. Dissertation, MIT, 1969).

35. George Usdansky and Loren J. Chapman, "Schizophrenic-like Response in Normal Subjects under Time Pressure," *Journal of Abnormal and Social Psychology*, LX (1960), 143–146; Pauline N. Pepinsky and William B. Pavlik, "The Effects of Task Complexity and Time Pressure Upon Team Productivity," *Journal of Applied Psychology*, XLIV (1960), 34–38; N. H. Mackworth and J. F. Mackworth, "Visual Search for Successive Decisions," *British Journal of Psychology*, IL (1958), 210–221; Birch, "Motivational Factors"; Bruner, Goodnow, and Austin, *Study of Thinking*; Peter Dubno, "Decision Time Characteristics of Leaders and Group Problem Solving Behavior," *Journal of Social Psychology*, LIX (1963), 259–282; Horvath, "Psychological Stress"; Donald R. Hoffeld and S. Carolyn Kent, "Decision Time and Information Use in Choice Situations," *Psychological Reports*, XII (1963), 68–70; and Frye and Stritch, "Effects of Timed vs. Non-timed Discussion."

36. Robert J. Albers, "Anxiety and Time Perspectives," *Dissertation Abstracts*, XXVI (1966), 4848; James D. Thompson and Robert W. Hawkes, "Disaster, Community Organization, and Administrative Process," in Baker and Chapman, *Man and Society*, p. 283.

37. David Rioch, quoted in Korchin, "Anxiety and Cognition," p. 63.

38. Morton Deutsch and Robert M. Krauss, "The Effects of Threat Upon Interpersonal Bargaining," *Journal of Abnormal and Social Psychology*, LXI (1960), 189.

39. Max Montgelas and Walther Schücking (eds.), *Outbreak of the World War, German Documents Collected by Karl Kautsky* (New York: Oxford University Press, 1924), #401.

40. Korchin, "Anxiety and Cognition," pp. 65–67; J. W. Moffitt and Ross Stagner, "Perceptual Rigidity and Closure as a Function of Anxiety," *Journal of Abnormal and Social Psychology*, LII (1956), 355; S. Pally, "Cognitive Rigidity as a Function of Threat," *Journal of Personality*, XXIII (1955), 346–355; Sheldon J. Korchin and Harold Basowitz, "Perceptual Adequacy in Life Stress," *Journal of Psychology*, XXXVIII (1954), 501.

41. Richard C. Snyder, *Deterrence, Weapons and Decision-Making* (China Lake, Calif.: US Naval Ordnance Test Station, 1961), p. 80.

42. Richard C. Snyder and Glenn D. Paige, "The United Nations Decision to Resist Aggression in Korea: The Application of an Analytical Scheme," *Administrative Science Quarterly*, III (1958), 245; and Glenn D. Paige, *The Korean Decision* (New York: The Free Press, 1968). See also March and Simon, *Organizations*, pp. 154 ff.

43. Leon Festinger, *A Theory of Cognitive Dissonance* (Evanston: Row, Peterson & Co., 1957), pp. 43–44. Italics added.

44. See, for example, Kenneth Boulding, "National Images and International Systems," *The Journal of Conflict Resolution*, III (1959), 120–131; Charles E. Osgood, "Suggestions for Winning the Real War with Communism," *The Journal of Conflict Resolution*, III (1959), 295–325; Raymond A. Bauer, "Problems of Perception and the Relations Between the United States and the Soviet Union," *The Journal of Conflict Resolution*, V (1961), 223–229; and Samuel F. Huntington, "Arms Races," in Carl Friedrich and Seymour Harris (eds.), *Public Policy, 1958* (Cambridge, Mass.: Harvard University Press, 1958).

45. Montgelas and Schücking, *Outbreak of the World War*, #480.

46. Ole R. Holsti and Robert C. North, "The History of Human Conflict," in Elton B. McNeil, *The Nature of Human Conflict* (Englewood Cliffs, N.J.: Prentice-Hall, 1965), pp. 165–166.

47. George A. Heise and George A. Miller, "Problem Solving by Small Groups Using Various Communication Nets," *Journal of Abnormal and Social Psychology*, XLVI (1951), 335.

48. For exceptions, see Charles F. Hermann, "Some Consequences of Crisis which Limit the Viability of Organizations," *Administrative Science Quarterly*, VIII (1963) 61–82; James G. Miller, "Information Input Overload," *Self Organizing Systems—1962* (n.p.); James G. Miller, "Information Input Overload and Psychopathology," *American Journal of Psychiatry*, CXVI (1960), 695–704; and Harry B. Williams, "Some Functions of Communication in Crisis Behavior," *Human Organization*, XVI (1957), 15–19.

49. Siegfried Streufert, Michael J. Driver, and Kenneth W. Haun, "Components of Response Rate in Complex Decision-Making," *Journal of Social Psychology*, III (1967), 286–295. See also George A. Miller, "The Magical Number Seven Plus or Minus Two: Some Limits on Our Capacity for Processing Information," *Psychological Review*, LXIII (1956), 81–97.

50. Sorensen, *Decision-Making in White House*, p. 38. See also, James G. Miller, "Information Input Overload and Psychopathology," *American Journal of Psychiatry*, CXVI (1960), 695–704. Theories of selective exposure to information are in dispute among psychologists, but they appear to fare better in field research than in the laboratory. See William J. McGuire, "Selective Exposure: A Sum-

ming Up," in Robert P. Abelson, *et al.*, (eds.), *Theories of Cognitive Consistency* (Chicago: Rand McNally & Co., 1968), pp. 797–800.

51. Richard A. Brody, "Some Systemic Effects of the Spread of Nuclear Weapons Technology: A Study Through Simulation of a Multi-Nuclear Future," *Journal of Conflict Resolution*, VII (1963), 663–753.

52. Snyder and Paige, "The United States Decision," 341–378; Glenn D. Paige, *The Korean Decision* (New York: The Free Press, 1968); C. M. Roberts, "The Day We Didn't Go to War," *Reporter*, 14 September 1954; Hedrick Smith, "Cambodian Decision: Why President Acted," *New York Times*, 30 June 1970, pp. 1, 14; Townsend Hoopes, *The Limits of Intervention* (New York: David McKay Co., Inc., 1969); and David R. Maxey, "How Nixon Decided to Invade Cambodia," *Look*, 11 August 1970.

53. Dean G. Pruitt, "Problem Solving in the Department of State" (Unpublished paper: Northwestern University, 1961), cited in Hermann, "Some Consequences of Crisis."

54. George M. Thomson, *The Twelve Days: July 24 to August 4, 1914* (New York: G. P. Putnam's Sons, 1964), pp. 44–45.

55. This example was suggested by Robert Jervis.

56. James G. Miller, "Information Input Overload," *Self Organizing Systems—* 1962 (n.p.).

57. Paul Smoker, "Sino-Indian Relations: A Study of Trade, Communication and Defence," *Journal of Peace Research* (1964), no. 2, 65–76.

58. Amia Lieblich, "Effects of Stress on Risk Taking," *Psychonomic Science*, X (1968), 303–304; Korchin and Levine, "Anxiety and Verbal Learning," p. 238; Leonard Berkowitz, "Repeated Frustration and Expectations in Hostility Arousal," *Journal of Abnormal and Social Psychology*, XL (1960), 422–429; and Bruce Dohrenwend, "The Social Psychological Nature of Stress," *Journal of Abnormal and Social Psychology*, LXII (1961), 294–302.

59. For a further development of this point, see Horvath, "Psychological Stress"; and the pertinent observations about crisis "gaming" in Bernard Brodie, *Escalation and the Nuclear Option* (Princeton: Princeton University Press, 1966), pp. 37–39.

60. Horvath, "Psychological Stress," p. 208.

61. Tirpitz, *My Memoirs* (London: Hurst and Blackett, 1919), pp. 279, 280. See also the kaiser's marginal notes during the crisis for dramatic evidence of the consequences of protracted stress.

62. Quoted in Luigi Albertini, *The Origins of the War of 1914*, vol. III (New York: Oxford University Press, 1953), p. 501.

CHAPTER TWO: THE 1914 CRISIS

1. The following paragraphs present a very sketchy overview of the crisis. For a fuller description, see Sidney B. Fay, *The Origins of the World War*, vol. II, 2nd ed., rev. (New York: Macmillan Co., 1930); Luigi Albertini, *The Origins of the War of 1914*, vols. II and III (New York: Oxford University Press, 1953); and a forthcoming study by Eugenia Nomikos and Robert C. North. The historical backgrounds of the crisis are discussed in volume I of both the Fay and the Albertini works cited above, as well as in a forthcoming volume by Robert C. North and Nazli Choucri.

2. David Lloyd George, *War Memoirs*, vol. I (London: Ivor Nicholson and Watson, 1933), p. 55.

3. Quoted in Edmund Taylor, *The Fall of the Dynasties* (Garden City: Doubleday, 1963), pp. 209, 222.

4. Barbara Tuchman, *The Guns of August* (New York: Macmillan Co., 1962).

5. Richard S. Lazarus, James Deese, and Sonia F. Osler, "The Effects of Psychological Stress Upon Performance," *Psychological Bulletin*, IL (1952), 294. Other definitions may be found in the psychological literature cited in Chapter 1.

6. Michael Haas, "Communication Factors in Decision Making," *Peace Research Society (International), Papers*, XII (1969), 65–86.

7. Austro-Hungarian Monarchy, Ministerium des k. and k. Hauses und des Aeusseren, *Oesterreich-Ungarns Aussenpolitik von der bosnischen Krise 1908 bis zum Kriegsausbruch 1914; Diplomatische Aktenstucke des Oesterreich-ungarischen Ministeriums des Aeussern*, vol. VIII, Ludwig Bittner, Alfred Pribram, Heinrich Srbik, and Hans Uebersberger (eds.) (Vienna and Leipzig, 1930). Hereafter cited as Austria-Hungary.

France, Commission de Publication des documents relatifs aux origines de la guerre, 1914, *Documents Diplomatiques Français (1871–1914)*, 3rd series, vols. X and XI (Paris, 1936). Hereafter cited as France.

Great Britain, Foreign Office, *British Documents on the Origins of the War, 1898–1914*, vol. XI G. P. Gooch and Harold Temperley (eds.); *Foreign Office Documents June 28th–August 4th 1914*, coll. by J. W. Headlam-Morley (London: HMSO, 1926). Hereafter cited as Great Britain.

Max Montgelas and Walther Schücking (eds.), *Outbreak of the World War, German Documents Collected by Karl Kautsky* (New York: Oxford University Press, 1924). Hereafter cited as Germany.

Russia, Komissiia po izdaiiu dokumentov spokhi imperializma: *Mozhdunarodnye otnosheniia v ipokhu imperializma; dokumenty iz arkhivov tsarkogo i vremennogo pravitel 'stv 1878–1915 gg.*, 3rd series, vols. IV and V (Moscow and Leningrad, 1931 and 1934). Hereafter cited as Russia.

8. For a more extensive description of the 1914 documents, as well as a more general discussion of systematic research using archival materials, see Dina A. Zinnes, "Documents as a Source of Data," in Robert C. North *et al.*, *Content Analysis; A Handbook with Applications for the Study of International Crisis* (Evanston, Ill.: Northwestern University Press, 1963), pp. 17–36.

9. J. W. Headlam-Morley, "Introduction," in Great Britain, *op. cit.*, vii, italics mine. This assessment has withstood the test of time, even though some new archival materials have become available since publication of the collections cited in footnote 7: "The British and French diplomatic archives do not add any startling new information to that contained in the earlier published volumes [of documents] on 1914." Samuel R. Williamson, Jr., *The Politics of Grand Strategy: Britain and France Prepare for War, 1904–1914* (Cambridge, Mass.: Harvard University Press, 1969), p. 343.

See also the "Preliminary Remarks" by the editors of the German collection, Max Montgelas and Walther Schücking, in Germany, pp. 41–46.

It is perhaps worth noting that even Fritz Fischer's recent work on German diplomacy during the July crisis is essentially based on the collections cited in footnote 7 above, rather than on newly discovered diplomatic documents. This may be verified by checking the references in Fischer, *Germany's Aims*, ch. 2.

10. For an elaboration of this definition, see my *Content Analysis for the Social Sciences and Humanities* (Reading, Mass.: Addison-Wesley, 1969), ch. 1.

11. Germany, #390. The full text of the telegram and the kaiser's annotations appear in Figure 3.

CHAPTER THREE: TWO VALIDITY EXPERIMENTS

1. *Times* (London), *Economist* (London), *Wall Street Journal*, *Le Temps* (Paris), and F. W. Hirst, *The Political Economy of War* (New York: E. P. Dutton and Co., 1915).
2. Germany, #271.
3. Winston S. Churchill, *The World Crisis, 1911–1914* (New York: Charles Scribner's Sons, 1928), p. 208.
4. *Economist*, 1 August 1914, p. 231.
5. *Economist*, 1 August 1914, p. 299; 29 August 1914, p. 383.
6. *Economist*, 18 July 1914, p. 126; 25 July 1914, p. 173; 19 December 1914, p. 13.
7. Ruth M. Jaeger, *Stabilization of the Foreign Exchange* (New York: Isaac Goldman Co., 1922).
8. Hirst, *Political Economy of War*, pp. 281, 290. *Economist*, 25 July 1914, p. 169; 15 August 1914, pp. 316, 321.
9. *Economist*, 1 August 1914, p. 229; 14 August 1914, p. 320; 19 December 1914 (Special War Supplement), p. 13.
10. *Economist*, 1 August 1914, pp. 230–231.
11. Hirst, *Political Economy of War*, p. 283.
12. *Economist*, 1 August 1914, p. 219.
13. *Economist*, 1 August 1914, p. 219.
14. *Economist*, 15 August 1914, p. 302.
15. *Economist*, 1 August 1914, p. 219.
16. Such a suggestion has in fact been made. Richard L. Merritt, "The Representational Model in Cross-National Content Analysis," in Joseph L. Bernd (ed.), *Mathematical Applications in Political Science* (Dallas: Southern Methodist University Press, 1966).
17. Michael Haas, "Bridge-Building in International Relations: A Neotraditional Plea," *International Studies Quarterly*, XI (1967), 320–338; Gordon Hilton, "The Stanford Studies of the 1914 Crisis: Some Comments" (London: mimeo., 1969); Robert Jervis, "The Costs of the Quantitative Study of International Relations," in Klaus Knorr and James N. Rosenau (eds.), *Contending Approaches to International Politics* (Princeton: Princeton University Press, 1969); and John Mueller, "Deterrence, Numbers and History" (Security Studies Project, UCLA, 1969). Studies of the 1914 crisis in which individual data are aggregated include: Dina A. Zinnes, Robert C. North, and Howard E. Koch, Jr., "Capability, Threat, and the Outbreak of War," in James N. Rosenau (ed.), *International Politics and Foreign Policy* (New York: The Free Press, 1961); Ole R. Holsti, Robert C. North, and Richard A. Brody, "Perception and Action in the 1914 Crisis," in J. David Singer (ed.), *Quantitative International Politics; Insights and Evidence* (New York: The Free Press, 1968); Dina A. Zinnes, "The Expression and Perception of Hostility in Prewar Crisis: 1914," *ibid.*; and Dina A. Zinnes, "A Comparison of Hostile Behavior of Decision-Makers in Simulate and Historical Data," *World Politics*, XVIII (1966), 474–502.
18. One of the few empirical analyses of this question in a foreign-policy context is James N. Rosenau, "Private Preferences and Public Responsibility: The Relative Potency of Individual and Role Variables in the Behavior of U.S. Senators," in Singer, *Quantitative International Politics*. For a more general research

approach to this and related problems of comparative foreign policy, see James N. Rosenau, "Pre-theories and Theories of Foreign Policy," in R. Barry Farrell (ed.), *Approaches to Comparative and International Politics* (Evanston, Ill.: Northwestern University Press, 1966).

19. Janet Coleman, R. R. Blake, and Jane Mouton, "Task Difficulty and Conformity Pressures," *Journal of Abnormal and Social Psychology*, LVII (1958), 120–122; Robert L. Hamblin, "Group Integration During a Crisis," *Human Relations*, XI (1958), 67–76; and Leonard Weller, "The Effects of Anxiety on Cohesiveness and Rejection," *Human Relations*, XVI (1963), 189–197. But, as Robert Jervis has pointed out in a personal communication, similar definitions of the situation—for example, that it involves high threat—need not result in agreement on strategies to cope with the problem.

CHAPTER FOUR: CRISIS COMMUNICATIONS

1. Edmund Taylor, *The Fall of the Dynasties* (Garden City: Doubleday, 1963), pp. 220–221.

2. C. W. Thayer, *Diplomat* (New York: Harper, 1959), p. 21, quoted in Charles F. Hermann, "International Crises: Theoretical Implications of Current Research," paper read at the 1967 annual meeting of the American Political Science Association.

3. Howard H. Lentner, "The Concept of Crisis as Viewed by the United States Department of State," in Charles F. Hermann (ed.), *Contemporary Research in International Crises* (New York: The Free Press, forthcoming); and W. A. Runge, *Analysis of the Department of State Communication Traffic During a Politico-Military Crisis*, Research Memorandum OAD RM 109, Stanford Research Institute (Menlo Park, California, 1963), quoted in Charles F. Hermann, "International Crises."

4. For an interesting attempt to make such an adjustment, see Dina A. Zinnes, "Expression and Perception of Hostility in International Relations" (Ph.D. Dissertation, Stanford University, 1963), pp. 137–143.

5. For evidence that channel capacity is higher in small groups which meet face-to-face than in large groups, see James G. Miller, "Information Input Overload," *Self Organizing Systems—1962* (n.p.).

6. A more comprehensive description of the normal patterns of diplomatic communication may be found in Zinnes, "Expression and Perception," pp. 20–24.

7. Miller, "Information Input Overload."

8. Birger Dahlerus, *The Last Attempt* (London: Hutchinson, 1947).

9. Samuel R. Williamson, Jr., *The Politics of Grand Strategy: Britain and France Prepare for War, 1904–1914* (Cambridge, Mass.: Harvard University Press, 1969), p. 317.

10. Miller, "Information Input Overload," James G. Miller, "Information Input Overload and Psychopathology," *The American Journal of Psychiatry*, CXVI (1960), 695–704; James G. Miller, "The Individual as an Information Processing System," in W. S. Fields and W. Abbott (eds.), *Information Storage and Neural Control* (Springfield, Illinois: Charles C. Thomas, 1963); and Siegfried Streufert, Michael J. Driver, and Kenneth W. Haun, "Components of Response Rate in Complex Decision-Making," *Journal of Social Psychology*, III(1967), 286–295.

11. Walter Görlitz (ed.), *The Kaiser and His Court: The Diaries, Notebooks and Letters of Admiral Georg Alexander von Müller, Chief of the Naval Cabinet, 1914–1918* (New York: Harcourt, Brace & World, Inc., 1964), p. 6.

12. Luigi Albertini, *The Origins of the War of 1914*, vol. III (New York: Oxford University Press, 1953), p. 476.

13. Germany, #323, 377, 383, 384, 385, and 395.

14. This example is drawn from Richard L. Meier, "Information Input Overload and Features of Growth in Communication-Oriented Institutions," in Fred Massarik and Philburn Ratoosh (eds.), *Mathematical Explorations in Behavioral Science* (Homewood, Illinois: Irwin-Dorsey, 1965).

15. David Kraslow and Stuart H. Loory, *The Secret Search for Peace in Vietnam* (New York: Vintage, 1968).

16. Germany, #349 and #368.

17. Lindsey Churchill, "Some Sociological Aspects of Message Load: Information Input Overload and Features of Growth in Communication-Oriented Institutions," in Massarik and Ratoosh, *Mathematical Explorations*, p. 279.

18. For evidence on this point from the Korean, Indo-Chinese, Cuban, and Cambodian crises, as well as various key decisions in the Vietnam war, see Glenn D. Paige, *The Korean Decision* (New York: The Free Press, 1966); C. M. Roberts, "The Day We Didn't Go to War," *Reporter*, 11 September 1954, pp. 11–12; Elie Abel, *The Missile Crisis* (New York: J. B. Lippincott Co., 1966); Kraslow and Loory, *Secret Search;* David R. Maxey, "How Nixon Decided to Invade Cambodia," *Look*, 11 August 1970, pp. 22–25; and Hedrick Smith, "Cambodia Decision: Why President Acted," *New York Times*, 30 June 1970, pp. 1, 14.

19. Herbert S. Dinerstein, "The Future of Ideology in Alliance Systems," paper read at the 66th Annual Meeting of the American Political Science Association, 9 September 1970, pp. 15–16. Some policy implications of the thesis that raw information does not ensure sound decisions are discussed in Chapter 8.

20. James G. Miller, "Information Input Overload," *Self Organizing Systems—1962* (n.p.) See also Churchill, "Sociological Aspects of Message Load"; and Meier, "Information Input Overload."

21. Personal Communication, August 1961.

22. Robert C. North, "Fact and Value in the 1914 Crisis" (Stanford University, mimeo., 1961).

23. Germany, #179.

24. *Ibid.*, #207.

25. Alfred von Tirpitz, *My Memoirs* (London: Hurst and Blackett, 1919), p. 275.

26. Germany, #382.

CHAPTER FIVE: CRISIS, TIME PRESSURE, AND POLICY MAKING

1. Robert C. North *et al.*, *Content Analysis: A Handbook with Applications for the Study of International Crisis* (Evanston, Ill.: Northwestern University Press, 1963), p. 173.

2. James G. March and Herbert A. Simon, *Organizations* (New York: John Wiley and Sons, 1958), p. 116.

3. *Ibid.*, p. 117.

4. Richard C. Snyder and Glenn D. Paige, "The United Nations Decision to Resist Aggression in Korea: The Application of an Analytical Scheme," *Administrative Science Quarterly*, III (1958), p. 229.

5. Richard C. Snyder, *Deterrence, Weapons and Decision-Making* (China Lake, Calif.: U.S. Naval Ordnance Test Station, 1961), p. 141.

6. *Ibid.*, p. 155.

7. Quoted in Luigi Albertini, *Origins of the War of 1914*, vol. II (New York: Oxford University Press, 1953), p. 122.

8. Austria-Hungary, #10118.
9. Germany, #48.
10. Russia, #35.
11. *Ibid.*, #23.
12. France, #121.
13. Great Britain, #99.
14. *Ibid.*, #411.
15. France, #550.
16. Germany, #343.
17. France, #32.
18. Winston S. Churchill, *The World Crisis, 1911–1914* (New York: Charles Scribner's Sons, 1928), pp. 230–231.
19. Germany, #390.
20. *Ibid.*, #433.
21. *Ibid.*, #182.
22. *Ibid.*, #451.
23. France, #305.
24. *Ibid.*
25. Germany, #529.
26. France, #401.
27. *Ibid.*, #473.
28. Churchill, "*The World Crisis,*" p. 211.
29. Great Britain, #368.
30. *Ibid.*, #446.
31. Albertini, *Origins of War*, vol. II, p. 558.
32. Germany, #221.
33. Russia, #221.
34. Germany, #874.
35. *Ibid.*, #661.
36. *Ibid.*, #491.
37. Great Britain, #348.
38. Germany, #600.
39. Great Britain, #594.
40. Germany, #702.

CHAPTER SIX: POLICY OPTIONS IN AN INTERNATIONAL CRISIS

1. Thomas Schelling, *The Strategy of Conflict* (Cambridge, Mass.: Harvard University Press, 1960), pp. 137–138.
2. Quoted in Elie Abel, *The Missile Crisis* (Philadelphia: J. B. Lippincott Co., 1966), p. 134.
3. Austria-Hungary, #10118.
4. Great Britain, #103.
5. Germany, #247.
6. Russia, #118.
7. Great Britain, #263.
8. Russia, #170.
9. Germany, #487.
10. *Ibid.*, #575.
11. Austria-Hungary, #11203; France, #532 and #725.
12. Winston S. Churchill, *The World Crisis, 1911–1914* (New York: Charles

Scribner's Sons, 1928), p. 230; *Economist*, 1 August 1914, p. 213; Great Britain, #239, #447, and #448. At best Grey's statements were half-truths because Britain had in fact undertaken certain secret naval commitments to France which would have made a policy of neutrality very difficult to pursue once France and Germany were drawn into the war.

13. Great Britain, #286.
14. Germany, #401.
15. France, #38.
16. Great Britain, #252.
17. Russia, #221.
18. Germany, #401.
19. Schelling, *Strategy of Conflict*, p. 37.
20. Virginia Cowles, *The Kaiser* (New York: Harper and Row, 1964), pp. 343–346).
21. This paragraph and the next two draw in part upon A. J. P. Taylor, "War by Time-Table," *History of the Twentieth Century*, vol. I, ch. 16 (1969), 443–448.
22. Sidney B. Fay, *The Origins of the World War*, vol. II, (2nd ed., rev.) (New York: Macmillan Co., 1930) p. 481.
23. Moltke, *Erinnerungen*, quoted in Cowles, *The Kaiser*, pp. 348–349.
24. Fay, *Origins of the World War*, vol. II, p. 207.
25. *Ibid.*, #368.
26. Great Britain, #264.
27. *Ibid.*, #447.
28. Great Britain, #101.
29. Germany, #395.
30. *Ibid.*, #396.
31. Fay, *Origins of the World War*, vol. II, p. 509.
32. The literature on this point is extensive. For an early statement of the limits of rationality, see Herbert Simon, *Administrative Behavior* (New York: Macmillan Co., 1945), Chapter 5.

CHAPTER SEVEN: OCTOBER 1962

1. Materials on the missile crisis have been drawn from: Elie Abel, *The Missile Crisis* (Philadelphia: J. B. Lippincott, 1966); Henry M. Pachter, *Collision Course: The Cuban Missile Crisis and Coexistence* (New York: Praeger, 1963); Theodore C. Sorensen, *Decision-Making in the White House* (New York: Columbia University Press, 1963); Theodore C. Sorensen, *Kennedy* (New York: Harper & Row, 1965); Arthur M. Schlesinger, *A Thousand Days* (New York: Houghton-Mifflin Co., 1965); Roger Hilsman, "The Cuban Crisis: How Close We Were to War," *Look*, 25 August 1964; Roger Hilsman, *To Move a Nation* (Garden City, N.Y.: Doubleday & Co., 1967); Robert F. Kennedy, "Thirteen Days: The Story About How the World Almost Ended," *McCalls*, November 1968, pp. 6–9, 148–173; Dean Acheson, "Dean Acheson's Version of Robert Kennedy's Version of the Cuban Missile Affair," *Esquire*, February 1969, pp. 76–77; Deadline Data on World Affairs, *Cuban Crisis* (New York: Keynote Publications Inc., 1963); and "The Cuban Crisis: 14 Days that Shook the World," special supplement to the *New York Times*, 3 November 1963. Unless otherwise indicated, all quotations from this chapter are drawn from the last source.
2. NBC, "Cuba: The Missile Crisis," 9 February 1964, mimeo. transcript, p. 8.
3. Quincy Wright, "The Cuban Quarantine of 1962," in John G. Stoessinger

and Alan F. Westin (eds.), *Power and Order* (New York: Harcourt, Brace & World, Inc., 1964), p. 186.

4. See, for example Roberta Wohlstetter, "Cuba and Pearl Harbor," *Foreign Affairs*, XLIII (1965), 691–707; and Cyril Black, "The Failure of National Intelligence Estimates: The Case of the Cuban Missiles," *World Politics*, XVI (1964), 455–67.

5. Sorensen, *Kennedy*, pp. 674–75.

6. Stewart Alsop and Charles Bartlett, "In Time of Crisis," *Saturday Evening Post*, 8 December 1962, p. 16.

7. The deployment of military forces during the crisis is discussed in more detail by Fletcher Knebel, "Inside Story of the War We Never Fought," in "This World," supplement of the *San Francisco Chronicle*, 10 February 1963, pp. 13–21; Curtis E. LeMay, "Deterrence in Action," *Ordnance*, XLVII (1963), 526–528; and Alain Joxe, "La Crise cubaine de 1962—Entrainement Contrôlé Vers la dissuasion réciproque," *Strategie* (Été, 1964), 60–88.

8. NBC, "Cuba," p. 36.

9. Alsop and Bartlett, "In Time of Crisis," p. 16.

10. See, for example, Sorensen, *Kennedy*, p. 714; and Kennedy, "Thirteen Days," pp. 152, 167.

11. Douglas Dillon, quoted in Abel, *Missile Crisis*, p. 48.

12. See, for example, Roman Kolkowicz, "Conflicts in Soviet Party-Military Relations: 1962–1963," Rand Corp. Memo, RM-3760-PR, 1963; and Arnold L. Horelick, "The Cuban Missile Crisis: An Analysis of Soviet Calculations and Behavior," *World Politics*, XVI (1964), 363–389.

13. Sorensen, *Decision-Making in the White House*, p. 31.

14. The need to measure decision time in relation to the task rather than in absolute terms is further discussed in James A. Robinson, "Crisis Decision-Making," in Charles F. Hermann (ed.), *Contemporary Research in International Crises* (New York: The Free Press, in press).

15. NBC, "Cuba," p. 19.

16. Hilsman, "Cuban Crisis," p. 19.

17. CBS, "A Conversation with President Kennedy," 17 December 1962, mimeo. transcript, pp. 2–3.

18. Schlesinger, *Thousand Days*, p. 804.

19. NBC, "Cuba," p. 14.

20. CBS, "Conversation with President Kennedy," p. 4.

21. Sorensen, *Decision-Making in the White House*, p. 60.

22. Sidney Verba, "Assumptions of Rationality and Non-rationality in Models of the International System," *World Politics*, XIV (1961), 93–117.

23. Acheson, "Dean Acheson's Version."

24. Schlesinger, *Thousand Days*, p. 808.

25. CBS, "Conversation with President Kennedy," p. 4.

26. *Ibid.*

27. NBC, "Cuba," p. 17.

28. Sorensen, *Kennedy*, p. 698.

29. Kennedy, "Thirteen Days," p. 149.

30. NBC, "Cuba," p. 42.

31. CBS, "Conversation with President Kennedy," p. 21.

32. Ben Bagdikian, "Press Independence and the Cuban Crisis," *Columbia Journalism Review*, Winter, 1965, p. 6.

33. An extended discussion of the problems of communicating with adversaries may be found in Robert Jervis, *The Logic of Images in International Relations* (Princeton: Princeton University Press, 1970).

34. ABC News, "John Scali, A.B.C. News," 13 August 1964, mimeo. transcript, p. 9.

35. CBS, "Conversation with President Kennedy," p. 3.

36. For example, Thomas Schelling, *Arms and Influence* (New Haven: Yale University Press, 1966), pp. 94–99.

37. W. S. Churchill, *The World Crisis: 1911–1914* (New York: Charles Scribner's Sons, 1928), p. 208.

38. Kennedy, "Thirteen Days," p. 8.

39. Quoted in Abel, *Missile Crisis*, p. 151.

40. In addition to the seminal works of Harold Lasswell, and Erik Erikson, see the essays in Fred I. Greenstein (ed.), "Personality and Politics," *Journal of Social Issues*, XXIV (July 1968), 1–163.

41. Roy Grinker and John Spiegel, quoted in John R. Raser, "The Failure of Fail-Safe," *Transaction*, VI (January 1969), 16.

CHAPTER EIGHT: CONCLUSION

1. George Zaninovich, "An Empirical Theory of State Response: The Sino-Soviet Case," (Stanford University, Ph.D. Dissertation, 1964); Bruce M. Russett, "Cause, Surprise and No Escape," *Journal of Politics*, XXIV (1962), 3–32; and Michael Haas, "Communication Factors in Decision-Making," *Peace Research Society (International), Papers*, XII (1969), 65–86.

2. See, for example, Charles F. Hermann, *Crisis in Foreign Policy* (Indianapolis; Bobbs-Merrill, 1969); James A. Robinson, "Crisis: An Appraisal of Concepts and Theories," in Charles F. Hermann (ed.), *Contemporary Research in International Crisis* (New York: The Free Press, forthcoming); Glenn D. Paige, "Comparative Analysis of Crisis Decisions: Korea and Cuba," in *ibid.*; and Kent Miller and Ira Iscoe, "The Concept of Crisis: Current Status and Mental Health Implications," *Human Organization*, XXII (1963), 195–201.

3. Davis Bobrow, "Communist China's Conflict System," *Orbis*, X (1966), 931. The impact of historical analogies on decision-making is well illustrated in the memoirs of Harry S Truman and Anthony Eden. See also, Glenn D. Paige, *The Korean Decision* (New York: The Free Press, 1968); and Philip M. Burgess, *Elite Images and Foreign Policy Outcomes* (Columbus, Ohio State University Press, 1967).

4. David Hackett Fischer, *Historians' Fallacies* (New York: Harper & Row, 1970), p. 157. See also "How Decision-Makers Learn from History" a chapter in Robert Jervis' forthcoming study of *Perception and International Relations*.

5. Robert F. Kennedy, "Thirteen Days: The Story About How the World Almost Ended," *McCalls*, November 1968, p. 148.

6. George Ball, "Lawyers and Diplomats," *Department of State Bulletin*, XLVII (31 December 1962), 990.

7. Dean Acheson, *Present at the Creation* (New York: W. W. Norton, 1969), p. 411.

8. See Roberta Wohlstetter, *Pearl Harbor: Warning and Decision* (Stanford: Stanford University Press, 1962); and David McLellan, "Dean Acheson and the Korean War," *Political Science Quarterly*, LXXXIII (1968), 16–39.

9. George Kennan, *Russia, the Atom and the West* (New York: Harper and Row, 1957), pp. 21–22.

10. Gilles Perrault, *The Secrets of D-Day* (Boston: Little, Brown & Co., 1965), pp. 52–53.

11. Haas, "Communication Factors," p. 73.

12. Richard E. Neustadt, *Alliance Politics* (New York: Columbia University Press, 1970), pp. 67, 71.

13. Cf. Paul Smoker, "Sino-Indian Relations: A Study of Trade, Communication and Defense," *Journal of Peace Research*, no. 2 (1964), 65–76.

14. This example was suggested by Robert Jervis. See also James A. Robinson, Charles F. Hermann, and Margaret G. Hermann, "Search Under Crisis in Political Gaming and Simulation," in Dean G. Pruitt and Richard C. Snyder (eds.), *Theory and Research on the Causes of War* (Englewood Cliffs, N.J.: Prentice-Hall, 1969).

15. Leonard Mosely, *On Borrowed Time* (New York: Random House, 1969), p. 229.

16. Wohlstetter, *Pearl Harbor*, pp. 302, 382. This point also emerges from Leon V. Segal, "The 'Rational Policy' Model and the Formosa Straits Crises," *International Studies Quarterly*, XIV (1970), 121–156.

17. Robert Jervis, "Hypotheses on Misperception," *World Politics*, XX (1968); and Joseph de Rivera, *The Psychological Dimension of Foreign Policy* (Columbus, Ohio: Charles E. Merrill Publishing Co., 1968), pp. 61–64, 209–211.
A 600-page report, "Diplomacy for the 1970's," prepared by 250 members of the US State Department and Foreign Service, suggests institutionalizing this function by means of a special planning group responsible for preparing the case against prevailing policies.

18. Perrault, *Secrets of D-Day*, p. 171.

19. Mosely, *On Borrowed Time*, p. 223. Similar episodes are reported in William L. Shirer, *The Collapse of the Third Republic* (New York: Simon and Schuster, 1969).

20. George Reedy, "Divided We Stand," NBC News Special, 10 May 1970. This point is developed further in Reedy's *The Twilight of the Presidency* (New York: World Publishing Co., 1970).

21. Townsend Hoopes, *The Limits of Intervention* (New York: David McKay Co., Inc., 1969), pp. 60, 219. In a paper read at the American Historical Association meeting in 1970, Professor John P. Roche challenged the accuracy of Hoopes' book. "The Jigsaw Puzzle of History," *The New York Times Magazine*, 24 January 1971. But most sources seem to support Hoopes' account. Both Roche and Hoopes served in the Johnson administration.

22. Hoopes, *Limits of Intervention*, pp. 204–205.

23. *Herald Tribune* (Paris ed.), 22 May 1970.

24. David R. Maxey, "How Nixon Decided to Invade Cambodia," *Look*, 11 August 1970, pp. 22–25.

25. Stewart Alsop, "On the President's Yellow Pad," *Newsweek*, 1 June 1970, p. 106.

26. See for example Richard M. Nixon, *Six Crises* (New York: Doubleday & Co., 1962); and James D. Barber, "The President and his Friends," paper read at the 65th Annual Meeting of the American Political Science Association, 3 September 1969.

27. Elie Abel, *The Missile Crisis* (Philadelphia: J. B. Lippincott, 1966), pp. 17–18; and Graham T. Allison, "Conceptual Models and the Cuban Missile Crisis," *American Political Science Review*, LXIII (1969), p. 713.

28. John Pierson, "Presidential Isolation is Part of the Job," *Wall Street Journal*, 5 June 1970, p. 8.

29. Bernard Brodie, *Strategy in the Missile Age* (Princeton: Princeton University Press, 1959), p. 59.

30. Allison, "Conceptual Models," p. 706.

31. Stewart Alsop, "A Lesson of the '60s," *Newsweek*, 6 October 1969, p. 134.

32. This point is developed more fully in Alexander L. George, David K. Hall, and William R. Simons, *The Limits of Coercive Diplomacy: Laos, Cuba, Vietnam* (Boston: Little, Brown and Co., 1971).

33. A. J. P. Taylor, "War by Time-Table," *History of the Twentieth Century*, vol. I, ch. 16 (1969), 443–448.

34. Hedrick Smith, "Cambodia Decision: Why President Acted," *New York Times*, 30 June 1970, p. 14.

35. W. E. Knox, "Close-up of Khrushchev During a Crisis," *New York Times Magazine*, 18 November 1962, p. 128; and Albert and Roberta Wohlstetter, "Controlling the Risks in Cuba," in Linda Miller (ed.), *Dynamics of World Politics* (Englewood Cliffs: Prentice-Hall, 1968), pp. 69–71.

36. Jervis, "Hypotheses on Misperception," p. 463; and Andrew M. Scott, *The Functioning of the International Political System* (New York: Macmillan Co., 1967), p. 129.

37. Germany, #401.

38. Mosely, *On Borrowed Time*, pp. 200, 379; Shirer, *Collapse of Third Republic*, p. 349.

39. Mosely, *On Borrowed Time*, p. 211.

40. Hoopes, *Limits of Intervention*, p. 58.

41. Neustadt, *Alliance Politics*, p. 128.

42. Roman Kolkowicz, *Conflicts in Soviet Party Military Relations: 1962–1963*, Rand Corp. Memo, RN-3760-PR, 1963.

43. I. L. Janis and S. Feshback, "Effects of Fear-Arousing Communication," *Journal of Abnormal and Social Psychology*, XLVIII (1953), 78–92; and Elliot Aronson, "Threat and Obedience," *Transaction*, III (March–April, 1966), 25–27.

44. A. J. P. Taylor, *Origins of the Second World War* (Harmondsworth, England: Penguin Books, 1964), p. 336.

45. Evan Luard, "Conciliation and Deterrrence: A Comparison of Political Strategies in the Interwar and Postwar Periods," *World Politics*, XIX (1967), 185.

46. Arthur M. Schlesinger, *A Thousand Days* (New York: Houghton-Mifflin Co., 1965), p. 391.

47. *Ibid.*, p. 425.

48. Henry Brandon, "An Untold Story of the Cuban Crisis," *Saturday Review*, 9 March 1963, 56–57.

49. Elements of this approach may be found in virtually all issues of *Orbis*, published by the Foreign Policy Research Institute. The present summary has relied heavily on Robert Strausz-Hupé *et al.*, *Protracted Conflict* (New York: Harper & Bros., 1959); Arleigh Burke, "Power and Peace," *Orbis*, VI (1962), 187–204; William Kintner and Stefan T. Possony, "Nato's Nuclear Crisis," *Orbis*, VI (1962), 217–243; John Ponturo, "The Deterrrence of Limited Aggression: Strategic and Non-Strategic Interaction," *Orbis*, VI (1963), 593–622; Chester C. Ward, "The 'New Myths' and 'Old Realities' of Nuclear War," *Orbis*, VIII (1964), 255–291; and Stefan T. Possony, "Foreign Policy and Rationality," *Orbis*, XII (1968), 132–160.

50. Ward, " 'New Myths,' " 278.

51. Possony, "Foreign Policy," 152.

52. Burke, "Power and Peace," 198.

53. Thomas C. Schelling, *The Strategy of Conflict* (New York: Oxford University Press, 1963).

54. J. David Singer, *Deterrence, Arms Control and Disarmament* (Columbus: Ohio State University Press, 1962). A somewhat different set of scenarios describing possible causes of war is presented in Herman Kahn, *On Thermonuclear War* (Princeton: Princeton University Press, 1960), pp. 524 ff.

55. The implications of vulnerability were first spelled out in Albert Wohlstet-

ter, "The Delicate Balance of Terror," *Foreign Affairs*, XXXVII (1959), 211–234.

56. For further details on Soviet thinking on the issue of pre-emptive strategies, see Herbert Dinerstein, *War and the Soviet Union*, rev. ed. (New York: Praeger, 1962); and Roman Kolkowicz, *The Soviet Military and The Communist Party* (Princeton: Princeton University Press, 1967).

57. Fay, *Origins of World War*, p. 480.

58. Quoted in Thomas C. Schelling, *Arms and Influence* (New Haven: Yale University Press, 1966), p. 224.

59. Samuel R. Williamson, Jr., *The Politics of Grand Strategy: Britain and France Prepare for War 1904–1914* (Cambridge, Mass.: Harvard University Press, 1969), pp. 126–7.

60. Robert Jervis, *The Logic of Images in International Relations* (Princeton: Princeton University Press, 1970), p. 107.

61. This argument is developed further in Bernard Brodie, "Technology and the Future International System," paper read to the 66th Annual Meeting of the American Political Science Association, Los Angeles, California, 9 September 1970. The point is also discussed in George, Hall, and Simons, *Limits of Coercive Diplomacy*, pp. 15–16.

APPENDIX

1. Robert C. North, *et al.*, *Content Analysis: A Handbook with Applications for the Study of International Crisis* (Evanston, Ill.: Northwestern University Press, 1963).

2. Sidney B. Fay, *The Origins of the World War* (New York: Macmillan Co., 1930); and Luigi Albertini, *The Origins of the War of 1914* (New York: Oxford University Press, 1953).

3. North *et al.*, *Content Analysis*, pp. 37–77.

4. "The 1914 Case," *American Political Science Review*, LIX (1965), 365–378.

5. Philip J. Stone, *et al.*, *The General Inquirer: A Computer Approach to Content Analysis in the Behavioral Sciences* (Cambridge: MIT Press, 1966); and Ole R. Holsti, "An Adaptation of the 'General Inquirer' for the Systematic Analysis of Political Documents," *Behavioral Science*, IX (1964), 382–388.

6. Ole R. Holsti, Richard A. Brody, and Robert C. North, "Measuring Affect and Action in International Reaction Models," *Journal of Peace Research*, III–IV (1964), 170–190.

INDEX